SOUPS AND STEWS

SAUSAGE AND POTATO STEW IN LEMON ROSEMARY BROTH, PAGE 275

SOUPS AND STEWS

Food & Wine
BOOKS

American Express Publishing Corporation
New York

Editorial Director: Judith Hill
Assistant Editors: Jacqueline Bobrow and Susan Lantzius
Copy & Production Editor: Terri Mauro
Wine Specialist: Richard A. Marmet
Designer: Nina Scerbo
Photographer: Eric Jacobson
Food Stylist: Deborah Mintcheff
Prop Stylist: Sara Abalan
Illustrator: Karen Scerbo

Cover Photo: Mexican Chicken Soup, page 115, and Navarin, page 283
Back Photo: Tomato Fennel Soup with Grilled Red Onion and Shrimp, page 23

AMERICAN EXPRESS PUBLISHING CORPORATION
©1994 American Express Publishing Corporation

Published by American Express Publishing Corporation
1120 Avenue of the Americas, New York, New York 10036

Library of Congress Catalog Card Number: 94-79572

ISBN 0-916103-25-0

Manufactured in the United States of America

CONTENTS

COLD CURRIED ZUCCHINI SOUP WITH CILANTRO, PAGE 171

FOREWORD

For all of us who love to cook, what could be a better addition to our cookbook shelf than *Soups & Stews*? This collection of over 150 recipes includes mouthwatering offerings from some of America's renowned chefs, as well as delicious dishes developed in *Food & Wine*'s test kitchen.

The soup section is a potpourri. There are many inventive ideas for vegetarians, ranging from Cauliflower and Buttermilk Soup with Dill to Wild-Mushroom Minestrone with Mascarpone Cappeletti, plus plenty of meat- and fish-based recipes. And when summer comes, you'll find cold soups that are perfect for sweltering days.

The stews gathered here are delightful meals in themselves. We circled the globe to make our selections, which include a spicy American catfish stew, a Moroccan-style chicken-and-sweet-potato combination and a Portuguese classic made with pork and clams.

Most of these recipes can be prepared ahead, making them felicitous solutions for those of you with hectic schedules. And they are as appropriate for dinner parties as they are for homey meals enjoyed with family. There are also wine suggestions, suited to each particular soup or stew, which will bring you added pleasure.

Welcome to our latest cookbook. May your soups and stews be delectable.

MARY SIMONS
Editor in Chief
Food & Wine Magazine

A WORD ABOUT CHOOSING WINE

Elegant or rustic, exotic or familiar, soups and stews are inherently convivial food, and what better to pass around the table along with them than an open bottle of wine.

What should that bottle be? The wine suggestions that follow were developed based on the ingredients in the various recipes and the flavors and textures of the final products, but consideration was also given to the personality of each dish. The recipes in this book represent a broad and diverse range of dishes from every corner of the globe, some of them among the gastronomic pillars of haute cuisine, others tracing their lineage to lowly peasant food, and many that are contemporary inventions.

Some of these dishes have such definite characters that certain wine choices seem inevitable. It's hard to argue with the pairing of an elegant, old world classic such as lobster bisque with a traditional, refined wine. And a rustic stew with a strong sense of its origins, such as daube or goulash, will resonate to a hearty bottle of wine from the same geographical area.

Dishes from non-European, in most cases non-wine-drinking, cultures can be paired with any number of unconventional wines—or, in some cases, beer. Another category, those familiar dishes that we grew up on, like chicken noodle soup or beef stew, just seem to go best with easygoing, unassuming wines (which may say something about the way we used to be).

Wine matches can be tougher for some of the more innovative American dishes, with their generally strong flavors sometimes from two or more very different cuisines. Ironically, it seems that these dishes work best with wines from regions that are often ignored by American wine drinkers such as chenin blanc from the Loire Valley in France, various Alsatian wines and especially German rieslings.

I hope that you'll try the dishes from all of the categories in this book, together with their wine suggestions. Explore the vast differences that producers, vineyards and vintages make within each broad category of a suggested wine, and, since experimenting with different combinations is what makes matching wine and food interesting, try some ideas of your own as well. Then pass the soup or stew and a good bottle of wine and enjoy the way that the food and drink play to, and off, each other.

RICHARD A. MARMET

CHAPTER 1 · VEGETABLE SOUPS

Southwest Vegetable Sou

Make this an even heartier soup by adding chicken or shrimp. If already cooked, they should be put in at the last minute to just heat through. Or cook raw shellfish or cubes of poultry in the soup during the last five minutes of simmering.

SERVES 6

½   pound chorizo or pepperoni, cut into thin slices
1   tablespoon cooking oil
1   onion, chopped
3   cloves garlic, minced
1   rib celery, chopped
2   teaspoons cumin seeds
2   quarts Chicken Stock, page 299, or canned low-sodium chicken broth
2   pounds tomatoes (about 4), peeled, seeded and chopped, or 3½ cups canned tomatoes (28-ounce can), drained and chopped
½   pound boiling potatoes (about 2 small), peeled and cut into ½-inch dice
1   red bell pepper, chopped
1   green bell pepper, chopped
2   tablespoons tomato paste
1   bay leaf
¼   teaspoon dried oregano
¼   cup chopped fresh parsley
1   teaspoon salt
3   cups fresh (cut from about 4 ears) or frozen corn kernels
½   teaspoon fresh-ground black pepper
¼   cup chopped fresh cilantro

WINE RECOMMENDATION: You'll need a rich and sturdy white wine to stand up to the strong flavors of the chorizo and cumin in this soup. Try a young chenin blanc or gewürztraminer from California.

1. In a large pot over moderate heat, cook the chorizo, stirring frequently, until brown, about 10 minutes. Transfer to paper towels to drain.

2. Reduce the heat to moderately low and add the oil. Add the onion, garlic, celery and cumin seeds and cook, stirring occasionally, until the onions are translucent, about 5 minutes.

3. Add the chorizo, stock, tomatoes, potatoes, bell peppers, tomato paste, bay leaf, oregano, 2 tablespoons of the parsley and the salt. Bring to a boil. Reduce the heat and simmer until the potatoes are tender, about 20 minutes.

4. Add the corn and simmer about 4 minutes. Remove the bay leaf and stir in the black pepper. Serve topped with the remaining 2 tablespoons parsley and the cilantro.

Gumbo z'Herbes

Traditionally, this Cajun specialty is served on Good Friday and prepared with at least seven different greens. Three is the minimum for Chef Spicer of Bayona in New Orleans. Here she tops each serving with crisp fried oysters.

SERVES 6

8   tablespoons olive oil
6   tablespoons flour
2   onions, chopped
2   green bell peppers, chopped
4   ribs celery, chopped
2   turnips, peeled and chopped
4   scallions including green tops, minced
3   cloves garlic, minced
1½ pounds mixed greens, at least 3 of the following: turnip greens, mustard greens, collard greens, spinach, arugula, escarole, endive, watercress or Swiss chard, stems removed, leaves washed and chopped fine
1   pint oysters in their liquor
1   tablespoon gumbo filé, optional
½   teaspoon dried thyme
2   quarts Chicken Stock, page 299, or canned low-sodium chicken broth
1   bouquet garni: 6 parsley stems, 3 sprigs fresh thyme or ½ teaspoon dried, and 1 bay leaf
¼   pound okra, chopped (about 1 cup)
2   tablespoons cider vinegar
1½ teaspoons Worcestershire sauce, or more to taste
½   teaspoon Tabasco sauce, or more to taste
2   teaspoons salt
½   teaspoon fresh-ground black pepper
½   cup yellow cornmeal
    Cooking oil, for frying oysters

WINE RECOMMENDATION:
THIS SLIGHTLY SPICY, VERY LEAFY AND OYSTER-RICH SOUP IS PERFECT WITH A LIGHT, FRESH WHITE WINE SUCH AS THE LATEST VINTAGE OF MUSCADET FROM FRANCE OR A VINHO VERDE FROM PORTUGAL.

1. In a large pot, heat 6 tablespoons of the olive oil over moderately low heat. Add the flour and cook, stirring frequently, until the roux turns the color of peanut butter, about 15 minutes. As the roux darkens, stir the mixture more frequently.

2. Add the onions, bell peppers, celery, turnips, scallions and garlic and stir until the vegetables are coated with the roux. Cook over moderate heat, stirring occasionally, until the vegetables begin to turn golden, about 5 minutes.

3. Add the greens and cook, stirring occasionally, until they wilt, about 8

minutes longer. With a slotted spoon, remove the oysters from their liquor. Pour the liquor into a bowl through a sieve lined with cheesecloth.

4. Stir the filé, if using, and thyme into the vegetable mixture and then whisk in the stock and oyster liquor. Bring to a simmer and add the bouquet garni. Cook the gumbo, partially covered, stirring occasionally, for 30 minutes.

5. Meanwhile, heat the remaining 2 tablespoons olive oil in a small frying pan over moderate heat. Add the okra. Cook until beginning to brown, about 5 minutes. Stir in the vinegar. Add the okra to

the gumbo with the Worcestershire sauce, Tabasco sauce, salt and ¼ teaspoon of the black pepper. Simmer about 10 minutes longer. Remove the bouquet garni.

6. Just before serving, fry the oysters: Combine the remaining ¼ teaspoon black pepper and the cornmeal. In a frying pan, heat about 1 inch of cooking oil until hot but not smoking. Meanwhile, toss the oysters with the cornmeal. Fry until golden, about 1 minute per side, and transfer to paper towels to drain. Top each serving of gumbo with fried oysters and serve at once.

—Susan Spicer
Bayona

Minestrone with Pesto

Many versions of this well-known vegetable soup from Italy exist. The popular one from Genoa, given here, has pesto stirred in at the end. In Rome, mint is added, and on hot summer days in Milan, minestrone is often served at room temperature. Most variations include cannellini beans and some type of pasta, and of course plenty of mixed fresh vegetables. Cheese and Herb Croutons, page 306, add an appealing finishing touch.

SERVES 6

½   cup dried white beans, preferably cannellini
2   tablespoons olive oil
¼   pound pancetta, chopped
1   onion, chopped
2   carrots, chopped
2   ribs celery, chopped
2   cloves garlic, minced
2   quarts Chicken Stock, page 299, or canned low-sodium chicken broth
1   bouquet garni: 6 parsley stems, 3 sprigs fresh thyme or ½ teaspoon dried, and 1 bay leaf
¼   cup ditalini or other small macaroni
¼   pound green beans, cut into 1-inch lengths
1   pound tomatoes (about 2), peeled, seeded and chopped
2   teaspoons salt
2   medium zucchini, quartered lengthwise, seeded and cut into ½-inch dice
2   tablespoons Pesto alla Genovese, page 305

¼   teaspoon fresh-ground black pepper
    Cheese and Herb Croutons, page 306
    Grated Parmesan cheese, for serving

WINE RECOMMENDATION: CHOCK FULL OF VEGETABLES, THIS ITALIAN CLASSIC SHOULD BE PAIRED WITH A YOUNG PINOT BIANCO OR OTHER SIMPLE WHITE WINE FROM ITALY.

1. Soak the white beans overnight in enough cold water to cover by at least 2 inches. Drain.

2. In a large pot, heat the oil over moderate heat. Add the pancetta and cook, stirring frequently, until brown and crisp, about 5 minutes. Remove with a slotted spoon.

3. Reduce the heat to moderately low. Add the onion, carrots, celery and garlic. Cook, stirring occasionally, until the onion is translucent, about 5 minutes. Add the white beans, stock and bouquet garni. Bring to a boil. Reduce the heat. Simmer, partially covered, for 40 minutes.

4. Add the pasta, green beans, tomatoes and salt. Simmer, uncovered, 10 minutes. Add the reserved pancetta and the zucchini. Simmer until the beans, pasta and all the vegetables are tender, about 10 minutes longer. Remove the bouquet garni.

5. Stir the pesto and pepper into the soup. Top with the croutons and pass the Parmesan.

SHORTCUT

If you haven't any pesto on hand, you needn't make a batch especially for this soup. Just add at the end: 12 minced fresh basil leaves, 3 tablespoons grated Parmesan cheese and 2 minced cloves garlic.

ONLY THE NAMES HAVE BEEN CHANGED

The French are as proud of their *soupe au pistou* as the Italians are of minestrone. *Soupe au pistou*, the Provençal version of vegetable soup, is thick with vegetables and is flavored with *pistou*, a blend of basil, olive oil and Parmesan made in the same way as Italian pesto. Sound familiar? The soups are virtually the same; only the names differ.

Wild-Mushroom Minestrone with Mascarpone Cappelletti

Minestrone, that hearty Italian favorite, gets a whole new look and flavor in this mushroom version. A perfect way to feature autumn's bounty of wild mushrooms, this soup is also great made with the domesticated white variety. This is a case where homemade chicken stock will make a big difference in the flavor of the soup. If you don't have the time to make the mascarpone pasta, though, just cook a quarter-pound of pasta shells instead. The soup will still taste delicious.

SERVES 6

1 head garlic
3 tablespoons olive oil
Salt
Fresh-ground black pepper
3 quarts Chicken Stock, page 299
12 parsley stems
3 sprigs fresh thyme, or ½ teaspoon dried
2 bay leaves
8 peppercorns
4 carrots, cut into ¼-inch dice
½ pound napa cabbage, cut into ½-inch squares
½ pound spinach, stems removed, leaves washed and cut into ½-inch squares
2 tablespoons butter
¾ pound mixed fresh wild mushrooms, such as morels, chanterelles, porcini and oyster mushrooms, cut into ½-inch dice
1 tomato, peeled, seeded and cut into ½-inch dice

3 tablespoons chopped fresh basil
24 wonton wrappers
¾ cup mascarpone cheese
3 tablespoons grated Parmesan cheese

WINE RECOMMENDATION:
THIS EARTHY BUT ARISTOCRATIC SOUP DESERVES A WINE WITH SIMILAR QUALITIES. TRY A FIVE- TO TEN-YEAR-OLD BARBARESCO OR BAROLO FROM PIEDMONT IN ITALY.

1. Heat the oven to 400°. Cut off the top third of the head of garlic and save it for another use. Rub the cut head of garlic with 1 tablespoon of the oil and sprinkle with a pinch each of salt and pepper. Wrap in aluminum foil and roast in the oven until the garlic is soft, about 45 minutes. When cool enough to handle, scoop out the flesh with a small knife.

2. In a large pot, bring the stock to a boil. Reduce the heat, add the roasted garlic, parsley stems, thyme, bay leaves and peppercorns and simmer until

reduced to 2 quarts, about 30 minutes. Strain the stock.

3. Meanwhile, in a large pot, heat the remaining 2 tablespoons oil over moderately high heat. Add the carrots and cook, stirring occasionally, for 5 minutes. Add the cabbage and cook, stirring, for 5 minutes. Add the spinach, ½ teaspoon salt and a pinch of pepper and cook, stirring, until all the vegetables are soft, about 5 minutes. Remove the vegetables.

4. In the same pot, melt the butter over moderate heat. Add the mushrooms, ¼ teaspoon salt and a pinch of pepper and cook, stirring, until beginning to brown, about 5 minutes. Add the tomato and basil and cook, stirring,

for 1 minute. Add the stock, carrots, cabbage and spinach to the pot.

5. On a clean work surface, lay out a few of the wonton wrappers and brush lightly with water. Put about 1½ teaspoons of the mascarpone in the center of each wonton, fold into a triangle and seal. Join the two bottom points and seal. Repeat with the remaining wonton wrappers.

6. In a pot of boiling, salted water, cook the mascarpone cappelletti until just done, about 3 minutes, and drain. Add the cappelletti to the soup and bring just to a simmer. Serve topped with the Parmesan.

—Charles Palmer
Aureole

18

Watercress Soup

The essence of watercress comes through in this easy soup thickened with potatoes. Because watercress is available all through the year, you can grace even wintertime tables with its vibrant color and fresh, spring-like flavor.

SERVES 6

3	tablespoons cooking oil
2	onions, chopped
2	quarts Chicken Stock, page 299, or canned low-sodium chicken broth
1	pound baking potatoes (about 2), peeled and cut into 1-inch cubes
½	pound watercress, leafy portion removed and reserved, half the stems reserved and tied together with string
1½	teaspoons salt
1½	cups heavy cream
¼	teaspoon fresh-ground black pepper Miniature Croutons, page 307, optional

WINE RECOMMENDATION:
Tame the peppery taste of this classic soup with a crisp Sauvignon Blanc-based wine from the Loire Valley in France. Look for a Sancerre or even a Pouilly-Fumé.

1. In a large pot, heat the oil over moderately low heat. Add the onions and cook, stirring occasionally, until translucent, about 5 minutes. Add the stock, potatoes, watercress stems and salt and bring to a boil. Reduce the heat and simmer, partially covered, until the potatoes are soft, about 20 minutes. Discard the watercress stems.

2. Reserve 18 watercress leaves for decoration. Bring a pot of salted water to a boil and add the remaining watercress leaves. Return just to a boil. Drain. Add the leaves to the soup and bring to a boil.

3. In a blender, puree the soup. Return the soup to the pot and add the cream and pepper. Bring to a simmer and serve topped with the reserved watercress leaves and the croutons, if you like.

Sorrel Soup with Smoked-Salmon Croûtes

Lemony sorrel makes a delectable, traditional French soup. Here it's given a crowning touch of smoked salmon piled on croûtes and floated on the surface. The classic combination of sorrel and salmon has never been better. Sorrel is available in many specialty stores and farmers' markets in the spring, summer and fall.

SERVES 6

4	tablespoons butter or cooking oil
2	onions, chopped
7½	cups Chicken Stock, page 299, or canned low-sodium chicken broth
1	½-pound baking potato, peeled and cut into 1-inch cubes
1	pound sorrel, stems removed
1	teaspoon salt
¼	pound sliced smoked salmon, cut into ¼-inch squares
1	tablespoon mixed fresh herbs, such as dill, basil, chives and chervil
	Fresh-ground black pepper
6	Rustic Croûtes, page 309
6	tablespoons heavy cream

WINE RECOMMENDATION:
Look for a tart wine with lots of character to match and contend with the sourness of the sorrel and the smokiness of the salmon croûtes. An excellent choice would be a young sauvignon blanc from California or Washington State.

1. In a large pot, heat the butter over moderately low heat. Add the onions and cook, stirring occasionally, until translucent, about 5 minutes. Add the stock, potato, sorrel and salt and bring to a boil. Reduce the heat and simmer, partially covered, until the potatoes are soft, about 20 minutes.

2. Meanwhile, combine the smoked salmon, herbs and a pinch of pepper. Top each croûte with a small mound of the salmon mixture.

3. In a blender, puree the soup. Return to the pot and add the cream and ¼ teaspoon pepper. Bring to a simmer and serve topped with the croûtes.

Summer Tomato Soup

When you have an abundance of garden tomatoes on hand, make them into this tasty soup. You can sprinkle it with whatever herbs happen to be growing at the time; basil and dill are particularly nice. Or top the soup with Polenta Croutons, either plain or herb, page 308.

SERVES 6

7½ pounds tomatoes, about 15
1   tablespoon butter
1   tablespoon cooking oil
3   onions, chopped
3   cloves garlic, minced
1½ quarts Chicken Stock, page 299, or canned low-sodium chicken broth
6   parsley stems
3   sprigs fresh thyme, or ½ teaspoon dried
1   bay leaf
1½ tablespoons chopped fresh summer savory, or 1½ teaspoons dried
1½ tablespoons tomato paste
2½ teaspoons salt
1½ teaspoons sugar
¼   teaspoon fresh-ground black pepper
    Polenta Croutons or Polenta and Herb Croutons, page 308, optional

WINE RECOMMENDATION: The straightforward flavors of this soup call for a simple, acidic white wine. Try a pinot grigio from Italy.

1. Cut 6 pounds of the tomatoes (about 12) into large chunks. Put in a food processor and chop.

2. In a large pot, heat the butter and oil over moderately low heat. Add the onions and garlic and cook, stirring occasionally, until translucent, about 5 minutes. Add the chopped tomatoes, stock, parsley stems, thyme, bay leaf, summer savory, tomato paste, salt and sugar. Bring to a boil. Reduce the heat and simmer the soup, partially covered, for 40 minutes.

3. Peel and seed the remaining tomatoes. Cut the flesh into ½-inch squares.

4. Strain the soup and push the soft vegetables through the strainer. Return the soup to the pot. Add the diced tomatoes and bring back to a boil. Reduce the heat and simmer 5 minutes. Add the pepper. If you like, serve the soup topped with the croutons.

Tomato Fennel Soup with Grilled Red Onion and Shrimp

From New Orleans comes an easy-to-make tomato soup flavored with garlic, fennel, basil and Pernod. Made with canned rather than fresh tomatoes, this is a homemade tomato soup you can enjoy any time of the year.

SERVES 6

6	tablespoons olive oil
2	yellow onions, chopped
2	fennel bulbs, chopped
2	cloves garlic, minced
½	cup Pernod
¾	cup fresh basil leaves, shredded
1	teaspoon saffron, optional
2	quarts canned tomatoes with their juice (two 35-ounce cans), chopped
1¾	cups water
	Salt
	Fresh-ground black pepper
1	red onion, cut into ½-inch slices
18	medium shrimp (about ½ pound), shelled

WINE RECOMMENDATION: Look for a white wine with refreshing acidity to go with the predominant flavors of tomato and fennel. Try a young bottle of Entre-Deux-Mers or Bordeaux blanc, based on sauvignon blanc and sémillon, both from France.

1. In a large pot, heat 4 tablespoons of the oil over moderately low heat. Add the yellow onions, fennel and garlic and cook, stirring occasionally, until the vegetables are soft, about 10 minutes. Add the Pernod, ½ cup of the basil and the saffron, if using. Bring to a boil, reduce the heat and simmer 1 minute. Add the tomatoes and their juice, the water, 1 teaspoon salt and ¼ teaspoon pepper and bring back to a boil. Reduce the heat and simmer for 30 minutes. Strain and press the vegetables firmly to get all the liquid. Return the soup to the pot.

2. Light a grill or heat a broiler. Brush both sides of the red-onion slices with 1 tablespoon of the oil and grill or broil until browned, about 12 minutes. When the onion slices are cool enough to handle, cut them into ¼-inch dice. ➤

3. Brush the shrimp with the remaining 1 tablespoon oil and sprinkle with ⅛ teaspoon salt and a pinch of pepper. Grill or broil just until cooked through, about 4 minutes.

4. Bring the soup to a simmer. Ladle into bowls and top with the shrimp, red onion and the remaining ¼ cup basil.
—Richard Benz
Gautreau's

DIFFERENT COOKING TECHNIQUES FOR DIFFERENT HERBS

Fresh herbs can be divided into two major categories—delicate and sturdy. Delicate herbs, such as basil, cilantro, tarragon, chervil, parsley and dill, have soft leaves that will lose much of their flavor if left to simmer in a soup or stew for longer than about half an hour. To maintain the vibrant color and distinctive flavors of these herbs, add them toward the end of cooking or stir them in just before serving. Sturdier herbs like rosemary and thyme, on the other hand, are usually added at the beginning of cooking so that they soften and their flavors have time to permeate the dish.

Rice and Peas in Broth with Prosciutto

Risi e bisi (rice and peas), a famous dish from Italy's Veneto region, is usually made as a rather soupy rice dish. This version qualifies as an actual soup. Because the chicken stock is so important to the taste, it's best to use homemade rather than canned. In fact we boil down even homemade stock to concentrate the flavor.

SERVES 6

¾ cup arborio rice

3 tablespoons butter

1 onion, chopped

1 rib celery, chopped

¼ cup dry white wine

3 quarts Chicken Stock, page 299, boiled down to 2 quarts

1 cup fresh or frozen petite peas

1 tablespoon chopped fresh flat-leaf parsley

1 teaspoon salt

¼ teaspoon fresh-ground black pepper

¼ pound prosciutto, fat removed, cut into matchstick strips

½ cup grated Parmesan cheese

WINE RECOMMENDATION: THE COMBINATION OF SWEET PEAS AND SALTY PROSCIUTTO IS BEST PAIRED WITH A LIGHT, REFRESHING WHITE WINE FROM ITALY. TRY A PINOT GRIGIO OR PINOT BIANCO.

1. In a large saucepan of boiling, salted water, cook the rice until just tender, about 15 minutes. Drain.

2. In a large pot, melt the butter over moderately low heat. Add the onion and celery and cook, stirring occasionally, until the onion is translucent, about 5 minutes. Add the wine and boil until it almost entirely evaporates. Add the stock and bring to a boil over moderately high heat. Add the fresh peas, if using, and cook until tender, about 4 minutes. Add the rice, the frozen peas, if using, the parsley, salt and pepper and bring to a simmer.

3. Distribute the prosciutto among individual bowls. Ladle on the soup, top with the Parmesan and serve.

—Erica De Mane

Garlic Soup

This smooth soup is a specialty of the house at Bayona in New Orleans. What seems like a prodigious quantity of garlic and onions is mellowed by the long, slow cooking. If you can, make the soup a day ahead; the flavor will be even better.

SERVES 6

2	tablespoons olive oil
2	tablespoons butter
2	pounds onions, about 4, chopped
2	cups garlic cloves, about 4 large heads, chopped
2	quarts Chicken Stock, page 299, or canned low-sodium chicken broth
½	loaf day-old French bread (about ¼ pound), cut into chunks
1	bouquet garni: 6 parsley stems, 9 sprigs fresh thyme or 1½ teaspoons dried, and 1 bay leaf
1½	teaspoons salt
2	cups half-and-half
¼	teaspoon fresh-ground black pepper Miniature Croutons, page 307, optional

WINE RECOMMENDATION: EXPERIMENT WITH EITHER A RED, SUCH AS ONE OF THE FRUITY WINES FROM THE CORBIÈRES REGION OF FRANCE, OR A WHITE, SUCH AS A FAIRLY HIGH-ALCOHOL WINE FROM THE CÔTES-DU-RHÔNE OR CÔTES DE PROVENCE IN FRANCE.

1. In a large pot, heat the oil and butter over low heat. Add the onions and garlic. Cover and cook, stirring occasionally, until very soft and beginning to turn golden, about 30 minutes. Raise the heat to moderate and continue cooking the onions and garlic, uncovered, stirring frequently, until deep golden, about 10 minutes longer.

2. Add the stock, bread, bouquet garni and salt. Bring to a boil. Reduce the heat and simmer about 15 minutes.

3. Remove the bouquet garni and puree the soup in a blender or food processor. Strain the soup back into the pot. Add the half-and-half and pepper and bring back to a boil. Serve topped with the croutons, if you like.

—Susan Spicer
Bayona

Zucchini and Lemon Soup with Couscous

The Greek egg-and-lemon theme of Avgolemono Soup, page 131, is expanded here to include couscous, zucchini and the distinctly Italian note of Parmesan cheese for a delicious mix of Mediterranean flavors.

SERVES 6

½   cup couscous
2   quarts Chicken Stock, page 299, or canned low-sodium chicken broth
3   tablespoons olive oil
4   medium zucchini, cut into small dice
1   teaspoon salt
2   cloves garlic, minced
3   tablespoons lemon juice
     Pinch cayenne
¼   teaspoon fresh-ground black pepper
2   eggs, beaten
½   cup grated Parmesan cheese
¼   cup chopped fresh flat-leaf parsley

 MAKE IT AHEAD

Because this soup doesn't reheat well, it's best served at once. But you can prepare it up to the last step well ahead of time.

WINE RECOMMENDATION: THE DIVERSE FLAVORS OF THIS SOUP ARE BEST PAIRED WITH A RICH WINE WITHOUT TOO MUCH FLAVOR INTENSITY, SUCH AS A YOUNG PINOT BLANC FROM ALSACE IN FRANCE.

1. Put the couscous in a large bowl. In a small saucepan, heat 1 cup of the stock and pour it over the couscous. Let the couscous sit until it absorbs all of the liquid, about 5 minutes. Fluff with a fork and set aside.

2. In a large pot, heat the oil over moderate heat. Add the zucchini and salt and sauté, stirring frequently, until tender but still firm, about 5 minutes. Add the garlic and cook until fragrant, about 1 minute. Add the remaining 7 cups stock, the lemon juice, cayenne and black pepper.

3. Stir the eggs, Parmesan and parsley into the couscous. Bring the soup just to a boil and slowly pour it into the couscous mixture, stirring constantly so that the eggs do not curdle. Serve at once.

—Erica De Mane

Asparagus and Leek Soup

Celebrate the arrival of spring with this velvety-smooth blend of leeks and tender young asparagus. Bright green, studded with asparagus tips and topped with crème fraîche and crisp fried leeks, this soup is as pretty as a picture.

SERVES 6

¼ cup olive oil
2 pounds leeks, white and light-green parts only, half chopped, half cut into 2-inch-long matchstick strips, washed well
1 ½-pound baking potato, peeled and chopped
3 pounds asparagus, stems cut into pieces, tips quartered lengthwise if large
2 quarts Chicken Stock, page 299, or canned low-sodium chicken broth
½ cup fresh flat-leaf parsley leaves
2½ teaspoons salt
¼ teaspoon fresh-ground black pepper
    Cooking oil, for frying
¾ cup crème fraîche or sour cream

1. In a large pot, heat the olive oil over moderately low heat. Add the chopped leeks and cook, stirring occasionally, for 3 minutes. Add the potato and asparagus stems and cook, stirring occasionally, for 3 minutes.

2. Add the stock and bring to a boil. Reduce the heat and simmer until the vegetables are soft, about 20 minutes. Add the parsley, salt and pepper and cook for 1 minute.

3. In a blender or food processor, puree the soup and then strain into a large pot. Press the vegetables firmly with a spoon to get all the puree.

4. In a medium pan of boiling, salted water, cook the asparagus tips for 2 minutes. Drain. Rinse with cold water and drain thoroughly. ➤

5. In a small saucepan, heat ½ inch of cooking oil until very hot, about 350°. Add half of the leek strips to the oil and fry until they are tinged with brown, about 1 minute. Remove with a slotted spoon and drain on paper towels. Repeat with the remaining leek strips.

6. Bring the soup to a simmer over moderate heat, stirring occasionally. Add the asparagus tips. Bring back to a simmer. Ladle into bowls and serve topped with the crème fraîche and fried leeks.

—Charles Palmer
Aureole

BOILING AND BAKING POTATOES

In supermarkets, potatoes are labeled as boiling, baking or all-purpose. **Boiling potatoes**, sometimes called round potatoes, are what we've called for in most of our recipes. They're lower in starch than bakers and have a thin red or brown skin and a waxy texture after cooking. They're dense and hold their shape well through boiling or simmering. Hence they're perfect for soups and stews. New potatoes are young boiling potatoes that have not yet converted all their sugar into starch and are therefore slightly sweeter than their larger relatives. **Baking potatoes**, also known as russet or Idaho, are oval rather than round and have a thicker, rougher skin than boiling potatoes. They have a high starch content and are fluffy once cooked. They're ideal for baking, mashing and frying. When cooked in liquid they tend to fall apart. We use them in pureed soups, such as the one on this page. We want them to fall apart in this case, and boiling potatoes often turn to glue when pureed. **All-purpose potatoes** are between the other two. They're either round or oval with a thin skin and are really better for boiling than baking.

Mushroom Barley Soup

Lots of mushrooms give this vegetarian soup a hearty, meaty flavor, and chewy barley adds to the effect.

SERVES 6

2   quarts Vegetable Stock, page 303, or water

1   ounce dried porcini mushrooms

2   pounds white mushrooms, 1 pound whole, 1 pound cut into thin slices

2   onions, quartered

2   ribs celery, cut into thirds

2   tablespoons olive oil

2   cups water

⅔   cup barley

1   teaspoon dried marjoram

2½   teaspoons salt

½   teaspoon fresh-ground black pepper

2   tablespoons chopped fresh chives, parsley or chervil

WINE RECOMMENDATION: PAIR THIS HEARTY SOUP WITH A FAIRLY RUSTIC ITALIAN RED WINE. TRY A FIVE-YEAR-OLD AGLIANICO DEL VULTURE OR SALICE SALENTINO, BOTH FROM SOUTHERN ITALY.

1. Bring 2 cups of the stock to a boil. Put the porcini in a bowl and pour the boiling stock over them. Soak until softened, about 20 minutes. Remove the porcini and strain their liquid through a sieve lined with a paper towel into a bowl. Rinse the porcini well to remove any remaining grit and chop them.

2. In a food processor, chop the whole mushrooms fine. Remove. Add the onions and celery and chop fine. In a large pot, heat the oil over moderate heat. Add the chopped vegetables and cook, stirring occasionally, until the liquid has evaporated and the vegetables have browned, about 15 minutes.

3. Add the remaining 6 cups stock to the pot, scraping the bottom to dislodge any brown bits. Stir in the porcini and soaking liquid, the sliced mushrooms, water, barley, marjoram and salt. Bring to a boil. Reduce the heat and simmer until the barley is done, about 1 hour. Stir in the pepper. If the soup thickens too much on standing, add more water. Serve sprinkled with the fresh herbs.

Creamy Grilled-Portobello-Mushroom Soup

Grilled mushrooms make classic cream of mushroom soup better than ever. It's a perfect first course for a dinner party, in which case it will serve eight. In winter you can broil rather than grill the mushrooms.

SERVES 6

2   pounds portobello mushrooms
     Oil, for brushing the grill
4   tablespoons butter
4   shallots, chopped
1   cup dry white wine
¼   cup flour
1½ quarts Chicken Stock, page 299, or canned low-sodium chicken broth
½   teaspoon dried rosemary, crumbled
1½ teaspoons salt
2   cups heavy or light cream
¼   cup chopped fresh parsley
¼   teaspoon fresh-ground black pepper

1. Trim the mushrooms. Cut the stems from the caps and chop the stems.

2. Light the grill. When hot, oil it and cook the mushroom caps 3 to 6 inches above the coals, turning occasionally, until done, 10 to 15 minutes. Or you can broil the mushrooms. Cut the mushrooms into thin slices and cut each of the slices in half.

3. In a large pot, heat the butter over moderate heat. Add the chopped mushroom stems and the shallots. Cook, stirring occasionally, until the vegetables are golden, about 10 minutes.

4. Add the wine and cook until almost evaporated. Add the flour and cook, stirring, for 2 minutes. Stir in the stock, rosemary and salt. Bring to a boil,

reduce the heat and simmer, stirring occasionally, for 10 minutes. Pour the soup into a food processor and process until almost, but not completely, smooth. Return the soup to the pot. Stir in the cream and bring the soup just to a simmer.

5. Stir the grilled and sliced portobello mushrooms, 3 tablespoons of the chopped parsley and the black pepper into the soup and heat through. Sprinkle each serving with some of the remaining chopped parsley.

WILD-MUSHROOM RUNDOWN

You can mix and match the mushrooms for this soup and, in fact, for most dishes that call for wild mushrooms. Among those you're most likely to see in stores are chanterelles, morels, oyster mushrooms, portobellos and shiitakes. Porcini (also known as cèpes and boletes) are more difficult to find. The best way to store mushrooms is in a shallow container in the refrigerator. If they're moist, put a paper towel between layers and on top. If on the dry side, cover with a damp paper towel. Don't store them in a plastic bag; they'll quickly rot in the trapped moisture.

◆ CHANTERELLES are trumpet-shaped with a color that ranges from golden yellow to orange. The flavor varies, too, from delicate to nutty or meaty.

◆ MORELS have a cone-shaped, spongy, honeycombed cap that averages two to four inches in length and can be off-white, yellow or dark brown. The darker the color, the more intense the earthy, nutty flavor.

◆ OYSTER MUSHROOMS grow in clusters and have light-gray, fan-shaped caps. Their flavor is mild.

◆ PORCINI are large, with round, brown caps averaging about six inches in diameter. Instead of gills, they have a spongy area under the cap. The bulbous stem is lighter in color than the cap. An especially meaty texture is their hallmark.

◆ PORTOBELLOS are related to the common white mushroom and the similar cremini. They have a large cap resembling an umbrella and usually range between four and eight inches in size.

◆ SHIITAKES, originally from Japan and Korea, are now cultivated in this country. They have gold or brown umbrella-shaped caps, usually two to three inches across. The cooked mushrooms are meaty in flavor and soft in texture.

Celeriac and Roasted-Garlic Soup with Scallion Oil and Grilled Scallops

A talented chef brings together a group of unlikely partners that work beautifully together. Celeriac (celery root) and roasted garlic make an earthy, flavorful soup that gets the glamour treatment with a drizzle of emerald-green scallion oil and a skewer of grilled scallops. Though the soup is wonderful even without the shellfish, the celery-root and scallop combination is nothing short of inspired.

SERVES 6

6   heads garlic
¾   cup plus 1 tablespoon olive oil
1¾   teaspoons salt
      Fresh-ground black pepper
1   bunch scallions, green tops only, chopped
½   teaspoon sugar
3   onions, chopped
2½   pounds celeriac, about 1 large, peeled and cut into 1-inch pieces
2   quarts Chicken Stock, page 299, or canned low-sodium chicken broth
3   ounces bay scallops or quartered sea scallops

 MAKE IT AHEAD

Prepare the soup and scallion oil whenever you like. The soup even freezes well. But wait to grill or broil the scallops until shortly before serving.

WINE RECOMMENDATION: THE SOPHISTICATED FLAVORS OF THIS DISH SHOULDN'T BE OVERWHELMED BY A WINE; SO LOOK FOR A LIGHT BUT ELEGANT WHITE WINE—POSSIBLY ONE OF THE NEW WHITES FROM SPAIN BASED ON THE ALVARIÑO GRAPE.

1. Soak 6 wooden skewers in water for ½ hour. Heat the oven to 400°. Cut off the top third of each head of garlic and save it for another use. Rub the cut heads of garlic with 2 tablespoons of the olive oil and sprinkle with ¼ teaspoon of the salt and ¼ teaspoon pepper. Wrap them all together in aluminum foil. Roast in the oven until the garlic is soft, about 45 minutes. When the garlic is cool enough to handle, scoop out the flesh with a small knife.

2. Bring a pot of salted water to a boil and add the scallions. Return just to a boil and drain. Rinse with cold water and drain thoroughly. In a food processor, puree the scallions with the sugar, ⅛

teaspoon of the salt and a pinch of pepper. With the machine running, add ½ cup of the oil in a thin stream.

3. In a large saucepan, heat 2 tablespoons of the oil over moderately low heat. Add the onions and cook, stirring occasionally, until translucent, about 5 minutes. Add the celeriac and cook, stirring occasionally, for 10 minutes. Stir in the roasted garlic, stock, 1¼ teaspoons of the salt and ¼ teaspoon pepper. Bring to a boil, reduce the heat and simmer, partially covered, until the celeriac is soft, about 45 minutes. In a food processor or blender, puree the soup and then strain into a large pot. Bring to a

simmer over moderate heat, stirring occasionally.

4. Light the grill or heat the broiler. Thread the scallops on the skewers, brush with the remaining tablespoon oil and sprinkle with the remaining ⅛ teaspoon salt and a pinch of pepper. Grill or broil the scallops, turning once, until just done, about 3 minutes.

5. Ladle the soup into bowls. Drizzle each serving with the scallion oil and serve with a scallop skewer on the edge of each bowl.

—Ming Tsai
Ginger Club

CELERIAC

Also called celery root, this knobby beige tuber has a dense white interior and a flavor that's like celery with a hint of pepper. The tough outer skin must be removed before cooking. Cut the celery root in a few chunks and then use a small paring knife to cut away the peel. Depending on the maturity of the vegetable, there may be a woody layer beneath the peel that you should also remove with a small knife. If you're not using the celeriac immediately, keep it in a bowl of acidulated water so that it doesn't discolor. Just squeeze half a lemon into the bowl or stir in a tablespoon or two of vinegar. Drain before using.

Celeriac Soup

Mellow and smooth, this classic French soup is elegant enough to serve to any guest. If you have it as a first course, this quantity will serve eight to ten.

SERVES 6

2   tablespoons butter
1   onion, chopped
2   quarts Chicken Stock, page 299, or canned low-sodium chicken broth
3   pounds celeriac, about 1 large, peeled and cut into 1-inch pieces
1   pound baking potatoes (about 2), peeled and cut into 1-inch pieces
1½   teaspoons salt
1   cup heavy cream
¼   teaspoon fresh-ground black pepper
¼   cup chopped fresh parsley
      Herb Croutons, page 306, optional

WINE RECOMMENDATION: THE SMOOTH, MELLOW TASTES OF THE CELERY ROOT AND POTATOES GO WITH A RANGE OF SIMPLE, REFRESHING WHITE WINES. TRY A CHARDONNAY FROM EITHER THE MÂCON OR BURGUNDY REGIONS IN FRANCE.

1. In a large pot, melt the butter over moderately low heat. Add the onion and cook, stirring occasionally, until translucent, about 5 minutes.

2. Add the stock, celeriac, potatoes and salt. Bring to a boil, reduce the heat and simmer, partially covered, until the vegetables are soft, about 55 minutes.

3. In a food processor or blender, puree the soup until smooth and return to the pot. Bring to a boil over high heat. Reduce to a simmer and stir in the cream and pepper. Continue cooking until heated through. Stir in the parsley. Serve topped with the croutons, if you like.

—Jan Newberry

French Onion Soup

The distinctive flavor of this longtime favorite comes from the caramelized onions. Let them get really brown and be sure to scrape the bottom of the pan after adding the wine to loosen all the flavorful bits. A little cognac is generally added shortly before the soup is done. If you don't have any around, bourbon or Canadian whiskey will make a fine, albeit untraditional, substitute.

SERVES 6

2   tablespoons butter
3   tablespoons cooking oil
2   pounds onions, about 4, cut into thin slices
2½ teaspoons salt
3   tablespoons flour
½   cup red wine
2   quarts Beef Stock, page 302, or canned low-sodium beef broth
½   teaspoon dried thyme
¼   cup cognac or other brandy
½   teaspoon fresh-ground black pepper
6   ½-inch-thick slices from a large loaf of French bread
½   pound Gruyère cheese, cut into very thin slices

WINE RECOMMENDATION: A PERFECT COMBINATION WITH THIS FRENCH CLASSIC WOULD BE A YOUNG BEAUJOLAIS-VILLAGES. THE FRUIT AND CHARM OF THAT RED WINE COMPLEMENT THE STRAIGHTFORWARD APPEAL OF THE ONIONS, BREAD AND CHEESE.

1. In a large pot, melt the butter with 2 tablespoons of the oil over low heat. Add the onions and ¼ teaspoon salt. Cover and cook, stirring occasionally, until the onions are very soft, about 20 minutes. Raise the heat to moderate and cook, stirring, until the onions are a rich brown, about 10 minutes. Be careful that the onions don't burn. Add the flour and cook, stirring, 2 minutes.

2. Add the wine and scrape the bottom of the pot to dislodge any brown bits. Add the stock, thyme and remaining 2¼ teaspoons salt. Bring to a boil. Reduce the heat and simmer, partially covered, 40 minutes. Add the cognac and pepper to the soup.

3. Meanwhile, trim the slices of bread to fit into the bowls. Heat the broiler. Put the bread on a baking sheet and

brush both sides with the remaining 1 tablespoon oil. Broil on both sides until golden brown.

4. Heat the oven to 375°. Put 6 ovenproof bowls on a baking sheet. Divide the soup among the bowls. Float the toasted bread on the soup and top it with the cheese. Bake the soup until the cheese is bubbling and golden brown, about 25 minutes. If you don't have any ovenproof bowls, bake the cheese-topped toast by itself and then set it on top of the soup.

Garlicky Roasted-Eggplant and Red-Pepper Soup with Chèvre

If you love eggplant, this is the soup for you. In fact, even people who aren't crazy about eggplant like it this way. Sweet red pepper mellows any hint of bitterness, and tangy cheese is an ideal complement.

SERVES 6

3	pounds eggplants (about 2 large)
1	red bell pepper
3	tablespoons olive oil
2	onions, chopped
6	cloves garlic, minced
7	cups Chicken Stock, page 299, or canned low-sodium chicken broth
1½	teaspoons fresh thyme, or ½ teaspoon dried
2½	teaspoons salt
¼	teaspoon fresh-ground black pepper
2	tablespoons chopped fresh basil
3	ounces fresh goat cheese, such as Montrachet, cut into 6 slices

WINE RECOMMENDATION:
A CRISP AND AGGRESSIVE YOUNG SAUVIGNON BLANC FROM CALIFORNIA OR NEW ZEALAND IS AN IDEAL MATE FOR THE EGGPLANT AND TANGY GOAT CHEESE IN THIS SOUP.

1. Heat the oven to 425°. Oil a baking sheet. Cut the eggplants in half lengthwise. With a sharp knife, cut 5 slashes, about ½ inch deep, on the cut side of each eggplant half. Arrange the eggplants, cut-side down, and the whole bell pepper on a baking sheet.

2. Roast the vegetables in the oven, turning the bell pepper occasionally, until the pepper is black on all sides and the eggplants are very soft, about 40 minutes.

3. In a medium frying pan, heat the oil over moderately low heat. Add the onions and garlic and cook, stirring occasionally, until the onions are translucent, about 5 minutes. Transfer to a food processor.

4. When the pepper is cool enough to handle, pull off the skin. Remove the

stem, seeds and ribs. Put the flesh in the food processor. Scrape the eggplants from their skin and add the flesh to the food processor. Puree until smooth.

5. Transfer the vegetable puree to a large pot. Add the stock, thyme and salt. Simmer, uncovered, 15 minutes. Stir in the black pepper. Ladle the soup into bowls, sprinkle with the basil and top with a slice of goat cheese.

SERVE IT COLD

Ravenous refrigerator raiders have discovered that some of our hot soups are just as good served cold. Asparagus and Leek Soup, page 29, is transformed into a refreshing spring soup when chilled for a few hours. When the Garlicky Roasted-Eggplant and Red-Pepper Soup with Chèvre on this page is served cold, the flavor resembles that of a Middle Eastern roasted-eggplant salad. The goat cheese won't melt into the soup but will still be a delicious addition crumbled on top. If you've prepared a hot soup and think it would be good served cold, try it. You'll have best luck with those made with little or no meat, and oil rather than butter.

Potato Soup with Ham and Scallions

Delicious, economical and quick to prepare—this hearty soup has so much going for it that it's bound to become a favorite. It's also a great way to use leftover ham.

SERVES 6

3   tablespoons butter
3   onions, chopped
4   pounds baking potatoes (about 8), peeled, quartered lengthwise and cut into ¼-inch slices
3   cups Chicken Stock, page 299, or canned low-sodium chicken broth
1½ cups water
1½ teaspoons salt
6   ounces baked ham, cut into ¼-inch dice
4   scallions including green tops, cut into thin slices
1½ cups light cream
¼   teaspoon fresh-ground black pepper
⅓   cup chopped fresh parsley

WINE RECOMMENDATION: THIS RUSTIC, CHUNKY SOUP, WITH ITS SMOKY HAM FLAVOR, WILL BE PERFECT WITH A PINOT GRIS FROM ALSACE IN FRANCE. AS AN ALTERNATIVE, TRY THE LESS RICH AND FLAVORFUL PINOT BLANC, ALSO FROM ALSACE.

1. In a large pot, melt the butter over moderately low heat. Add the onions and cook, stirring occasionally, until translucent, about 5 minutes.

2. Add the potatoes, stock, water and salt and bring to a boil. Reduce the heat and simmer, covered, until the potatoes are tender, about 20 minutes.

3. Add the ham and scallions and cook until the potatoes are very soft, about 10 minutes.

4. Add the cream, pepper and parsley and bring just to a simmer, stirring.
                                        —Annette Lantzius

Mexican Potato Soup

Both fresh and canned chile peppers are used in this recipe, each lending its distinctive flavor. The soup is spicy, but for an even hotter dish, add the seeds from the jalapeño pepper.

SERVES 6

2	tablespoons cooking oil
¼	pound chorizo, quartered lengthwise and cut into ¼-inch slices
1	onion, chopped
3	cloves garlic, minced
1	jalapeño pepper, seeds and ribs removed, minced
½	teaspoon ground cumin
½	teaspoon dried oregano
2	pounds boiling potatoes (about 6), peeled and cut into ¼-inch dice
1½	quarts Chicken Stock, page 299, or canned low-sodium chicken broth
1	4-ounce can chopped green chiles
2	teaspoons salt
¼	cup chopped fresh cilantro
½	cup sour cream, optional

WINE RECOMMENDATION:
THE SPICINESS HERE GOES WELL WITH A RICHER STYLE OF WHITE WINE, SUCH AS A CHENIN BLANC FROM CALIFORNIA. BEER IS ALSO A GOOD CHOICE.

1. In a large pot, heat the oil over moderately high heat. Add the chorizo and cook until well browned, about 3 minutes. Remove with a slotted spoon and set aside.

2. Reduce the heat to moderately low. Add the onion, garlic, jalapeño, cumin and oregano. Cook, stirring occasionally, until the onion is translucent, about 5 minutes. Stir in the potatoes, stock, canned chiles and salt. Bring to a boil, reduce the heat and simmer, partially covered, until the potatoes are very tender, about 30 minutes. Add the chorizo. Just before serving, stir in the cilantro. Serve with sour cream, if you like.

—Jan Newberry

Cauliflower and Buttermilk Soup with Dill

Buttermilk's tangy, creamy flavor sets off the earthiness of cauliflower.
If you like a soup with body, add a boiled potato before pureeing.

SERVES 6

3   tablespoons butter
1   onion, chopped
1   head cauliflower, about 1½ pounds, cored and chopped
5   cups Chicken Stock, page 299, or canned low-sodium chicken broth
2   cups buttermilk
¾   teaspoon salt
¼   teaspoon fresh-ground black pepper
2   tablespoons chopped fresh dill, plus dill sprigs for garnish
     Oven-Baked Croutons, page 306, optional

WINE RECOMMENDATION:
THE TANGINESS OF THE BUTTERMILK AND THE PRONOUNCED FLAVOR OF THE DILL WORK BEST WITH AN AGGRESSIVELY FLAVORED SAUVIGNON BLANC. IF YOU CAN, GET ONE FROM NEW ZEALAND; IF NOT, TRY A CALIFORNIA VERSION.

1. In a large pot, melt 2 tablespoons of the butter over moderately low heat. Add the onion and cook, stirring occasionally, until translucent, about 5 minutes. Add the cauliflower and cook, stirring occasionally, about 5 minutes.

2. Add the stock, buttermilk and salt and bring to a simmer. Simmer, partially covered, until the cauliflower is very tender, about 30 minutes.

3. In a food processor or blender, puree the soup until smooth. Reheat if necessary and stir in the pepper, chopped dill and the remaining 1 tablespoon butter. Garnish with the dill sprigs. Serve topped with the croutons, if you like.

—Charles Pierce

Creamy Carrot Soup

Simple and straightforward, this typical French pureed-vegetable soup can be made several days before serving. The choice of water over stock lets the carrot flavor come through loud and clear.

SERVES 6

4	tablespoons butter
½	pound carrots, sliced
2	ribs celery, chopped
2	onions, sliced
1	pound boiling potatoes (about 3), peeled and sliced
1½	quarts water
2½	teaspoons salt
1	cup heavy cream or milk
½	teaspoon fresh-ground black pepper
	Croutons, page 306, optional

 WINE RECOMMENDATION: THIS SWEET AND CREAMY SOUP IS GOOD WITH A PINOT BLANC FROM ALSACE IN FRANCE.

1. In a large pot, melt the butter over low heat. Add the carrots, celery and onions. Cover and cook, stirring occasionally, until the vegetables are soft, about 20 minutes. Add the potatoes, water and salt. Cover and bring to a boil. Reduce the heat and simmer, uncovered, until the potatoes are very tender, about 30 minutes.

2. In a blender or food processor, puree the soup. Return it to the pot. Stir in the cream and pepper and bring to a simmer. Serve the soup topped with the croutons, if you like.

—Jane Sigal

Cream of Spinach Soup

You can make this classic soup with virtually any green vegetable; broccoli and asparagus work particularly well. Simply adjust the cooking time depending on the vegetable you choose.

SERVES 6

6   tablespoons butter
2   onions, chopped
1   rib celery, chopped
½   cup flour
1   quart Chicken Stock, page 299, or canned low-sodium chicken broth
1   quart milk
2   teaspoons salt
2   pounds spinach, stems removed, leaves washed
½   teaspoon fresh-ground black pepper

WINE RECOMMENDATION:
THE CREAMINESS OF THIS SOUP IS WELL SUITED TO A LIGHT, CRISP, REFRESHING WHITE, SUCH AS THE NEW STYLE OF UGNI BLANC-BASED WINES BEING PRODUCED IN THE CÔTES DE GASCOGNE AND THE PROVENCE REGIONS OF FRANCE.

1. In a large pot, melt the butter over moderately low heat. Add the onions and celery and cook, stirring occasionally, until the onions are translucent, about 5 minutes. Add the flour and cook, stirring, for 2 minutes.

2. Whisk in the stock, milk and salt and bring to a boil. Reduce the heat and simmer, stirring occasionally, until thickened, about 10 minutes.

3. Stir in the spinach and simmer until the leaves wilt, about 5 minutes. Puree the soup in a blender or food processor. Return the soup to the pot. Reheat if necessary and add the pepper.

Hearty Cabbage Soup with Bacon

Full of flavor and stick-to-your-ribs goodness, this is winter soup at its best. Cooking time for the cabbage will vary according to the age of the individual head. It should be cooked through but still have some body.

SERVES 6

½ pound bacon, chopped

2 carrots, cut into ½-inch dice

2 onions, cut into thin slices

1½ pounds green cabbage, shredded

¼ cup red-wine vinegar

1½ quarts Chicken Stock, page 299, or canned low-sodium chicken broth

½ teaspoon salt

¼ teaspoon fresh-ground black pepper

2 teaspoons caraway seeds

AS YOU LIKE IT

◆ Omit the carrots if you prefer. They're here mostly to give color to a delicious but drab-looking soup.

◆ If you have access to good slab bacon, use it instead of the sliced kind. Cut it like the French do in small sticks that measure about an inch long and quarter-inch wide.

◆ You can substitute water or white wine for some of the stock.

◆ Add a couple of medium-size potatoes, peeled, cubed and boiled, to make the soup even heartier.

WINE RECOMMENDATION: The leafy richness of this soup, with its slight smokiness from the bacon, is ideally suited to a rich pinot gris from Alsace in France. Look for one with three to five years of age.

1. In a large pot, cook the bacon until crisp. Remove and drain on paper towels. Pour off all but one tablespoon of the bacon fat.

2. Add the carrots and onions and cook, stirring occasionally, until the onions are translucent, about 5 minutes. Add the cabbage and cook, stirring, until slightly wilted, about 5 minutes. Stir in the vinegar and cook an additional 3 minutes. Add the stock and salt and bring to a boil. Reduce the heat and simmer, partially covered, until the cabbage is soft but not mushy, about 20 minutes.

3. Add the pepper, caraway seeds and bacon. Simmer until the soup is warmed through, about 5 minutes.

—Charles Pierce

Butternut-Squash and Leek Soup

Perfect for autumn, this bright-orange soup looks as right for the season as it tastes. You can make it with pumpkin as well and can substitute one or two onions for the leeks if you prefer.

SERVES 6

3   pounds butternut squash (about 1 large), halved lengthwise
4   tablespoons butter
3   large leeks, white and light-green parts only, split lengthwise, cut crosswise into ½-inch pieces and washed well
6   fresh thyme sprigs, or 1 teaspoon dried
3   ounces bacon, chopped
2   quarts Chicken Stock, page 299, or canned low-sodium chicken broth
2   teaspoons salt
¼   teaspoon fresh-ground black pepper
½   cup sour cream
2   tablespoons chopped fresh chives

WINE RECOMMENDATION: THE MILD FLAVOR OF BUTTERNUT SQUASH, COMBINED WITH SMOKY BACON, IS GOOD WITH A PINOT BLANC OR PINOT GRIS FROM ALSACE IN FRANCE.

1. Heat the oven to 350°. Put the squash, cut-side down, on a baking sheet and bake until tender, about 40 minutes. Let cool slightly. Scoop out and discard the seeds. Scrape the squash from the skin.

2. In a large pot, melt the butter over low heat. Add the leeks and thyme and cook, stirring occasionally, until the leeks are soft and browned, about 40 minutes. Discard the thyme sprigs, if using.

3. Meanwhile, fry the bacon until crisp. Drain on paper towels.

4. Stir the squash, stock and salt into the leek mixture. Simmer over moderate heat for 20 minutes. In a blender or food processor, puree the soup until smooth. Pour the soup back into the pot and add the pepper. Reheat and serve topped with the sour cream, chives and bacon.

Sweet-Potato and Carrot Soup with Ginger

Crystallized ginger adds a bit of bite and just the right amount of sweetness to this smooth, slightly spicy soup. The soup thickens on standing; add more water if it becomes too thick.

SERVES 6

2	tablespoons butter
2	onions, chopped
2	pounds sweet potatoes (about 3), peeled and cut into 1-inch pieces
1	pound carrots, cut into 1-inch pieces
5	cups Chicken Stock, page 299, or canned low-sodium chicken broth
1	teaspoon salt
1¼	teaspoons ground ginger
¼	teaspoon fresh-ground black pepper
2	tablespoons finely chopped crystallized ginger

WINE RECOMMENDATION:
TRY PAIRING THE ROOT VEGETABLES AND THE GINGER WITH A FAIRLY RICH BUT NOT STRONG-FLAVORED WHITE WINE, SUCH AS A PINOT BLANC FROM ALSACE IN FRANCE.

1. In a large pot, melt the butter over moderately low heat. Add the onions and cook, stirring occasionally, until translucent, about 5 minutes. Add the sweet potatoes and carrots and cook, covered, for 5 minutes. Add the stock and salt and bring to a boil. Reduce the heat and simmer, partially covered, until the vegetables are tender, about 25 minutes.

2. In a food processor or blender, puree the soup until very smooth. Return the soup to the pot and stir in the ground ginger and pepper. Reheat the soup until very hot. If it's thicker than you like, stir in up to ¾ cup water. Sprinkle each serving of soup with the crystallized ginger.

—Charles Pierce

Pumpkin Sage Soup

Reserve this tasty soup for autumn when fresh pumpkins are abundant. Or make it with butternut squash. If you like, serve with crisp croutons to contrast with the smooth and creamy soup.

SERVES 6

4	tablespoons butter
4	onions, chopped
4	cloves garlic, chopped
6	pounds pumpkin, peeled and cut into 2-inch pieces
5	cups Chicken Stock, page 299, or canned low-sodium chicken broth
2	teaspoons salt
2	tablespoons chopped fresh sage, or 1½ teaspoons dried
3	cups light cream
¼	teaspoon fresh-ground black pepper
	Black-Pepper Croutons, page 306, optional

WINE RECOMMENDATION:
PAIR THIS CREAMY SOUP WITH A BOTTLE OF THE SOMEWHAT RICH, SLIGHTLY ACIDIC BUT NOT TOO FLAVORFUL PINOT BLANC FROM ALSACE IN FRANCE.

1. In a large pot, heat the butter over moderately low heat. Add the onion and garlic and cook, stirring occasionally, until translucent, about 5 minutes.

2. Add the pumpkin, stock, salt and dried sage, if using. Bring to a boil. Reduce the heat and simmer, covered, until the pumpkin is tender, about 30 minutes. Stir in 1 tablespoon of the fresh sage, if using, and simmer 5 minutes longer.

3. Puree the soup in a blender or food processor until smooth. Strain the puree back into the pot and add the cream. Stir in the pepper. Simmer over low heat for 5 minutes. Top with the remaining 1 tablespoon chopped fresh sage, if using, and croutons, if you like.

Creamy Rutabaga Soup

The French serve delicious, smooth pureed soups any time of year using whatever vegetables may be in season. Julia Child's recipe is a fine model on which to build any number of soups—broccoli, carrot and cauliflower, for starters. Just adjust the cooking time to suit the main ingredient. She uses rice as a thickener, and to ensure that the rice is completely smooth, she recommends using a blender rather than a food processor to puree the soup.

SERVES 6

1½   tablespoons butter
1   onion, sliced
2   ribs celery, sliced
⅓   cup rice
3   pounds rutabagas, peeled and cut into ½-inch pieces
1   quart Chicken Stock, page 299, or canned low-sodium chicken broth
3   cups water
2½   teaspoons salt
2½   cups milk
¼   teaspoon fresh-ground black pepper
½   cup sour cream
3   tablespoons chopped fresh chives

WINE RECOMMENDATION:
THE MILDNESS OF THIS SOUP ALLOWS PAIRING WITH ANY NUMBER OF WHITE WINES. TRY A YOUNG, ACIDIC AND SLIGHTLY AGGRESSIVE WHITE SUCH AS A DRY RIESLING FROM ALSACE OR A WHITE BORDEAUX FROM THE GRAVES REGION OF FRANCE.

1. In a large pot, melt the butter over moderately low heat. Add the onion and celery and cook, stirring occasionally, until the onions are soft, about 8 minutes. Stir in the rice, rutabagas, stock, water and salt. Bring to a boil. Reduce the heat and simmer, partially covered, until the rutabagas are very tender, about 1 hour.

2. In a blender, puree the soup in batches, adding a little of the milk if needed. Return the soup to the pot, stir in the remaining milk and the pepper and heat. Top each serving with a dollop of sour cream and a sprinkling of chives.

—Julia Child

Cheddar Cheese Soup

The flavor of this soup will vary depending on the sharpness and quality of the cheese you choose. We like it best made with a very sharp, aged cheddar. To ensure that the cheese melts without turning into rubbery strands, add a little of the hot soup to it first, whisk until smooth, and then pour in the rest.

SERVES 6

2	tablespoons butter
2	carrots, chopped fine
2	onions, chopped fine
2	ribs celery, chopped fine
¾	cup beer
½	cup flour
1	teaspoon salt
1	quart Vegetable or Chicken Stock, page 303 or 299, or canned low-sodium chicken broth
1	quart milk
1	pound cheddar cheese, grated
½	teaspoon fresh-ground black pepper Black-Pepper Croutons, page 306, optional

 VARIATIONS

Cheddar Cheese Soup with Fresh-Tomato Dice: Stir ½ cup diced tomatoes into the soup before serving.

Pimiento and Cheese Soup: For the flavor of Southern pimiento and cheese salad, add ½ cup diced pimientos.

WINE RECOMMENDATION: ALTHOUGH THIS SOUP GOES WITH ANY NUMBER OF RED WINES, THE DEEP FLAVORS OF THE CHEDDAR, BEER AND ONIONS ARE PERFECTLY ACCOMPANIED BY THE LUSH, SILKY FRUIT FLAVORS OF A SLIGHTLY CHILLED YOUNG MERLOT FROM CALIFORNIA OR WASHINGTON STATE. BEER IS GOOD WITH THIS, TOO.

1. In a large pot, melt the butter over low heat. Add the carrots, onions and celery. Cover and cook, stirring occasionally, until the vegetables are very soft, about 15 minutes. Increase the heat to moderate. Add the beer and simmer until almost completely evaporated, about 5 minutes. Add the flour and salt. Cook, stirring, 2 minutes.

2. Add the stock and milk slowly, whisking. Bring to a boil, reduce the heat and simmer 5 minutes. Transfer the soup to a blender and puree until smooth. Put the cheese in a large bowl. Add about a quarter of the hot soup, whisking constantly. Add the remaining soup and whisk until smooth. Return the soup to the pot. Add the pepper and reheat if necessary. Top each serving with croutons, if you like.

CHAPTER 2 · PEA & BEAN SOUPS

Curried Red-Lentil Soup

Adjust the amount of curry powder to suit your taste. We think this amount is perfect, but some curry enthusiasts might like a more intense effect. If you're in a hurry, buy a small jar of red peppers or pimientos rather than charring and peeling a fresh one.

SERVES 6

1	red bell pepper
2	tablespoons cooking oil
1	onion, chopped
1	tablespoon curry powder, or to taste
1	pound (about 2⅓ cups) red lentils
7	cups Chicken Stock, page 299, or canned low-sodium chicken broth
1½	teaspoons tomato paste
1	teaspoon salt
¼	teaspoon fresh-ground black pepper
2	tablespoons chopped fresh chives or scallion tops

WINE RECOMMENDATION:
A WHITE WINE WITH A SLIGHT TOUCH OF SWEETNESS WILL PLAY AGAINST THE SPICINESS OF THE CURRY HERE. GEWÜRZTRAMINER OR PINOT BLANC, WHICH IS LESS SWEET, ARE GOOD CHOICES. LOOK FOR ONE OF THESE FROM THE ALSACE REGION IN FRANCE AND SERVE IT VERY COLD.

1. Roast the pepper over an open flame or broil 4 inches from the heat, turning with tongs until charred all over, about 10 minutes. When the pepper is cool enough to handle, pull off the skin. Remove the stem, seeds and ribs. Cut the pepper into small dice.

2. In a medium pot, heat the oil over moderately low heat. Add the onion. Cook, stirring occasionally, until translucent, about 5 minutes. Add the curry powder and cook, stirring, until fragrant, about 30 seconds.

3. Stir in the roasted pepper, the lentils, stock and tomato paste. Bring to a boil. Reduce the heat and simmer 15 minutes. Add the salt and continue cooking until the lentils are very tender, about 15 minutes longer. ➤

4. Transfer half the soup to a food processor or blender and puree. Return the pureed soup to the pot and add the pepper. Heat and serve topped with the chives. If the soup thickens too much on standing, stir in some water.

—Charles Pierce

RED LENTILS

The bright orangey-red lentils turn ochre in color when cooked. Because they're skinless, they fall apart quickly. Though they usually need to cook about thirty minutes, start checking for doneness after ten minutes, especially if you want to serve them whole. While red lentils are sold in some supermarkets, they're more commonly found in Middle Eastern or Indian markets.

Lentil Soup

Thick with vegetables and smoky bacon, this winter favorite makes a wonderful one-dish meal. For a vegetarian version, replace the bacon with two tablespoons olive oil and use water or Vegetable Stock, page 303, instead of the chicken stock.

SERVES 6

6	slices bacon, cut crosswise into thin strips
2	onions, chopped
3	carrots, chopped
2	ribs celery, chopped
3½	cups canned tomatoes (28-ounce can), drained and chopped
1	pound (about 2⅓ cups) lentils
1	bouquet garni: 6 parsley stems, 3 sprigs fresh thyme or ½ teaspoon dried, and 2 bay leaves
2½	quarts Chicken Stock, page 299, or canned low-sodium chicken broth
1¾	teaspoons salt
½	teaspoon fresh-ground black pepper
6	tablespoons chopped fresh parsley
1	teaspoon lemon juice

WINE RECOMMENDATION:
CONTRAST THE HEARTINESS OF THE LENTILS WITH A FRUITY, SLIGHTLY CHILLED BOTTLE OF YOUNG RED WINE, SUCH AS THE GAMAY-BASED BEAUJOLAIS-VILLAGES FROM FRANCE OR A PASSETOUTGRAINS, A BLEND OF GAMAY AND PINOT NOIR FROM THE BURGUNDY REGION IN FRANCE.

1. In a large pot, cook the bacon over moderate heat until crisp. Remove. Pour off all but 2 tablespoons of the fat. Reduce the heat to moderately low. Add the onions, carrots and celery. Cook, stirring occasionally, until the onions are translucent, about 5 minutes.

2. Add the tomatoes, lentils, bouquet garni and stock and bring to a boil. Reduce the heat and simmer, partially covered, for 30 minutes. Add the salt and continue cooking until the lentils are tender, about 15 minutes longer. Discard the bouquet garni.

3. Before serving, stir in the pepper, half of the parsley and the lemon juice. Top with the bacon and the remaining 3 tablespoons parsley. If the soup thickens too much on standing, stir in some water.

Mushroom and Lentil Soup

With its earthy flavors of mushrooms and Vertes du Puy lentils, this soup is far from ordinary. We love the strong taste of these small green lentils, but regular brown ones make a milder soup that's also very good. At Terra in the Napa Valley, Chef Sone tops this soup with cubes of foie gras terrine and a drizzle of white-truffle oil. Though we recommend his garnish heartily, we've substituted sautéed mushrooms here and find they make an excellent final touch.

SERVES 6

7   tablespoons butter

3   onions, chopped

3   cloves garlic, minced

1   pound mushrooms, sliced

2   quarts Chicken Stock, page 299, or canned low-sodium chicken broth

1   quart water

¾   cup Vertes du Puy or brown lentils

2¼   teaspoons salt
     Fresh-ground black pepper

1   tablespoon chopped fresh chives or scallion tops

WINE RECOMMENDATION: THE DEEP, RICH FLAVORS OF THIS SOUP BEG FOR A WINE OF SIMILAR PROPORTIONS. LOOK FOR AN AGED (SEVEN TO TEN YEARS) BARBARESCO OR BAROLO, NEIGHBORS IN ITALY'S PIEDMONT REGION.

1. In a large pot, melt 6 tablespoons of the butter over moderately low heat. Add the onions and garlic and cook, stirring occasionally, until the onions are translucent, about 5 minutes. Raise the heat to moderate, add three-quarters of the mushrooms and cook, stirring, until brown, about 7 minutes.

2. Add the stock, water and lentils and bring to a boil. Reduce the heat and simmer, partially covered, for 30 minutes. Add 2 teaspoons of the salt and ¼ teaspoon pepper and continue cooking until the lentils are tender, about 15 minutes longer.

3. In a frying pan, melt the remaining 1 tablespoon butter over moderately high heat. Add the remaining mush-

rooms and ¼ teaspoon salt and a pinch of pepper and cook, stirring, until browned, about 5 minutes.

4. In a blender or food processor, puree half of the soup and pour it back into the pot. Heat and serve, topped with the sautéed mushrooms and the chives. If the soup thickens too much on standing, stir in more water.

—Hiro Sone
Terra

VERTES DU PUY LENTILS

Tiny, dark-green Vertes du Puy are top-of-the-line lentils that grow in the volcanic soil around Le Puy, France. Smaller than their regular brown counterparts, Vertes du Puy are renowned for their full, earthy flavor and ability to maintain their shape rather than getting mushy. Many specialty stores now carry them. As you might guess, they're not cheap, but we think they're worth it.

White-Bean Soup with Pesto

Simple white-bean soup is a perfect backdrop for swirls of zesty, emerald-green pesto. You'll be surprised how much flavor a spoonful of pesto per bowl will add to this or any bean soup.

SERVES 6

1	pound (about 2 cups) dried white beans, preferably cannellini
1	tablespoon olive oil
2	onions, chopped
3	cloves garlic, minced
2½	quarts Vegetable or Chicken Stock, page 303 or 299, or canned low-sodium chicken broth
¾	teaspoon dried rosemary, crumbled
1¾	teaspoons salt
3	carrots, chopped
4	ribs celery, chopped
1	turnip, peeled and chopped
¼	teaspoon fresh ground black pepper
½	cup Pesto alla Genovese, page 305
3	tablespoons grated Parmesan cheese

WINE RECOMMENDATION:
THIS SATISFYING SOUP WITH ITS ROOT-VEGETABLE FLAVORS IS PERFECT WITH AN ASSERTIVE YOUNG BOTTLE OF SAUVIGNON BLANC FROM SANCERRE OR A VOUVRAY SEC (BASED ON THE CHENIN BLANC GRAPE), ALSO FROM THE LOIRE VALLEY IN FRANCE.

1. Soak the beans overnight in enough cold water to cover by at least 2 inches. Drain.

2. In a large pot, heat the oil over moderately low heat. Add the onions and garlic and cook, stirring occasionally, until the onions are translucent, about 5 minutes. Add the beans, stock and rosemary. Bring to a boil, reduce the heat and simmer, partially covered, for 1 hour. Add the salt and continue cooking until the beans are tender, about 15 minutes longer. Add the carrots, celery, turnip and pepper and continue simmering until the vegetables are tender, about 10 minutes.

3. Puree 2 cups of the beans with some of the liquid in a blender or food processor. Return the puree to the soup. Top each bowl of soup with a swirl of the pesto. Sprinkle with the Parmesan. If the soup thickens too much on standing, stir in some water.

White-Bean and Sausage Soup with Sage

A hearty, satisfying soup, this can be varied to suit your taste. Try hot or smoked sausage rather than the mild Italian called for here. If you're not a sage lover, experiment with the herb, too. Rosemary, thyme and marjoram would all be good.

SERVES 6

¾ pound (about 1½ cups) dried white beans, preferably cannellini
1 pound mild Italian sausages
1 tablespoon olive oil
2 large onions, chopped
3 ribs celery, chopped
1 red bell pepper, chopped
3 cloves garlic, minced
2 quarts Chicken Stock, page 299, or canned low-sodium chicken broth
4 tablespoons chopped fresh sage, or 1 tablespoon dried
4 tablespoons chopped fresh flat-leaf parsley
2½ teaspoons salt
¼ teaspoon fresh-ground black pepper
   Garlic and Parsley Croutons, page 306, optional

WINE RECOMMENDATION:
A SIMPLE, RUSTIC RED WINE FROM THE SOUTH OF FRANCE, SUCH AS A CÔTES-DU-RHÔNE OR MINERVOIS, WILL ACCOMPANY THIS HEARTY DISH NICELY.

1. Soak the beans overnight in enough cold water to cover by at least 2 inches. Drain.

2. Prick the sausages in several places. In a large pot, heat the oil over moderately high heat. Add the sausages. Cook until well browned and cooked through, about 10 minutes. Remove the sausages. When they are cool enough to handle, cut them into ¼-inch slices and set aside.

3. Add the onions, celery, bell pepper and garlic to the pot. Cover and cook over moderately low heat, stirring occasionally, until the vegetables are soft, about 10 minutes.

4. Add the beans, stock, 2 tablespoons of the fresh sage, if using, or all of the dried sage, and 2 tablespoons of the parsley. Bring to a boil. Reduce the heat and simmer until the beans are almost tender, about 1 hour.

64

5. Add the sausages and salt to the pot and continue cooking until the beans are very tender, about 15 minutes longer. Puree about 1½ cups of the beans with some of the liquid in a blender or food processor.

6. Return the bean puree to the soup. Add the remaining 2 tablespoons fresh sage and 2 tablespoons parsley and the pepper. If the soup thickens too much on standing, stir in some water. Serve topped with the croutons, if using.

VARIETIES OF WHITE BEANS

Cannellini, white kidney, Great Northern and navy, among others, are all haricot beans—the seeds found inside fully developed string beans. While these white beans are similar in color, they differ slightly in size, shape, flavor and cooking time. **Cannellini** beans, imported from Italy, are one of the larger haricots, about half an inch long. They're kidney-shaped, have a firm skin and are especially flavorful. Cooking time ranges from one to one and a half hours. The American approximation of cannellini is the **white kidney** bean, which is slightly smaller and milder in flavor and has a tender skin. It takes about the same time to cook. **Great Northern** beans, smaller still, have a delicate flavor and usually require only about an hour to cook. **Navy** beans are the smallest of all, about a quarter-inch long, yet take longer than any of the others to cook, about two hours. One bean easily substitutes for another. Just adjust the cooking time.

Cabbage and White-Bean Soup

Garlic, rosemary and prosciutto give the popular combination of cabbage and beans a wonderful, country Italian accent. Served with crusty peasant bread and a salad, this hearty soup makes a great winter meal.

SERVES 6

½   pound (about 1 cup) dried white beans, preferably cannellini

2   quarts Chicken Stock, page 299, or canned low-sodium chicken broth

4   teaspoons chopped fresh rosemary, or 1½ teaspoons dried, crumbled

2   teaspoons chopped fresh thyme, or ¾ teaspoon dried

2   bay leaves

2   teaspoons salt

¼   cup olive oil

4   onions, chopped

4   cloves garlic, minced

¼   pound thin-sliced prosciutto, cut crosswise into 1-inch strips

1½   pounds cabbage, preferably Savoy, shredded

2   ribs celery, chopped

2   pounds tomatoes (about 4), peeled, seeded and chopped

¼   teaspoon fresh-ground black pepper

1. Soak the beans overnight in enough cold water to cover by at least 2 inches. Drain.

2. Put the beans, stock, rosemary, thyme and bay leaves in a large pot. Bring to a boil, reduce the heat and simmer, partially covered, for 1 hour. Add the salt and continue cooking until the beans are just tender, about 15 minutes longer. Discard the bay leaves. In a blender or food processor, puree 1½ cups of the beans with some of the cooking liquid and return the mixture to the pot.

3. In a large frying pan, heat the oil over moderately low heat. Add the onions, garlic and prosciutto and cook, stirring occasionally, until the onions are translucent, about 5 minutes. Raise the heat to moderately high. Add the cabbage, celery and tomatoes and cook, stirring, until the cabbage wilts, about 7 minutes.

4. Add the cooked vegetables to the beans and simmer, partially covered, until the cabbage is just tender, about 15 minutes. Stir in the pepper. If the soup thickens too much on standing, stir in some water.

—Charles Palmer
Aureole

COOKING TIMES

Dried legumes can take anywhere from thirty minutes to three hours to cook. The big range in cooking time is due primarily to the great variety among legumes. Hard water can increase cooking time substantially, as can the age of the bean. Older, dryer beans take longer to cook, though even very old beans are still good. To test beans for doneness, eat one. If it is to be served whole in a soup, the skin of the bean should be slightly chewy and the interior soft. For pureed soups, the whole bean should be soft.

Bean, Butternut-Squash and Corn Soup

Our contemporary vegetable soup is based on a traditional one made by North and South American Indians. If fresh pumpkin is available, try it in place of the squash.

SERVES 6

½ pound (about 1 cup) Great Northern beans

1 dried ancho chile or fresh jalapeño pepper

1 tablespoon cooking oil

1 onion, chopped

1 rib celery, chopped

1 green bell pepper, chopped

3 cups Chicken Stock, page 299, or canned low-sodium chicken broth

1 bay leaf

1 teaspoon dried oregano

2 pounds butternut squash (about 1), peeled and cut into 2-inch chunks

1 tomato, chopped

2 teaspoons salt

1½ cups fresh (cut from about 2 ears) or frozen corn kernels

3 scallions including green tops, chopped

¼ teaspoon fresh-ground black pepper

3 tablespoons chopped fresh cilantro

WINE RECOMMENDATION:
Look for a fresh, lively white wine to accompany the flavors of this dish. Two good choices from the Pacific Northwest are an Oregon pinot gris or a Washington State sémillon.

1. Soak the beans overnight in enough cold water to cover by at least 2 inches. Drain.

2. Soak the ancho chile in 1 cup boiling water until soft, about 20 minutes. Reserve the soaking liquid. Stem, core and seed the chile. Chop it into small pieces. If using a fresh jalapeño, remove the ribs and seeds and mince it.

3. In a large pot, heat the oil over moderate heat. Add the onion, celery and bell pepper and cook, stirring occasionally, until the vegetables are golden, about 10 minutes.

4. Add the beans, ancho chile and soaking liquid (or fresh jalapeño with ¾ cup water), stock, bay leaf and oregano. Simmer for 30 minutes. Add the squash, tomato and salt and cook until the beans are tender, about 45 minutes longer. ➤

5. Add the corn and three-quarters of the scallions and simmer until the corn is done, about 4 minutes longer. Discard the bay leaf. Stir in the black pepper. Serve topped with the remaining scallion and the cilantro.

QUICK-SOAKING METHOD FOR BEANS

If you forget to soak the beans ahead of time or are pressed for time, you can reduce the soaking time to a little over an hour. Rinse the beans, put them in a large pot and cover with cold water by about two inches. Bring to a boil and cook for two minutes. Remove from the heat, cover and soak for one hour. Drain, rinse and cook in fresh water.

SORTING THROUGH DRIED LEGUMES

It's a good idea to sort through dried legumes to remove any grit or pebbles before cooking. The prepackaged ones that you find in supermarkets are relatively clean and need only rinsing to remove any dust. But legumes sold in bulk, as in health-food stores, are not usually picked through in advance and may contain pebbles, leaves or twigs. Discard these intruders and rinse thoroughly. Pay particularly close attention to lentils and chickpeas, in which small stones can easily be camouflaged.

Black-Bean Soup with Cilantro Yogurt

A delicious change from the usual thick-and-chunky black-bean soup, this one's thinner than usual, velvety smooth and full of Southwestern flavor from jalapeño pepper, poblano chile and cumin. A tangy and refreshing topping of cilantro and yogurt is an attractive finishing touch.

SERVES 6

½   pound (about 1 cup) dried black beans
2   tablespoons olive oil
¼   pound bacon, chopped
1   red onion, chopped
1   head garlic, separated, cloves peeled
2   red bell peppers, chopped
1   poblano chile, seeds and ribs removed, chopped
1   jalapeño pepper, seeds and ribs removed, minced
1   tablespoon cumin seeds
½   teaspoon chopped fresh thyme, or ¼ teaspoon dried
2   bay leaves
7   cups Chicken Stock, page 299, or canned low-sodium chicken broth
    Salt
½   cup chopped fresh cilantro
    Fresh-ground black pepper
1   cup plain yogurt

WINE RECOMMENDATION:
A COLD BEER IS IDEAL WITH THIS COMPLEX, SPICY SOUP. YOU MIGHT ALSO TRY A YOUNG GEWÜRZTRAMINER FROM CALIFORNIA OR WASHINGTON STATE, EITHER OF WHICH SHOULD HAVE A BIT OF SWEETNESS AND BE SERVED QUITE COLD.

1. Soak the beans overnight in enough cold water to cover by at least 2 inches. Drain.

2. In a large pot, heat the oil over moderately low heat and cook the bacon until crisp. Add the onion, garlic, bell peppers, poblano, jalapeño, cumin seeds, thyme and bay leaves and cook, stirring occasionally, until the onion is translucent, about 5 minutes.

3. Add the beans and stock and bring to a boil. Reduce the heat and simmer, covered, for 1 hour. Add 2¼ teaspoons salt and simmer, covered, until the beans are very tender, about 15 minutes longer. Stir in ¼ cup of the cilantro and ¼ teaspoon black pepper.

4. In a small bowl, combine the remaining ¼ cup cilantro with the yogurt

and a pinch of salt and pepper. Chill in the refrigerator for half an hour.

5. Discard the bay leaves. Puree the soup in a blender. Then push it through a sieve. Reheat and serve topped with the cilantro yogurt.

—Scott Cohen
The Stanhope

WHAT IS HOMINY?

Mexicans use hominy a great deal in their hearty soups and stews. It's simply dried corn kernels that have been soaked in a caustic solution, usually lye, to make them swell so that they're soft and easy to hull. Hominy is always hullless. Whole hominy is readily available canned. It can be added to soups or stews and simmered anywhere from a few minutes to several hours without changing its texture. When the dried hominy kernels are ground to a gritty consistency, they become hominy grits.

TOUGH LEGUMES

Don't add salt to the cooking water of beans, lentils or chickpeas until they're nearly done, or you may wait all day for them to soften. Salt toughens the skin of legumes, making them less soluble, and this slows the tenderizing process. Therefore, the best time to add salt is about ten to fifteen minutes before the beans are done. That way the salt brings out the flavor of the beans but doesn't inhibit cooking. This is even more true when adding beans to an acidic sauce, such as tomato. Do it after the beans are cooked; don't expect them to soften noticeably after they're combined with a very acidic ingredient. The only exceptions are split peas and red lentils. Since they're skinless, salt and acid don't affect their cooking.

20-Minute
Black-Bean Soup

Spicy with hot-pepper sauce and cumin, this hearty Mexican-inspired soup is blessedly simple to put together yet absolutely delicious. Serve with a salad and either crusty bread or warm flour tortillas.

SERVES 6

5	15-ounce cans black beans, drained and rinsed
5	cups Chicken Stock, page 299, or canned low-sodium chicken broth
2	tablespoons olive oil
2	onions, minced
3	cloves garlic, minced
6	ounces smoked ham, cut into ½-inch dice
5	teaspoons ground cumin
2	16-ounce cans yellow or white hominy, drained and rinsed
1½	cups water
5	teaspoons Worcestershire sauce
1½	teaspoons Tabasco sauce
1½	teaspoons salt
¾	cup chopped fresh cilantro
¼	teaspoon fresh-ground black pepper

WINE RECOMMENDATION:
SERVE THIS STRAIGHTFORWARD DISH WITH A SLIGHTLY CHILLED YOUNG RED WINE, SUCH AS A BEAUJOLAIS-VILLAGES FROM FRANCE OR A REASONABLY PRICED RIOJA FROM SPAIN.

1. Puree half of the black beans with the stock in a blender or food processor.

2. In a large pot, heat the oil over moderately low heat. Add the onions and garlic and cook, stirring occasionally, until the onions are translucent, about 5 minutes. Add the ham and cumin and cook, stirring, for 30 seconds. Add the pureed bean and stock mixture, the remaining whole black beans, hominy, water, Worcestershire sauce, Tabasco sauce and salt. Bring to a boil, reduce the heat and simmer 10 minutes.

3. Add the cilantro and pepper and serve.

—Grace Parisi

Southwest-Style Bean Soup with Avocado Salsa

Between bean soup and chili in flavor, this hearty dish is spicy with cumin but not hot. Add more cayenne if you like.

SERVES 6

¾   pound (about 1½ cups) dried red kidney beans

⅓   pound bacon, cut crosswise into thin strips

1   onion, chopped

3   ribs celery, chopped

3   carrots, chopped

3   cloves garlic, minced

¾   teaspoon dried thyme

2½   tablespoons ground cumin

1½   teaspoons dried oregano

1½   tablespoons tomato paste

3   quarts Chicken Stock, page 299, or canned low-sodium chicken broth

1   bay leaf

1½   teaspoons salt

¾   teaspoon fresh-ground black pepper
    Pinch cayenne

½   cup sour cream

1½   cups Avocado Salsa, next page

WINE RECOMMENDATION: A YOUNG BOTTLE OF GEWÜRZTRAMINER FROM CALIFORNIA OR YOUR FAVORITE BEER WILL GO BEST WITH THE SPICY FLAVORS OF THIS SOUP.

1. Soak the beans overnight in enough cold water to cover by at least 2 inches. Drain.

2. In a large pot, cook the bacon until crisp. Add the onion, celery, carrots, garlic, thyme, cumin and oregano. Cook, stirring occasionally, until the onions are translucent, about 5 minutes.

3. Stir in the tomato paste. Add the beans, stock and bay leaf. Bring to a boil. Reduce the heat and simmer, partially covered, about 1 hour. Add the salt and simmer until the beans are very tender, about 15 minutes longer.

4. Discard the bay leaf. Add the black pepper and cayenne. Serve topped with the sour cream and salsa. If the soup thickens too much on standing, add some water.

AVOCADO SALSA

MAKES 1½ CUPS

1   onion, chopped
1   tomato, seeded and
    chopped
1½ teaspoons minced jalapeño
    pepper
¼   teaspoon salt
1   tablespoon chopped fresh
    cilantro
4   teaspoons lime juice
1   avocado, preferably Hass, cut
    into ¼-inch dice

Put all the ingredients in a medium glass or stainless-steel bowl and stir to blend.

SOAKING DRIED BEANS

Although soaking beans is not necessary, there are two reasons to do it: to replace moisture lost in drying, thereby reducing cooking time, and to leach out many of the complex sugars that cause intestinal gas. Add water to cover the beans by two inches, about three times the volume of the beans. They'll usually absorb as much water as they can in about four hours, but soaking them overnight is often recommended for convenience. Discard the soaking water, rinse the beans well and cook them in fresh water.

Black-Eyed-Pea Soup with Greens

Black-eyed peas and flavorful greens simmer together with a ham hock to make this savory soup with a Southern accent.

SERVES 6

½   pound (about 1 cup) dried black-eyed peas
2   tablespoons cooking oil
1   onion, chopped
1   green bell pepper, chopped
1½ quarts Chicken Stock, page 299, or canned low-sodium chicken broth
1   meaty smoked ham hock, about ¾ pound
1   teaspoon salt
1   pound collard, mustard or turnip greens, tough stems removed, leaves chopped
¾   pound spinach, kale or sorrel, tough stems removed, leaves chopped
¼   teaspoon fresh-ground black pepper

WINE RECOMMENDATION:
A SLIGHTLY ACIDIC WHITE WINE WITH PLENTY OF CHARACTER, SUCH AS A BONE-DRY RIESLING FROM FRANCE'S ALSACE REGION, BRINGS OUT THE BEST IN THE LEAFY-GREEN AND SMOKED-HAM FLAVORS OF THIS SOUP.

1. Soak the black-eyed peas overnight in enough cold water to cover by at least 2 inches. Drain.

2. In a large pot, heat the oil over moderately low heat. Add the onion and bell pepper. Cook, stirring occasionally, until the onion is translucent, about 5 minutes. Add the black-eyed peas, stock and ham hock. Bring to a boil. Reduce the heat, cover and simmer for 45 minutes. Add the salt and cook until the black-eyed peas are very tender, about 10 minutes longer.

3. Remove the ham hock. When the ham hock is cool enough to handle, pull the meat from the bone and cut it into small pieces. Return the meat to the soup. Discard the bone. Stir in all the greens and the black pepper and simmer, uncovered, 10 minutes. If the soup thickens on standing, stir in some water.
—Charles Pierce

Old-Fashioned Split-Pea Soup

A meaty ham bone adds smoky flavor to hearty split-pea soup. With just a crusty loaf of bread, the soup makes a satisfying meal on a cold winter's night.

SERVES 6

2	tablespoons cooking oil
2	onions, chopped
2	carrots, chopped
2	ribs celery, chopped
4	cloves garlic, minced
1	pound (about 2⅓ cups) green split peas
1	meaty smoked ham hock, about ¾ pound
1	quart Chicken Stock, page 299, or canned low-sodium chicken broth
1	quart water
1	teaspoon dried thyme
1¾	teaspoons salt
¼	teaspoon fresh-ground black pepper

WINE RECOMMENDATION:
THE FLAVOR OF THE PEAS AND HAM WILL BE ENLIVENED BY A YOUNG, FRESH WHITE WINE, SUCH AS A PINOT GRIS FROM ALSACE OR A SAUVIGNON BLANC FROM NEW ZEALAND.

1. In a large pot, heat the oil over moderate heat. Add the onions, carrots, celery and garlic and cook until the vegetables begin to brown, about 5 minutes.

2. Add the split peas, ham hock, stock, water, thyme and salt. Bring the soup to a boil. Reduce the heat and simmer, partially covered, until the peas fall apart and thicken the soup, about 1¼ hours. Add the pepper.

3. Remove the ham hock. When the ham hock is cool enough to handle, pull the meat from the bone and cut it into small pieces. Return the meat to the soup. If the soup thickens too much on standing, stir in more water.

Barley, Split-Pea, Lima-Bean and Dried-Mushroom Soup

Dried mushrooms give this low-fat vegetable soup, rich with grains, beans and peas, an almost beefy taste. Time only improves its flavor.

SERVES 6

3 quarts water
2 tablespoons dried mushrooms, such as porcini or shiitakes
2 tablespoons cooking oil
2 carrots, chopped
2 onions, cut into thin slices
2 ribs celery, chopped
½ cup barley
½ cup yellow split peas
½ cup green split peas
¾ cup dried lima beans, or 1 cup frozen lima beans
1 bouquet garni: 6 parsley stems, 3 sprigs fresh thyme or ½ teaspoon dried, and 1 bay leaf
2½ teaspoons salt
½ teaspoon fresh-ground black pepper
3 tablespoons chopped fresh parsley

WINE RECOMMENDATION:
A YOUNG, SLIGHTLY CHILLED BOTTLE OF BARBERA D'ALBA OR CHIANTI, BOTH FROM ITALY, WILL WORK WELL WITH THE EARTHY FLAVORS OF THIS SOUP.

1. Bring 1 cup of the water to a boil. Put the mushrooms in a small bowl and pour the boiling water over them. Soak until softened, about 20 minutes. Remove the mushrooms and strain their liquid through a sieve lined with a paper towel into a bowl. Rinse the mushrooms well to remove any remaining grit and chop them.

2. In a large pot, heat the oil over moderate heat. Add the carrots, onions and celery and cook, stirring occasionally, until the vegetables begin to brown, about 5 minutes.

3. Add the remaining 11 cups water, the mushrooms and soaking liquid, the barley, split peas, dried lima beans, if using, and the bouquet garni. Bring to a boil. Reduce the heat and simmer, partially covered, for 1 hour. Add the salt and continue cooking until the barley, peas and beans are tender, ½ to 1 hour

longer. If using frozen lima beans, add them 30 minutes before the end of cooking.

4. Discard the bouquet garni. Stir in the pepper. Serve the soup topped with the parsley. If the soup thickens too much on standing, stir in more water.

—Jane Sigal

SERVING SIZE

Most of the soup recipes in this book make about nine cups, or one and a half cups per person. This is the right amount for lunch or a light supper. If you're serving a soup as a first course, the same recipe will serve nine or ten. Or you can cut the recipe by one-third so that it still serves six. (Or enjoy the extra soup the next day.) For a main course at dinner, you may want to increase the quantities for some soups, or figure that the recipe serves four rather than six. The occasional recipes that seem inappropriate as anything but a first course are so marked and generally make six cups for six people.

BOUQUET GARNI

Parsley stems, thyme sprigs and a bay leaf are the constants in a traditional bouquet garni. If you use dried thyme leaves instead of sprigs, toss them into the soup or stew on their own rather than trying to get them to stay in the bouquet. Leek greens and celery tops, rosemary and citrus zest are common additions to this bundle of flavorings. Quantity as well as contents may be adjusted according to the dish. The whole thing is tied together with string so that it can be removed easily at the end of cooking. If this seems fiddly to you, wrap the herbs in cheesecloth or stuff them into a tea ball. And if a recipe includes cloves or peppercorns, add them to the cheesecloth or tea ball so that you don't have to fish them out one by one later.

CHAPTER 3 · FISH & SHELLFISH SOUPS

Creamy Crab and Shrimp Soup with Spinach

Scallions, garlic and sherry, mellowed with light cream, set the stage for fresh crabmeat and shrimp in this delightful and quick-to-prepare soup. You can also make a clear version by replacing the cream with clam juice (see next page).

SERVES 6

2¼ cups Chicken Stock, page 299, or canned low-sodium chicken broth

2½ cups bottled clam juice

¾ pound medium shrimp, shells removed and reserved, shrimp cut in half lengthwise

2 tablespoons butter

2 onions, chopped

2 scallions including green tops, chopped

2 cloves garlic, minced

1½ teaspoons salt

2 carrots, cut into ⅛-inch diagonal slices

¾ cup light cream

¾ pound lump crabmeat, picked free of shell

½ pound spinach, stems removed, leaves washed and cut into ½-inch slices
   Large pinch fresh-ground black pepper

½ teaspoon dry sherry

WINE RECOMMENDATION:
PAIR THE FLAVORS OF JUST-COOKED SPINACH AND SLIGHTLY SWEET CRAB WITH THE GRASSY QUALITIES OF A CALIFORNIA OR NEW ZEALAND SAUVIGNON BLANC.

1. In a medium saucepan, combine the stock, clam juice and reserved shrimp shells and bring to a boil over high heat. Reduce the heat and simmer, covered, for 10 minutes. Strain and press the shells firmly to get all the liquid.

2. In a large pot, melt the butter over moderately low heat. Add the onions, scallions and garlic and cook, stirring occasionally, until the onions are translucent, about 5 minutes.

3. Add the reserved stock mixture and the salt and bring to a boil. Add the carrots, reduce the heat and simmer until the carrots are almost tender, about 4 minutes.

4. Add the cream and return to a simmer. Add the shrimp and simmer until almost cooked through, about 2

minutes. Add the crab, spinach and pepper and simmer until heated through, about 1 minute. Do not cook longer or the shrimp will overcook. Stir in the sherry and serve.

 ## AHEAD OF TIME

Overcooking shrimp to the rubbery state is all too easy. For that reason, we don't recommend completing this soup ahead of time. But you can make the recipe up to the point of adding the shrimp. Then finishing up will just take two or three minutes.

 ## VARIATION

For a brothy, garlicky soup rather than a creamy one, use bottled clam juice in place of the light cream, omit the sherry and reduce the salt to 1 teaspoon. Make Rouille, page 304. Stir 2 tablespoons of the rouille into the soup. Serve topped with Rustic Croûtes, page 309, spread with the remaining rouille.

She-Crab Soup

Creamy seafood broth studded with chunks of crabmeat, rounded out with sherry and a touch of paprika, make this traditional specialty from South Carolina and Georgia both refined and satisfying. Originally this soup was prepared with the meat and roe from female blue crabs. If you're able to get them and prefer cooking them yourself, you'll need eight or nine large crabs to get a pound and a half of meat and roe. Since the crabs can be hard to find, we offer a recipe using lump crabmeat. Our version is as quick and easy as it is delicious.

SERVES 6

2   hard-cooked eggs, optional
3   tablespoons butter
1   scallion including green top, minced
1   rib celery, minced
2   tablespoons flour
2   cups Fish Stock, page 303, or bottled clam juice
2   cups milk
2   cups heavy cream
1½   pounds lump crabmeat, picked free of shell
¼   cup dry sherry
1½   teaspoons salt
¼   teaspoon fresh-ground black pepper
½   teaspoon paprika
6   thin slices lemon

WINE RECOMMENDATION: THIS CREAMY SOUP IS PERFECTLY CONTRASTED WITH THE DRY, SLIGHTLY NUTTY TASTE OF A FINO OR MANZANILLA SHERRY FROM SPAIN. AN ALTERNATIVE IS A RICH CHARDONNAY, SUCH AS A MEURSAULT FROM FRANCE'S BURGUNDY REGION.

1. If using the eggs, separate the yolks from the whites and save the whites for another use. Press the yolks through a sieve and reserve.

2. In a large pot, melt the butter over moderately low heat. Add the scallion and celery and cook, stirring occasionally, until the vegetables are soft, about 4 minutes. Add the flour and cook, stirring, for 2 minutes. Stir in the stock, milk and cream. Bring to a simmer, stirring.

3. Add the sieved egg yolks, if using, the crabmeat, sherry, salt and pepper and bring almost to a simmer. Ladle into bowls and top each serving with a pinch of paprika and a lemon slice.

Lobster Bisque

French chefs not only learn to find a good use for every last bit of their ingredients, they even know how to make a luxury out of kitchen scraps. Lobster bisque, made from the usually discarded body section, is a delicious case in point.

SERVES 6

8	raw lobster bodies (without tails or large front legs with claws)
2	tablespoons cooking oil
2	onions, chopped
2	carrots, chopped
2	ribs celery, chopped
½	cup flour
½	cup cognac or other brandy
1½	quarts Chicken Stock, page 299, or canned low-sodium chicken broth
1	cup dry white wine
2	tablespoons tomato paste
½	teaspoon salt
3	sprigs fresh parsley
1	bay leaf
½	cup heavy cream
	Pinch cayenne

WINE RECOMMENDATION: THE LOBSTER FLAVOR AND CREAMY TEXTURE HERE ARE DELIGHTFUL WITH TWO VERY DIFFERENT WINES. TRY A RICH, PREFERABLY NOT-TOO-OAKY CHARDONNAY FROM CALIFORNIA OR A FINO OR MANZANILLA SHERRY FROM SPAIN.

1. With a pair of sharp kitchen scissors, start at the tail end and snip through the shell of the lobster body, top and bottom, leaving about 1 inch attached. The inch of shell is a safety margin so that you don't cut into the stomach sack at the head of the lobster. Pull apart the two halves of the lobster. You'll see a small sack on one side of the shell near the head. This is the stomach sack. Pull it out and discard. Snip or chop the bodies and legs into 1- to 2-inch pieces. Save any liquid that comes out of the lobster. Put the cut-up lobster, with its innards, in a bowl and repeat with the remaining bodies.

2. In a large pot, heat the oil over moderately high heat. Add the lobster pieces and cook until red, about 5 minutes. Add the vegetables and cook 5 minutes longer. Sprinkle the flour over the lobsters and vegetables and cook, stirring, 2 minutes. Pour in the cognac

and simmer 1 minute. If you like, you can turn off the heat and pound the lobster shells with the end of a French rolling pin, or a wine bottle, to extract as much of their flavor as possible.

3. Stir in the stock, wine, tomato paste, salt, parsley and bay leaf. Bring to

a simmer. Cover and cook, about 15 minutes. Strain the bisque into a large pot in batches, pressing the shells and vegetables firmly to get as much of the liquid as possible.

4. Stir the cream and cayenne into the bisque. Reheat.

LOBSTER BODIES

Every cook has a different method for making lobster bisque. The braver chef lops the tails and large front legs with claws off live lobsters and uses the bodies for the soup. Others use leftover cooked bodies. To taste the difference ourselves, we tested lobster bisque two ways. First, we used cooked lobster bodies, basically the leftovers you'd have after serving steamed lobsters for dinner. We thought this was a great way to get something for nothing. The soup was good. Then we used raw lobster bodies. Prepared exactly the same way as the first, this bisque was exceptional; its full, fresh flavor was a significant improvement. Unfortunately, fresh, raw lobster bodies without their appendages can be difficult to find. Here are a couple of suggestions:

◆ If you don't want to cut up a live lobster, you can ask your fish market to separate the tails and claws from the bodies for you. Use the bodies for bisque. Steam the meat and reserve some to garnish the soup. Save the rest to make a great salad, pasta or stir-fried dish.

◆ Most fish stores sell cooked lobster meat. Some cook the lobsters whole while others just cook the tails and claws to save space in the pot. Call a few fish stores to find one that will set a few raw lobster bodies aside for you. You may even get them for free.

Billi-Bi

An essence of mussels enriched with cream, billi-bi is a simple and elegant dish that resembles oyster stew. The French favorite is named for a customer at Maxim's in Paris who first requested it back in the 1920s. As the story goes, he wanted mussel soup without the mussels. So the mussels were strained out. We like them in the soup. You can follow tradition if you like, though, and then serve the mussels cold, dressed with vinaigrette, the next day. The egg yolks whisked in at the last minute add a velvety smoothness, but billi-bi is very good without them.

SERVES 6

1½ cups dry white wine
2 cups Fish Stock, page 303, or 1 cup bottled clam juice and 1 cup water
1 onion, chopped
2 ribs celery, minced
½ pound mushrooms, minced
1 bay leaf
4 pounds small mussels, scrubbed and debearded
3 cups heavy cream
   Pinch fresh-ground black pepper
¼ teaspoon salt, if needed
¼ cup chopped fresh parsley
2 egg yolks

WINE RECOMMENDATION: THIS RICH DISH WILL BENEFIT FROM A FRESH WHITE WINE WITH PLENTY OF ACIDITY, SUCH AS A MUSCADET FROM FRANCE.

1. In a large pot, combine the wine, stock, onion, celery, mushrooms and bay leaf. Bring to a boil over moderately high heat and continue boiling until reduced to 4 cups, about 10 minutes.

2. Discard any mussels that have broken shells or that do not clamp shut when tapped. Add the mussels to the pot. Cover, raise the heat to high and bring to a boil. Cook, shaking the pot occasionally, just until the mussels begin to open, about 3 minutes. Remove the open mussels. Continue to cook, uncovering the pot as necessary to remove the mussels as soon as their shells open. Discard any that do not open. When cool enough to handle, remove the mussels from their shells, holding them over the pot to catch all the juices.

3. Pour the cooking liquid through a sieve lined with a paper towel into a

medium saucepan. Add the cream and pepper and bring just to a simmer over moderate heat, stirring occasionally. Taste and add the salt if necessary. Add the mussels and 3 tablespoons of the parsley. Return to a simmer, stirring, and immediately remove from the heat so that the mussels won't toughen.

4. In a small bowl, whisk the egg yolks until combined and then whisk in 1 cup of the hot soup in a thin stream. Pour back into the soup, whisking constantly. Return to moderate heat and cook, whisking, until the soup thickens slightly. Do not boil, or it will curdle. Serve sprinkled with the remaining tablespoon of parsley.

AHEAD OF TIME

You can prepare this soup in advance, up to the point where you add the cooked mussels to the broth and cream mixture. To serve, reheat the soup, add the mussels and parsley and continue with the egg-yolk enrichment.

Tuscan Mussel Soup with White Beans and Garlic

A wonderful country soup from Tuscany, this is a happy blend of briny mussels, plump white beans, flavorful tomatoes and plenty of garlic. With a tossed green salad and crusty bread, this *zuppa* makes an ideal supper. As a main course, the recipe serves four rather than six.

SERVES 6

¾   cup dried white beans, preferably cannellini

1   onion, cut in half

2   carrots, cut in half

1   bay leaf

2   quarts water

¼ to ¾ teaspoon salt

3   pounds small mussels, scrubbed and debearded

2   tablespoons olive oil

2   tablespoons butter

4   cloves garlic, minced

2   cups dry white wine
    Large pinch dried red-pepper flakes

3   pounds tomatoes (about 6), peeled, seeded and cut into ¼-inch dice

2   tablespoons chopped fresh flat-leaf parsley

¼   teaspoon fresh-ground black pepper
    One-Inch Croutons, page 306

WINE RECOMMENDATION: SERVE THIS TUSCAN SOUP WITH A BASIC WHITE WINE FROM THE SAME REGION IN ITALY. TRY A YOUNG BOTTLE OF GALESTRO OR VERNACCIA DI SAN GIMIGNANO. BOTH OFFER CRISP, QUAFFABLE REFRESHMENT—PERFECT FOR THE HEARTY FLAVORS OF THE SOUP.

1. Soak the beans overnight in enough cold water to cover by at least 2 inches. Drain.

2. In a medium saucepan, combine the beans with the onion, carrots, bay leaf and water. Bring to a boil, reduce the heat and simmer, partially covered, for 1 hour. Add ¼ teaspoon of the salt and continue cooking until the beans are tender, about 15 minutes longer. Drain, reserving the liquid. Discard the onion, carrots and bay leaf.

3. Discard any mussels that have broken shells or that don't clamp shut when tapped. In a large pot, heat the oil and the butter over moderately low heat. Add the garlic and cook until soft but not brown, about 2 minutes. Add the wine, mussels and red-pepper flakes. Cover,

raise the heat to high and bring to a boil. Cook, shaking the pot occasionally, just until the mussels begin to open, about 3 minutes. Remove the open mussels and continue to cook, uncovering the pot as necessary to remove the mussels as soon as their shells open. Discard any mussels that do not open. When the mussels are cool enough to handle, remove them from their shells, holding them over the pot to catch all the juices.

4. Pour the cooking liquid through a sieve lined with a paper towel into a large measuring cup. Add enough of the bean liquid to make 4½ cups in all. Put the liquid in a large pot. Add the beans, tomatoes, parsley and black pepper. Taste for salt and, if necessary, add ¼ to ½ teaspoon salt.

5. Bring to a boil over moderately high heat and add the mussels. Return just to a simmer and remove from the heat immediately so that the mussels don't toughen. Top with the croutons.

—Paul Bartolotta
Spiaggia

Corn and Shrimp Chowder

An outstanding example of all-American chowder, this version is popular at Tribeca Grill in New York City. Chef Pintabona makes it with rock shrimp. Use them if you can find them easily, but medium shrimp work perfectly, too.

SERVES 6

1   tablespoon cooking oil
1   carrot, chopped
7   ribs celery, chopped
2   medium onions, chopped
1½   pounds medium shrimp, shells removed and reserved
3   cups water
¼   pound bacon, chopped
3   cups dry white wine
¼   cup flour
2¼   cups bottled clam juice
1½   teaspoons salt
2½   cups fresh (cut from about 4 ears) or frozen corn kernels
1½   cups heavy cream
¼   teaspoon fresh-ground black pepper

WINE RECOMMENDATION:
ANY NUMBER OF SIMPLE WHITES WOULD DO HERE, BUT CORN SEEMS TO CALL FOR AN AMERICAN WINE. TRY A YOUNG BOTTLE OF EITHER RIESLING OR CHENIN BLANC FROM WASHINGTON STATE.

1. In a medium pot, heat the oil over moderately low heat. Add the carrot, ¾ cup of the celery and ½ cup of the onions. Cook, stirring occasionally, until the onions are translucent, about 5 minutes. Add the shrimp shells and cook, stirring, until pink. Stir in the water and bring to a boil. Reduce the heat and simmer until the liquid is reduced to 2¼ cups, about 10 minutes. Strain the shrimp stock into a small bowl. Press the vegetables and shrimp shells firmly to get all the liquid.

2. In a large pot, cook the bacon over moderate heat until crisp. Remove the bacon with a slotted spoon and reserve. Reduce the heat to moderately low and add the remaining celery and onions. Cook, stirring occasionally, until the onions are translucent, about 5 minutes. Add the wine. Raise the heat to moderate and boil until the wine almost evaporates, about 10 minutes. ➤

3. Stir in the flour and cook, stirring, about 3 minutes. Whisk in the shrimp stock, clam juice and salt. Bring the mixture back to a boil, whisking, then reduce the heat and simmer, stirring occasionally, for about 5 minutes.

4. Puree the shrimp-stock mixture in a blender or food processor with half the shrimp and half the corn.

5. Return the soup to the pot. Bring back to a boil and add the remaining corn. Cook 2 minutes, then stir in the remaining shrimp. Cook until the shrimp are pink and the corn is tender, about 3 minutes longer. Stir in the cream and pepper and heat. Serve topped with the reserved bacon.

—Don Pintabona
Tribeca Grill

 ## THERE'S FLAVOR IN THEM THAR SHELLS

For the tastiest shrimp, cook them in their shells. Not only do the shrimp stay more moist, but they absorb much of the good flavor that's in the shell. When a dish such as the one on this page calls for peeled shrimp, you can still take advantage of those flavorful shells by using them to enhance the broth. Add the shells to the cooking liquid and strain them out before serving.

 ## MILKING THE CORN

Nothing beats eating summer corn just hours after it's picked. The sugars in the small kernels have not yet had a chance to turn into starch, and so they're crisp and sweet. But don't settle for just the cut kernels. Be sure to get all the good stuff left after slicing the corn from the cob. Using the back of a knife, scrape against the cob to extract all of the corn "milk" left behind and add this mixture to the soup or stew along with the kernels.

Fish Chowder with Scallops and Shrimp

Vary this good basic chowder recipe as you like. Make it extra special with chunks of lobster in place of the shrimp, or a mixture of both. Or simplify it by adding a pound of fish in place of the shellfish. Some people prefer it this more traditional way. If you don't want the smoky taste of bacon, use two tablespoons of butter in its place. And if you like a richer chowder, replace the light cream with heavy cream.

SERVES 6

¼	pound bacon, chopped
2	onions, chopped
1½	cups Fish Stock, page 303, or bottled clam juice
1½	cups water
2	pounds boiling potatoes (about 6), peeled and cut into ½-inch dice
1½	teaspoons salt
½	pound white fish fillet, such as cod, scrod, haddock or halibut, cut into 1-inch chunks
½	pound sea scallops, cut in half if large
¼	pound medium shrimp, shelled
1	cup light cream
¼	teaspoon fresh-ground black pepper Pinch paprika
1	tablespoon chopped fresh parsley

WINE RECOMMENDATION: MANY DRY WHITE WINES WOULD COMPLEMENT THE MELLOW FLAVOR OF THIS CHOWDER. TWO RELIABLE CHOICES: A PINOT BLANC FROM ALSACE OR A RICH (BUT NOT OAKY) CHARDONNAY FROM CALIFORNIA.

1. In a large pot, cook the bacon over moderate heat until crisp. Remove with a slotted spoon and drain on paper towels.

2. Pour off all but 2 tablespoons of the bacon fat from the pan and reduce the heat to moderately low. Add the onions and cook, stirring occasionally, until translucent, about 5 minutes. Add the stock, water, potatoes and salt and bring to a boil. Reduce the heat and simmer until the potatoes are almost tender, about 15 minutes.

3. Add the fish, scallops and shrimp to the pot. Simmer, covered, until the fish and seafood are just cooked, about 3 minutes. Add the cream and pepper. Bring just to a simmer. Serve sprinkled with the bacon, paprika and parsley.

Shrimp and Sausage Gumbo

Spicy and smoky andouille sausage frequently flavors Cajun dishes. Here it adds authenticity to a delectable gumbo. If andouille isn't available in your area, use chorizo instead, or thin slices of pepperoni.

SERVES 6

5   tablespoons cooking oil or lard

¼   cup flour

1   pound medium shrimp, shells removed and reserved

2   quarts plus 3 cups water

1   bay leaf

⅛   teaspoon dried red-pepper flakes

1   teaspoon dried thyme

½   teaspoon Tabasco sauce

2¾   teaspoons salt

¾   teaspoon fresh-ground black pepper

2   onions, chopped

1   green bell pepper, chopped

3   ribs celery, chopped

3   cloves garlic, minced

2   jalapeño peppers, seeds and ribs removed, minced

1   pound fresh okra, or 10-ounce package frozen okra, cut into thin slices

3½   cups canned tomatoes (28-ounce can), drained and chopped

½   pound andouille sausage, cut into ½-inch slices

1½   cups rice

WINE RECOMMENDATION:
POP OPEN A BEER WITH THIS SPICY, IN-FORMAL DISH. IF YOU MUST SERVE WINE, LOOK FOR A GEWÜRZTRAMINER FROM CALIFORNIA.

1. In a small saucepan, heat 2 tablespoons of the oil over moderately low heat. Add the flour and cook, stirring frequently, until the roux turns the color of peanut butter, about 15 minutes. As the roux darkens, stir the mixture more often so that it doesn't burn. Transfer to a small bowl and set aside.

2. In a large pot, combine the shrimp shells, 2 quarts of the water, the bay leaf, red-pepper flakes, thyme, Tabasco sauce, 2 teaspoons of the salt and ½ teaspoon of the black pepper. Bring to a boil, lower the heat and simmer 20 minutes. Strain the stock and press the shrimp shells firmly to get all the liquid.

3. In a large pot, heat the remaining 3 tablespoons oil over moderately low heat. Add the onions, bell pepper, celery, garlic and jalapeños. Cook, covered, stirring occasionally, until the vegetables are soft, about 10 minutes. Stir in the okra, tomatoes and ¼ teaspoon of the salt and cook, stirring,

until the juices have almost evaporated, 10 to 15 minutes.

4. Stir in the roux. Slowly pour in the reserved stock, stirring constantly. Add the sausage. Bring to a boil. Reduce the heat. Simmer, uncovered, for 1 hour.

5. Meanwhile, bring the remaining 3 cups water to a boil with the remaining ½ teaspoon salt. Add the rice. Reduce the heat, cover and simmer until the rice is tender and all the water is absorbed, about 25 minutes.

6. Bring the soup to a rolling boil. Add the shrimp and the remaining ¼ teaspoon black pepper, cover and remove the pot from the heat. Let the gumbo sit, stirring once or twice, until the shrimp are cooked through, about 3 to 5 minutes.

7. Pack ⅓ cup of the rice into a measuring cup or small ramekin. Unmold in the center of a bowl. Repeat with the remaining rice. Ladle the gumbo around the rice.

—Jan Newberry

WHAT IS GUMBO?

Gumbo is the quintessential Creole soup. Made with any combination of shrimp, crayfish, oysters, chicken, sausage or ham, the real thing *must* include a roux. Made by cooking flour with either lard or oil, a Creole roux is brown and has a nutty aroma. Unlike most roux, its purpose is not so much to thicken the soup (flour loses its thickening power as it browns) as to lend the distinctive flavor typical of gumbo. Okra or filé—dried and ground sassafrass leaves—is frequently added to gumbo and gives it an almost gelatinous texture. In some cases, such as Gumbo z'Herbes, page 12, both are used.

Scallop, Leek and Potato Chowder

Refined yet substantial, colorful with red bell peppers and mildly hot with jalapeños, this easy-to-make chowder is bound to become a favorite. Various fish and shellfish combinations can be used in place of some or all of the scallops. Cod, whitefish and shrimp would all be good.

SERVES 6

1½ pounds boiling potatoes (about 4), cut into large chunks
1½ tablespoons butter
4   leeks, white and light-green parts only, split lengthwise, cut crosswise into thin slices and washed well
3   red bell peppers, cut into ½-inch squares
2   jalapeño peppers, seeds and ribs removed, minced
2½ cups Chicken Stock, page 299, or canned low-sodium chicken broth
1½ cups bottled clam juice
¾   teaspoon chopped fresh thyme, or ¼ teaspoon dried
1½ teaspoons salt
⅛   teaspoon fresh-ground black pepper
1½ pounds sea scallops, halved horizontally
¾   cup light cream
¼   cup chopped fresh flat-leaf parsley

WINE RECOMMENDATION:
A FULL-BODIED BUT DEFINITELY ACIDIC WHITE WINE WILL WORK WELL WITH THE SWEETNESS OF THE SCALLOPS AND CREAM AND THE HEAT OF THE JALAPEÑOS. AN IDEAL CHOICE WOULD BE A KABINETT RIESLING FROM THE MOSEL-SAAR-RUWER REGION OF GERMANY.

1. Put the potatoes in a medium saucepan. Cover with salted water and bring to a boil. Continue boiling until tender, about 20 minutes. Drain. When cool enough to handle, peel and cut into bite-size pieces.

2. In a large pot, melt the butter over moderately low heat. Add the leeks, bell peppers and jalapeños. Cook, covered, stirring occasionally, until soft, about 10 minutes. Add the stock, clam juice and thyme and bring to a simmer. Stir in the potatoes, salt and black pepper.

3. Bring the soup back to a simmer and add the scallops and cream. Simmer gently, stirring occasionally, until the scallops are just cooked through, about 2½ minutes. Stir in the parsley and serve.

—Ann Clark

Manhattan
Clam Chowder

New Englanders may scoff at this "unauthentic" chowder, but we like their creamy style and New York's tomato-based version equally well.

SERVES 6

3   dozen littleneck or cherrystone clams, scrubbed
1½ cups water
6   ounces bacon, chopped
2   onions, chopped
2   ribs celery, chopped
1   green bell pepper, chopped
1   pound boiling potatoes (about 3), peeled and cut into ½-inch dice
    Pinch cayenne
¼ to ¾   teaspoon salt
5   cups canned tomatoes with their juice, chopped
¼   cup chopped fresh parsley
¼   teaspoon fresh-ground black pepper

WINE RECOMMENDATION: A VERY YOUNG ROSÉ FROM PROVENCE WILL WORK HERE. IF YOU CAN FIND A BOTTLE FROM LIRAC, GIVE IT A TRY.

1. Put the clams in a large pot with the water. Cover and bring to a boil over high heat. Cook, shaking the pot ocasionally, just until the clams begin to open, about 3 minutes. Remove the open clams and continue to cook, uncovering the pot as necessary to remove the clams as soon as their shells open. Discard any clams that do not open.

2. When cool enough to handle, remove the clams from their shells, holding them over the pot to catch all the juices. Chop the clams. Pour the broth through a sieve lined with a paper towel into a large measuring cup. Add enough of the water to measure 4½ cups.

3. In a large pot, cook the bacon until crisp. Remove the bacon with a slotted spoon and drain on paper towels. Pour off all but 1 tablespoon of the fat.

4. Add the onions, celery and bell pepper to the pot and cook, stirring occasionally, until the vegetables are soft and beginning to brown, about 10 minutes.

5. Add the reserved clam broth, potatoes, cayenne and ¼ teaspoon of the salt. Bring to a simmer, reduce the heat to moderately low and cook, covered, until the potatoes are soft, about 12 minutes. Add the tomatoes and their juice and simmer 10 minutes longer. Taste for salt and, if necessary, add ¼ to ½ teaspoon salt. Add the bacon, parsley and black pepper to the chowder. Divide the clams among individual bowls and ladle the soup over the clams.

AVOID RUBBERY CLAMS

To keep the clams in chowder tender, don't cook them again in the soup. Instead, after steaming them open, simply put the clams in the bowls and ladle the hot chowder over them. The heat of the soup will warm them enough. You can cook the clams and make the chowder ahead and then simply reheat the soup and combine the two at the last minute.

New England
Clam Chowder

Thick with clams, potatoes and cream, this American classic, originally made by fishermen off the New England coast, is now popular from one end of the country to the other. If you prefer a lighter version, use milk in place of one cup of the cream.

SERVES 6

4	dozen littleneck or cherrystone clams, scrubbed
2	cups water
2	cups Fish Stock, page 303, or bottled clam juice, more if needed
½	pound salt pork or bacon, chopped
2	onions, chopped
2	ribs celery, chopped
1½	pounds boiling potatoes (about 4), peeled and cut into ½-inch dice
1	bay leaf
1	teaspoon dried thyme
1 to 1½	teaspoons salt
2	cups heavy cream
½	teaspoon fresh-ground black pepper

1. Put the clams in a large pot with the water. Cover and bring to a boil over high heat. Cook, shaking the pot occasionally, just until the clams begin to open, about 3 minutes. Remove the open clams and continue to cook, uncovering the pot as necessary to remove the clams as soon as their shells open. Discard any clams that do not open.

2. When the clams are cool enough to handle, remove them from their shells, holding them over the pot to catch all the juices. Chop the clams. Pour the broth through a sieve lined with a paper towel into a large measuring cup. Add enough of the fish stock to the clam broth to measure 5 cups.

3. In a large pot, cook the salt pork over moderate heat until golden, about 6 minutes. Remove with a slotted spoon

and set aside. Pour off all but 1 tablespoon of the fat from the pan.

4. Add the onions and celery and cook, stirring occasionally, until translucent, about 5 minutes. Add the reserved clam broth, potatoes, bay leaf, thyme and 1 teaspoon of the salt and bring to a boil. Reduce the heat to moderately low, cover and cook until the potatoes are very tender, about 20 minutes. With a fork, mash about a third of the potatoes against the side of the pan.

5. Stir in the salt pork, cream and pepper and heat the soup just until it comes to a simmer. Remove the bay leaf. Taste the chowder and add ¼ to ½ teaspoon salt if needed.

6. Divide the chopped clams among individual bowls and ladle the chowder over them.

WHAT IS CHOWDER?

Nowadays virtually any chunky fish or vegetable soup that includes pieces of potato is considered a chowder, but traditionally the word referred to something more specific. The original chowders were fish soups. Though the variety of fish might change, three ingredients remained constant: salt pork, onions and potatoes. On the Northeast seaboard, clams came to dominate the soup, and New England Clam Chowder was born. It's still the best-known version.

Bouillabaisse

The famous fisherman's soup from the south of France, bouillabaisse boasts a rich-flavored fish broth, redolent of saffron, fennel and olive oil and brimming with chunks of fish and shellfish. Traditional bouill- abaisse calls for a number of Mediterranean fish, few of which are avail- able here. This version, based on a typical one from Marseilles, uses hal- ibut, monkfish and orange roughy, but you can substitute whatever firm fish are available. Top crisp croûtes with garlicky rouille and drop them in the soup to complete the medley of flavors and textures.

SERVES 6

1 pound monkfish fillet, cut into 2-by-3-inch chunks

1 pound halibut steak, about 1 inch thick, central bone removed, skin and side bone left on, cut into 2-by-3-inch chunks

1 pound orange roughy fillets, cut into 1-by-3-inch chunks

½ pound medium shrimp, shells removed and reserved

6 cloves garlic, minced

¾ teaspoon saffron

½ cup plus 2 tablespoons olive oil

2 onions, 1 chopped, 1 cut into thin slices

4 leeks, split lengthwise, green tops chopped, white and light-green parts cut crosswise into thin slices, washed well

4 pounds fish bones, heads and trimmings, including some from the above fish, if possible, rinsed well

2 quarts water

12 parsley stems

6 sprigs fresh thyme, or 1 teaspoon dried

2 bay leaves

8 peppercorns

2 ribs celery, cut into thin slices

2 fennel bulbs, cut into thin slices

3½ cups canned tomatoes with their juice (28-ounce can), seeded and chopped

1 3-inch strip orange zest

2¾ teaspoons salt

½ teaspoon fresh-ground black pepper

2 tablespoons Pernod

¼ cup chopped fresh flat-leaf parsley
Rustic Croûtes, page 309
Rouille, page 304

WINE RECOMMENDATION: PAIR THIS MEDITERRANEAN CLASSIC WITH ONE OF THE MANY INCREASINGLY INTER- ESTING WHITE WINES COMING OUT OF FRANCE'S PROVENCE REGION. TRY A BOTTLE OF CASSIS FROM THE VINEYARDS AROUND THE FISHING TOWN OF THE SAME NAME OR LOOK FOR ONE OF THE BETTER WHITES FROM CÔTES DE PROVENCE. ➤

1. In a large bowl, combine the monkfish, halibut, orange roughy, shrimp, half of the garlic, ½ teaspoon of the saffron and ¼ cup of the oil. Marinate the fish and shrimp for 1 hour, stirring once or twice.

2. In a large pot, heat 2 tablespoons of the oil over moderate heat. Add the chopped onion and the leek greens and cook, stirring occasionally, until the onion is translucent, about 8 minutes. Add the shrimp shells, the fish bones, heads and trimmings, the water, parsley stems, thyme, bay leaves and peppercorns and bring to a boil. Skim, reduce the heat and simmer for 30 minutes. Strain and press the bones and vegetables firmly to get all the liquid.

3. In a large pot, heat the remaining ¼ cup olive oil over moderate heat and add the sliced onion and leeks, the remaining garlic, the celery and fennel. Cook, covered, stirring occasionally, until soft, about 10 minutes.

4. Add the reserved stock, the tomatoes with their juice, the orange zest, the remaining ¼ teaspoon saffron, the salt and pepper. Bring to a boil, reduce the heat and simmer for 30 minutes. Remove the zest.

5. Add the fish and shrimp and simmer until they're all done, about 3 minutes. Stir in the Pernod. Sprinkle the soup with the parsley and serve with the croûtes and rouille.

Bourride

A classic from Provence, this soup features a medley of fish in a flavorful seafood broth. You can use any firm-fleshed fish in place of the ones called for here. Aioli, the luscious garlic mayonnaise that is the crowning glory of bourride, both flavors and thickens the soup and also tops the crisp croûtes that float on the surface.

SERVES 6

3   tablespoons olive oil
1   onion, chopped
2   cloves garlic, minced
2   leeks, white and light-green parts only, split lengthwise, cut crosswise into thin slices and washed well
1   fennel bulb, cut into thin slices
3   carrots, cut in half lengthwise and then crosswise into thin slices
5   cups Fish Stock, page 303, or bottled clam juice
¾   cup dry white wine
1   bouquet garni: two 3-inch strips orange zest, 3 sprigs fresh thyme or ½ teaspoon dried, and 1 bay leaf
½   teaspoon fennel seeds
2½ teaspoons salt
1   pound monkfish fillet, cut into 2-by-3-inch chunks
1   pound halibut steak, about 1-inch thick, central bone removed, skin and side bone left on, cut into 2-by-3-inch chunks
1   pound cod fillet, cut into 1-by-3-inch chunks
½   pound sea scallops

Aioli, page 304
2   egg yolks
¼   teaspoon fresh-ground black pepper
3   tablespoons chopped fresh flat-leaf parsley
    Rustic Croûtes, page 309

WINE RECOMMENDATION:
A FULL-BODIED, BUT NOT TOO OAKY, YOUNG CHARDONNAY FROM EITHER CALIFORNIA OR THE MÂCON REGION OF FRANCE WILL WORK JUST FINE ALONGSIDE THIS FLAVORFUL DISH LOADED WITH FISH. LOOK FOR A YOUNG BOTTLE OF EITHER WINE.

1. In a large pot, heat the oil over moderate heat. Add the onion, garlic, leeks, fennel and carrots and cook, stirring occasionally, until the onions are translucent, about 8 minutes. Add the stock, wine, bouquet garni, fennel seeds and salt and bring to a boil. Reduce the heat and simmer, partially covered, for 20 minutes. Discard the bouquet garni.

2. Add the monkfish, halibut, cod and scallops and simmer until they're all done, about 3 minutes longer. Remove the seafood and keep warm. ➤

3. Put 1 cup of the aioli into a medium bowl and whisk in the egg yolks. Add 1 cup of the hot soup in a thin stream, whisking, and then pour it back into the pot, whisking constantly. Heat, stirring, just until thickened. Do not bring to a simmer or the soup will curdle. Add the seafood and pepper.

4. Sprinkle the soup with the parsley and serve with the croûtes and remaining aioli.

BONY BOURRIDE

Traditionally, fisherman's soups such as this one and Bouillabaisse, page 105, are made with small, flavorful fish that are cut into pieces but are not boned. While the bones provide flavor, they are a nuisance to deal with at the table. So we've adapted these dishes by using fish fillets, with the exception of halibut, and making a fish stock with the bones and trimmings in advance. We recommend leaving the side bones and skin on the halibut both because they're easy to eat around and because they add traditional character. But if you prefer, fillet and skin the halibut.

Oyster Soup with Fennel

Oysters and fennel are both good in late autumn and early winter, making this soup ideal for holiday celebrations.

SERVES 6

2   dozen fresh-shucked medium oysters with their liquor (3 cups)
6   tablespoons butter
2   small fennel bulbs, chopped fine, plus the feathery tops, chopped for garnish
2⅔ cups milk
2   cups heavy cream
½ to 1 teaspoon salt
1   teaspoon Worcestershire sauce
½   teaspoon paprika

WINE RECOMMENDATION: THERE ARE FEW MORE CLASSIC FOOD-AND-WINE PAIRINGS THAN FRESH OYSTERS AND A BOTTLE OF CHABLIS FROM FRANCE. DESPITE THE FACT THAT THE OYSTERS HERE ARE COOKED AND IN A SOUP, A YOUNG PREMIER CRU CHABLIS WILL WORK WONDERFULLY. A CHEAPER ALTERNATIVE IS A BOTTLE OF MUSCADET, ALSO FROM FRANCE.

1. With a slotted spoon, remove the oysters from their liquor. Strain the liquor through a sieve lined with cheesecloth. In a medium saucepan, melt 4 tablespoons of the butter over moderate heat. Add the fennel and cook, stirring occasionally, until the fennel is tender, about 5 minutes.

2. Add the milk, cream and ½ teaspoon of the salt. Bring to a simmer, stirring constantly.

3. Reduce the heat to low, add the oysters, the reserved oyster liquor and the Worcestershire sauce and bring just to a simmer, stirring constantly. Simmer just until the oysters plump and begin to curl, about 1 minute. Do not boil or the cream will curdle. Taste and add ¼ to ½ teaspoon salt if needed. Stir in the remaining 2 tablespoons butter. Serve sprinkled with the paprika and chopped fennel tops.

Salmon and Smoked-Trout Chowder

A rich and luxurious soup, this makes a perfect first course for a dinner party or a star attraction at lunch. The salmon gives it a beautiful color and the trout imparts a delicious, smoky flavor. This recipe was inspired by a salmon chowder made by Bruce Tillinghast of New Rivers in Providence, Rhode Island.

SERVES 6

1½ quarts Fish Stock, page 303, or 3 cups bottled clam juice and 3 cups water
1 pound salmon bones, heads and trimmings, rinsed well
1 tablespoon cooking oil
2 onions, chopped
3 ribs celery, chopped
1 cup dry white wine
1½ pounds boiling potatoes (about 4), peeled and cut into ¼-inch slices
1 bouquet garni: 12 parsley stems, 6 sprigs fresh thyme or 1 teaspoon dried, and 2 bay leaves
½ teaspoon salt
1 whole boneless smoked trout, about ½ pound, skin removed, flesh broken into bite-size pieces
1 pound salmon fillet, skinned and cut into bite-size pieces
1 cup milk
1 cup light cream
1 cup frozen petite peas
1 teaspoon lemon juice
¼ teaspoon fresh-ground black pepper
2 tablespoons chopped fresh parsley

WINE RECOMMENDATION:
MATCH THE CREAMY, SMOKY TASTE OF THIS DISH WITH A RICH BUT LIVELY WHITE WINE FROM THE PACIFIC NORTHWEST, SUCH AS A PINOT GRIS FROM OREGON OR A SÉMILLON FROM WASHINGTON STATE.

1. Put the fish stock and the salmon bones, heads and trimmings in a large pot. Bring to a boil over moderately high heat and skim. Reduce the heat and simmer for 30 minutes. Strain and press the bones firmly to get all the liquid.

2. In a large pot, heat the oil over moderately low heat. Add the onions and celery and cook, stirring occasionally, until the onions are translucent, about 5 minutes. Add the reserved fish stock, wine, potatoes, bouquet garni and salt and bring to a boil. Reduce the heat and add the trout. Simmer until the potatoes are done, about 20 minutes. Remove the bouquet garni. ➤

3. Add the salmon and simmer until almost cooked through, about 1 minute. Add the milk, cream and peas and heat gently. Do not boil or the cream will curdle. Stir in the lemon juice and pepper. Serve sprinkled with the parsley.

AHEAD OF TIME

You can make this soup ahead of time, but wait to add the peas, salmon and lemon juice until after you've reheated it. Otherwise, the peas will lose their color, the salmon will overcook and the lemon will taste flat.

FISH STOCK SHORTCUT

Salmon bones add a distinct and delicious flavor to the final soup when simmered with the fish stock, as suggested in this recipe. If you're putting together fish stock specifically for this soup, you needn't make it and then simmer it again with the salmon bones. Add them with the other fish bones when making the stock and simmer for just half an hour. Or, if you can get enough of them, use all salmon bones, trimmings and heads to make the fish stock.

CHAPTER 4 · POULTRY SOUPS

Mexican Chicken Soup

Chock-full of zucchini, carrots, pepper and corn, this soup is spiced with cumin and brightened with fresh cilantro and a squeeze of lime juice. Cubes of mellow avocado add a touch of richness.

SERVES 6

2	pounds chicken parts
7	cups Chicken Stock, page 299, or canned low-sodium chicken broth
2	onions, 1 quartered, 1 chopped
2	carrots, 1 quartered, 1 cut into ¼-inch dice
1	bay leaf
2½	teaspoons salt
2	tablespoons cooking oil
3	cloves garlic, minced
1	teaspoon ground cumin
1	teaspoon dried oregano
1	zucchini, quartered lengthwise, seeded and cut into ¼-inch dice
1	red bell pepper, cut into ¼-inch dice
1	cup canned tomatoes, drained and chopped
1	avocado, preferably Hass
1½	cups fresh (cut from about 2 ears) or frozen corn kernels
¼	teaspoon fresh-ground black pepper
⅓	cup chopped fresh cilantro
3	tablespoons lime juice, from about 2 limes, or to taste

WINE RECOMMENDATION: THE WEALTH OF MEXICAN FLAVORS PACKED INTO THIS SOUP GO VERY NICELY WITH THE FRESH, GRASSY TASTE OF A YOUNG CALIFORNIA OR WASHINGTON STATE SAUVIGNON BLANC.

1. Put the chicken in a large pot. Add the stock, the quartered onion and carrot, the bay leaf and 2 teaspoons of the salt. Bring to a boil. Reduce the heat and simmer, skimming occasionally, until the chicken is cooked through, about 45 minutes.

2. Remove the chicken. When the chicken is cool enough to handle, remove the meat from the skin and bones and tear it into shreds. Strain the stock. Press the vegetables firmly to get all the liquid. Skim the fat from the stock. You should have 1½ quarts of stock.

3. Heat the oil in a large pot over moderately low heat. Add the chopped onion, the garlic, cumin and oregano. Cook, stirring occasionally, until the onion is translucent, about 5 minutes.

4. Add the stock, the diced carrot, zucchini and bell pepper, the tomatoes and the remaining ½ teaspoon salt. Bring to a boil, reduce the heat and sim-

mer until the vegetables are tender, about 10 minutes.

5. Cut the avocado into ¼-inch dice. Add the fresh corn, if using, to the soup and cook about 4 minutes longer. Add the shredded chicken, frozen corn, if using, and pepper and cook until heated through. Just before serving, stir in the avocado, cilantro and lime juice.

—Jan Newberry

SEASON TO TASTE

A chef wouldn't consider serving anything before first tasting it, and you shouldn't either. All of our recipes have been developed with specific quantities of salt and pepper. However, ingredients vary and, therefore, so does the amount of seasoning you need. Taste the dish before serving and add enough salt and pepper to bring out maximum flavor. Sprinkling seasonings on top of food after it reaches the table is never so effective.

Mexican Tortilla Soup

Piquant with garlic and jalapeños and brimming with chicken, vegetables and Jack cheese, this festive *sopa* is a slightly refined version of the traditional tortilla soup from Mexico. The broth is cooked with chopped corn tortillas, which give it a distinctive tortilla flavor and thicken it slightly. Then they're strained out, and fresh ones are added.

SERVES 6

¼ cup cooking oil

6 corn tortillas, 4 chopped, 2 cut into 1-inch-long matchstick strips

2 onions, chopped

1 head garlic, separated, cloves peeled

2 jalapeño peppers, seeds and ribs removed, minced

1 teaspoon cumin seeds

2 quarts Chicken Stock, page 299, or canned low-sodium chicken broth

4 pounds tomatoes (about 8), or 7 cups canned tomatoes with their juice (two 28-ounce cans), chopped

2 sprigs fresh epazote, optional

1¾ teaspoons salt

1 pound boneless, skinless chicken breasts, cut crosswise into ⅛-inch strips

¼ teaspoon fresh-ground black pepper

1 avocado, preferably Hass

¼ pound Monterey Jack cheese, grated (about 1 cup)

½ cup fresh cilantro leaves

WINE RECOMMENDATION: IT'S HARD TO IMAGINE PAIRING THIS LIVELY SOUP WITH ANYTHING MORE DEMANDING THAN A BEER OR A VERY FRUITY YOUNG WINE SUCH AS A GAMAY FROM California.

1. In a large pot, heat the oil over moderately low heat. Add the chopped tortillas, onions, garlic, jalapeños and cumin and cook, stirring occasionally, until the onions are translucent, about 5 minutes. Add the stock, tomatoes, the epazote, if using, and the salt. Bring to a boil. Reduce the heat and simmer for 45 minutes. Strain the stock into a large pot and press the vegetables firmly to get all the liquid.

2. Bring the soup to a simmer over moderate heat. Add the chicken and pepper and simmer, stirring, until the chicken is just done, about 1 minute.

3. Cut the avocado into ¼-inch dice. Distribute the remaining tortilla matchsticks, the avocado and the cheese among individual bowls. Ladle on the soup and top with the cilantro leaves.

—Scott Cohen
The Stanhope

Chicken Noodle Soup with Root Vegetables

Thick with vegetables, noodles and chunks of chicken, this is a homey, comforting soup like Grandma used to make. Parsnips, carrots and leeks give rich flavor, and a finishing touch of dill is a refreshing note.

SERVES 6

1	3-pound chicken
3	onions, 2 quartered, 1 chopped
4	carrots, 1 quartered, 3 cut into ¼-inch slices
4	ribs celery, 2 quartered, 2 cut into ¼-inch slices
4	cloves garlic, minced
2	quarts Chicken Stock, page 299, or canned low-sodium chicken broth
2	cups dry white wine
1	quart water
12	parsley stems
3	sprigs fresh thyme, or ½ teaspoon dried
2	bay leaves
5	peppercorns
3	tablespoons butter
2	medium parsnips, cut into 1-inch matchstick strips
2	leeks, white and light-green parts only, split lengthwise, cut crosswise into thin slices and washed well
2	teaspoons salt
1½	cups (3 ounces) wide egg noodles
¼	teaspoon fresh-ground black pepper
3	tablespoons chopped fresh dill

WINE RECOMMENDATION: CONTRAST THE MILDNESS OF THIS SOUP WITH SOMETHING A BIT EXCITING. TRY A RIESLING FROM ALSACE IN FRANCE, WITH ITS HIGH ACIDITY AND FULL FLAVOR. WHILE A YOUNGER VINTAGE WILL DO, A BOTTLE FROM AN OLDER VINTAGE WON'T BE WASTED ON THIS DISH.

1. Remove excess fat from the chicken. Put the chicken in a large pot. Add the quartered onions, carrot and celery, half of the garlic, the stock, wine, water, parsley, thyme, bay leaves and peppercorns. Bring to a boil over moderately high heat. Reduce the heat. Simmer, partially covered, skimming occasionally, for about 2 hours. Remove the chicken when it's cooked through, after about 1 hour.

2. When the chicken is cool enough to handle, separate the meat from the skin and bones. Return the chicken bones and skin to the simmering stock for added flavor. Tear the meat into shreds and set aside.

3. Strain the stock. Press the bones and vegetables firmly to get all the liquid. Skim off the fat. You should have about 2½ quarts of stock.

4. In a large pot, melt the butter over moderate heat. Add the chopped onion, the sliced carrots and celery, the remaining garlic, the parsnips and leeks. Cook, covered, stirring occasionally, for 5 minutes. Raise the heat to moderately high and cook, uncovered, until the vegetables are lightly browned, about 5 minutes. Add the stock and salt and bring to a boil. Reduce the heat and simmer, partially covered, for 15 minutes. Add the noodles and simmer, partially covered, until just done, about 10 minutes longer.

5. Add the shredded chicken, the pepper and dill to the soup and simmer just until heated through.

—Bob Chambers

THE HOMEMADE SOUP DIFFERENCE

Homemade soup is better than canned in lots of ways, but when it comes to noodle and rice soups, one difference stands out: the flabby noodles or bloated rice in the canned versions. When you spend the time to make a batch of soup from scratch, avoid the canned-soup phenomenon. You can still make the soup a few days ahead, just wait to add the noodles or rice until shortly before serving.

Grandma's Matzo-Ball Soup

One of our editors says that in her family no holiday meal is complete without Grandma's soup. Her grandmother, Mrs. Salzman, uses chicken feet for additional flavor and body. You can sometimes buy them from kosher butchers, but simply omit them if they're hard to find.

SERVES 6

1	4-pound chicken
5	pounds chicken backs, wings, necks and feet
3	onions, quartered
5	ribs celery, quartered
5	carrots, cut in half
2	parsnips, quartered
24	parsley stems
2	parsley roots, cut in half, optional
2	tomatoes, cut in half, or 2 teaspoons tomato paste
2	cloves garlic
3½	quarts water
2¼	teaspoons salt
½	cup matzo meal
	Small pinch ground cinnamon
2	eggs
2	tablespoons melted chicken fat or cooking oil

1. Remove excess fat from the chicken. Put the chicken in a large pot with the chicken parts. Add the onions, celery, carrots, parsnips, parsley stems, the parsley roots, if using, the tomatoes, garlic, water and 1¼ teaspoons of the salt. Bring to a boil. Reduce the heat and simmer, skimming occasionally, for 2 hours. Remove the whole chicken when it's cooked through, after about 1 hour.

2. When the chicken is cool enough to handle, separate the meat from the skin and bones. Return the chicken bones and skin to the simmering stock for added flavor. Cut enough of the chicken into bite-size pieces to make 1 cup. Reserve the remaining chicken for another use. Remove the carrots and cut enough of them into ¼-inch slices to make 1 cup.

3. Strain the soup and press the bones and vegetables firmly to get all the liquid. Skim off the fat. You should have about 7 cups of soup. ➤

4. In a bowl, combine the matzo meal, the remaining 1 teaspoon salt and the cinnamon. Beat the eggs to mix. Add the eggs, chicken fat and 2 tablespoons of the warm soup to the matzo meal and stir until well mixed. Chill for 30 minutes.

5. Bring a large pot of salted water to a boil. Wet your hands and scoop up a sixth of the matzo-meal mixture and shape it into a ball. Carefully drop the ball into the boiling water. Continue shaping the remaining matzo balls and dropping them into the soup, wetting your hands when the mixture begins to stick. Cover the pot and simmer 25 minutes.

6. Put the soup in a large pot. Add the cut up chicken and carrots. Bring to a boil. Transfer the matzo balls to the soup with a slotted spoon and simmer 10 minutes longer.

—Shirley Salzman

MAKE IT AHEAD

This soup is best made a day in advance so that you can chill it and remove the fat easily. But make the matzo balls the day you serve the soup so that they stay light and fluffy.

CHICKEN-SOUP VARIATIONS

This epitome of homemade chicken soup is so full-flavored and satisfying that it makes the ideal base for any number of variations. Skip the matzo balls and add noodles, rice, egg or whatever you like.

Chicken Noodle Soup
Break 3 ounces of noodles into 1-inch pieces. Bring the soup to a boil. Add the noodles and simmer until just done, about 8 minutes. Cooking time will vary depending on the noodles you choose. Stir in 1 tablespoon chopped fresh parsley with the chicken and carrots.

Chicken and Rice Soup
Bring the soup to a boil. Add ½ cup rice and simmer, covered, until cooked, about 25 minutes. Add the chicken and carrots and simmer until heated through.

Egg-Drop Soup
Omit the pieces of cooked chicken and sliced carrots. In a small bowl, lightly beat 3 eggs. Bring the soup to a boil. Add 1 tablespoon soy sauce and 3 chopped scallions including the green tops. Add the eggs to the soup in a thin stream. Let sit 1 minute and then stir the soup once or twice.

Cream of Chicken Soup with Mushrooms

Brimming with mushrooms and chunks of chicken, this modern version of an old favorite uses only a little cream to round out a great combination. Full-flavored chicken stock provides the base for this velvety soup, and sherry gives it a distinctive finish.

SERVES 6

1	3-pound chicken
3	onions, 2 quartered, 1 chopped
1	carrot, quartered
2	ribs celery, quartered
3	cloves garlic, 2 whole, 1 minced
1½	quarts Chicken Stock, page 299, or canned low-sodium chicken broth
1	quart water
2	cups dry white wine
12	parsley stems
3	sprigs fresh thyme, or ½ teaspoon dried
2	bay leaves
5	peppercorns
6	tablespoons butter
½	pound shiitake mushrooms, stems discarded, caps cut into thick slices
½	pound white mushrooms, cut into thick slices
2¼	teaspoons salt
¼	cup flour
½	cup heavy cream
1½	teaspoons dry sherry, optional
½	teaspoon fresh-ground black pepper

WINE RECOMMENDATION:
PAIR THIS SIMPLE, CREAMY SOUP WITH A YOUNG, HEARTY RED SUCH AS A CROZES-HERMITAGE OR ST.-JOSEPH FROM THE RHÔNE VALLEY IN FRANCE. NOTE HOW THE SLIGHT PEPPERY KICK OF THE SOUP IS COMPLEMENTED BY THE PEPPERY TASTE OF THE SYRAH GRAPE USED IN THESE TWO WINES.

1. Remove excess fat from the chicken. Put the chicken in a large pot. Add the quartered onions, carrot and celery, the 2 whole garlic cloves, the stock, water, wine, parsley, thyme, bay leaves and peppercorns and bring to a boil over moderately high heat. Reduce the heat and simmer, partially covered, skimming occasionally, for 2 hours. Remove the chicken when it's cooked through, after about 1 hour.

2. When the chicken is cool enough to handle, separate the meat from the skin and bones. Return the chicken bones and skin to the simmering stock for added flavor. Tear the meat into shreds.

3. Strain the chicken stock. Press the bones and vegetables firmly to get all the

liquid. Skim off the fat. You should have about 2 quarts stock.

4. In a large pot, melt 2 tablespoons of the butter over moderately high heat. Add the chopped onion and cook, stirring, until lightly browned, about 3 minutes. Stir in the minced garlic and cook for 30 seconds longer. Add the mushrooms and ¾ teaspoon of the salt. Cook over moderately high heat, stirring frequently, until the mushrooms are browned, about 10 minutes.

5. Add the remaining 4 tablespoons butter to the mushrooms and stir until melted. Add the flour and cook for 1 minute. Stir in the stock and the remaining 1½ teaspoons salt and bring to a boil. Reduce the heat and simmer,

skimming occasionally, until slightly thickened, about 10 minutes.

6. Add the shredded chicken, the cream, the sherry, if using, and the pepper and simmer until heated through.
—Bob Chambers

 ## TO SAVE TIME

Peeling onions for stock is wasted effort. Chefs leave the skin on not only to save time but to help color the stock. If the onions have dirty roots, cut them off, and, if you're finicky, remove a layer of the skin. You needn't peel carrots, either, though they should be washed.

Chicken and Escarole Soup

Bright green escarole and nutty Parmesan turn basic chicken soup into a delicious new dish with an Italian accent.

SERVES 6

2½ pounds chicken parts
7   cups Chicken Stock, page 299, or canned low-sodium chicken broth
3   onions, 1 quartered, 2 cut into thin slices
1   carrot, quartered
1   bay leaf
2½ teaspoons salt
2   tablespoons butter
1   head escarole (about 1 pound), cut into ½-inch pieces
¼   teaspoon fresh-ground black pepper
⅓   cup grated Parmesan cheese

WINE RECOMMENDATION:
THE LEAFY TASTE AND TEXTURE OF THE ESCAROLE AND THE NUTTINESS OF THE PARMESAN CHEESE ARE COMPLEMENTED BY THE TART, AGGRESSIVE TASTE OF SAUVIGNON BLANC. TRY A WINE BASED ON THAT GRAPE FROM EITHER GRAVES, WHERE IT IS MIXED WITH SÉMILLON, OR POUILLY-FUMÉ IN FRANCE.

1. Put the chicken in a large pot. Add the stock, the quartered onion and carrot, the bay leaf and salt. Bring to a boil. Reduce the heat and simmer, skimming occasionally, until the chicken is cooked through, about 45 minutes.

2. Remove the chicken. When the chicken is cool enough to handle, remove the meat from the skin and bones and cut it into bite-size pieces. Strain the stock. Press the vegetables firmly to get all the liquid. Skim off the fat. You should have 1½ quarts stock.

3. Melt the butter in a large pot over moderately low heat. Add the sliced onions and cook, stirring occasionally, until soft, about 10 minutes. Add the stock and bring to a boil. Stir in the escarole and simmer until tender, about 7 minutes. Add the chicken and pepper and simmer until heated through. Serve topped with the Parmesan cheese.

—Jan Newberry

125

Home-Style Italian Chicken Soup with Tiny Meatballs

Enriched chicken broth adds to the robust flavor of this hearty soup packed with chicken, meatballs, vegetables and pasta.

SERVES 6

1   3-pound chicken
2   onions, quartered
4   carrots, 2 quartered, 2 cut into ¼-inch dice
2   ribs celery, quartered
2   cloves garlic
1½   quarts Chicken Stock, page 299, or canned low-sodium chicken broth
1½   quarts water
2½   teaspoons salt
½   pound ground beef
6   tablespoons chopped fresh flat-leaf parsley
3   tablespoons grated Parmesan cheese, plus more for serving
2   tablespoons dry bread crumbs
1   egg, beaten
¼   pound green beans, cut into ½-inch lengths
1   medium zucchini, quartered lengthwise, seeded and cut into ¼-inch dice
⅔   cup tiny pasta, such as stars or orzo
1   cup canned tomatoes, drained and chopped
¼   teaspoon fresh-ground black pepper

WINE RECOMMENDATION:
THIS SIMPLE SOUP, WITH ITS MILD VEGETABLE AND CHICKEN FLAVORS, PAIRS WELL WITH A STRAIGHTFORWARD, REFRESHING WHITE WINE. TRY A YOUNG PINOT GRIGIO OR PINOT BIANCO FROM ITALY'S VENETO REGION.

1. Remove excess fat from the chicken. Put the chicken in a large pot. Add the quartered onions, carrots and celery, the garlic, stock, water and 2 teaspoons of the salt. Bring to a boil. Reduce the heat and simmer, partially covered, skimming occasionally, for 2 hours. Remove the chicken when it's cooked through, after about 1 hour.

2. When the chicken is cool enough to handle, separate the meat from the skin and bones and cut it into ½-inch pieces. Return the chicken bones and skin to the simmering stock for added flavor.

3. Strain the stock. Press the vegetables firmly to get all the liquid. Skim the fat from the stock. You should have 2 quarts of stock.

4. Meanwhile, make the meatballs: In a medium bowl, mix together the ground

beef, 4 tablespoons of the parsley, the Parmesan, bread crumbs, egg and the remaining ½ teaspoon salt. Shape the mixture into small meatballs, about ¾ inch in diameter. You should have about 50 meatballs.

5. Put the stock in a pot. Add the diced carrots and the green beans and bring to a boil. Reduce the heat and simmer for 5 minutes. Add the zucchini and simmer 5 minutes longer.

6. In a small saucepan of boiling, salted water, cook the pasta until just done, about 7 minutes. Drain and add to the soup with the reserved chicken, the meatballs, tomatoes and pepper. Bring back to a boil and simmer until the meatballs are cooked through, about 4 minutes.

7. Stir in the remaining 2 tablespoons parsley. Serve with additional Parmesan.
—Tracey Seaman

Chicken Consommé

Here chicken stock is transformed into a sparkling and intense soup. Our basic stock recipe is cooked down until it's bursting with flavor. Egg whites are added to clarify the soup. All the tiny particles floating in the soup catch in the whites. Then the eggs are strained out, leaving a brilliantly clear, light-as-can-be first course.

SERVES 6 AS A FIRST COURSE

3 quarts chilled Chicken Stock, page 299, made with 8 pounds chicken carcasses, backs, wings and/or necks, plus gizzards (optional)
1¼ teaspoons salt
3 egg whites

WINE RECOMMENDATION: AN UNCOMPLICATED YET SOPHISTICATED SOUP SUCH AS THIS CAN BE A SPLENDID BACKDROP FOR A LAVISH WHITE WINE, SUCH AS A PREMIUM CHARDONNAY FROM CALIFORNIA THAT HAS BEEN FERMENTED AND AGED IN OAK, OR A VILLAGES-LEVEL WINE FROM THE CÔTE DE BEAUNE IN BURGUNDY, SUCH AS A MEURSAULT, PULIGNY-MONTRACHET OR CHASSAGNE-MONTRACHET.

1. Scrape all of the fat from the top of the chilled stock. In a large, wide pot, bring the stock to a boil. Boil, uncovered, until reduced to 1½ quarts, about 30 minutes. Add the salt. Transfer the stock to a medium saucepan. If there is any sign of fat floating on top of the soup, remove it. The best way is to drag a clean, dry paper towel over the surface of the soup. Repeat with additional paper towels until no fat remains.

2. In a medium bowl, whisk the egg whites until frothy. Whisk them into the soup. Bring the soup back to a boil, still whisking. Turn off the heat and let the soup stand undisturbed for 10 minutes.

3. Rinse a dish towel several times in water to remove any residual soap. Set a

sieve over a large bowl and line it with the rinsed dish towel. Pour the soup through the lined sieve and leave it to strain undisturbed. Gently lift the towel away, being careful not to squeeze any of its contents into the soup. Serve the soup alone or with any of the garnishes on page 145.

NOTHING BUT THE BEST

While canned broth works well for many soups and is a great time-saver, we don't recommend it for clear soups with few ingredients, such as the Chicken Consommé on this page or Avgolemono Soup, opposite page. The intention of soups like these is simplicity, in order to savor the pure and delicious flavor of homemade stock. Convenient as it is, canned broth is not the real thing, and as a rule using it in thin, clear soups yields second-rate results.

Avgolemono Soup

The combination of lemon and eggs is a long-standing Greek favorite. Avgolemono sauce, made with whipped eggs and lemon juice, enhances meat, fish or vegetables. Here the duo adds flavor and richness to chicken soup. Serve it plain or with rice; either way is authentic.

SERVES 6

3 quarts Chicken Stock, page 299, boiled down to 9 cups
⅔ cup rice
1½ teaspoons salt
¼ cup lemon juice, from about 2 lemons
3 tablespoons chopped fresh parsley or dill
¼ teaspoon fresh-ground black pepper
4 eggs

WINE RECOMMENDATION: THIS CREAMY SOUP WILL PAIR WELL WITH THE ACIDITY, FRUIT AND SLIGHT SWEETNESS OF A KABINETT RIESLING FROM THE MOSEL-SAAR-RUWER REGION IN GERMANY.

1. In a large saucepan, bring the stock to a boil over moderately high heat. Add the rice and salt. Reduce the heat and simmer, covered, until the rice is just tender, about 25 minutes. Add the lemon juice, parsley and pepper.

2. In a large bowl, whisk the eggs until frothy. Bring the soup just to a boil and slowly pour it into the eggs, whisking constantly so that the eggs do not curdle. Serve at once.

VARIATION

Orzo, the tiny rice-shaped pasta, makes a great alternative to rice in this soup. Use the same quantity of orzo as rice and simmer just until the orzo is done, about 12 minutes.

Thai Coconut Chicken Soup

If you're new to Thai cooking, this classic soup's a good place to start.
It combines many basic Thai flavorings—ginger, lemongrass, chiles,
fish sauce and cilantro—to make a spicy and full-flavored dish.

SERVES 6

3¾	cups canned unsweetened coconut milk
1½	cups Chicken Stock, page 299, or canned low-sodium chicken broth
1	¾-inch piece fresh ginger, cut into thirds
3	stalks lemongrass,* bottom third only, cut into 3-inch lengths, or three 3-inch strips lemon zest
1½	pounds boneless, skinless chicken breasts, cut into thin strips
3	tablespoons Asian fish sauce (nam pla or nuoc mam)*
1½	tablespoons lime juice
3	small, fresh red chile peppers, seeds and ribs removed, minced, or 1½ teaspoons dried red-pepper flakes
¼	teaspoon sugar
1½	tablespoons chopped fresh cilantro

*Available at Asian markets

WINE RECOMMENDATION:
THE EXOTIC, SPICY FLAVORS OF THIS SOUP GO WELL WITH A GEWÜRZTRAMINER FROM THE ALSACE REGION IN FRANCE. BEER IS ALSO A POSSIBILITY.

1. In a large pot, combine the coconut milk, stock, ginger and lemongrass. Bring to a boil, reduce the heat and simmer 10 minutes. Add the chicken and simmer until cooked through, about 2½ minutes. Discard the ginger and lemongrass.

2. Add the fish sauce, lime juice, chiles and sugar. Serve sprinkled with the cilantro.

—Jan Newberry

COCONUT MILK

Coconut milk is made by soaking ground coconut in water and then squeezing it out, a time-consuming process. For many dishes a good canned brand works equally well. Taste of Thailand is our favorite. Also good are Chef's Choice, Chaokoh and Goya. Some recipes call for thick coconut milk. This, the richest part of the milk, rises and can be spooned off the top.

Thai Hot and Sour Soup

This clear soup should be distinctly hot and noticeably acidic at the same time. The heat comes from the fresh chile peppers, which vary in intensity. If yours aren't very spicy, include some of the seeds. If you reheat the soup, you may find you need to boost the sourness with more fresh lime juice.

SERVES 6

2	tablespoons cooking oil
3	shallots, chopped
3	cloves garlic, minced
9	cups Chicken Stock, page 299, or canned low-sodium chicken broth
½	pound mushrooms, cut into thin slices
6	stalks lemongrass,* bottom third only, cut into 1-inch lengths
3	small, fresh red chile peppers, seeds and ribs removed, minced
6	fresh or dried kaffir lime leaves, optional
½	cup lime juice, from about 6 limes
3	tablespoons Asian fish sauce (nam pla or nuoc mam)*
¾	pound boneless, skinless chicken breasts, cut into the thinnest possible slices
3	tablespoons whole cilantro leaves, for garnish

*Available at Asian markets

WINE RECOMMENDATION: UNCORK A BOTTLE OF GEWÜRZTRAMINER FROM ALSACE IN FRANCE TO STAND UP TO THE SPICINESS OF THIS SOUP. A COLD BOTTLE OF BEER IS ALSO A SPLENDID CHOICE.

1. In a large pot, heat the oil over moderate heat. Add the shallots and cook, stirring, until golden brown, about 5 minutes. Add the garlic and cook 1 minute longer. Stir in the stock, mushrooms, lemongrass, chile peppers and lime leaves, if using, and simmer, partially covered, for 10 minutes.

2. Stir in the lime juice, fish sauce and chicken. Turn off the heat and let the soup sit until the chicken is just done, about 2 minutes. Serve topped with the cilantro leaves.

Mulligatawny Soup

This mildly spiced soup originated in India, was adopted by the British and has evolved into a savory combination of chicken and vegetables with red lentils, or sometimes rice, and a splash of cream.

SERVES 6

2	tablespoons butter
3	carrots, chopped
2	ribs celery, chopped
4	cloves garlic, minced
3	onions, chopped
2	quarts Chicken Stock, page 299, or canned low-sodium chicken broth
⅔	cup red lentils
1	tablespoon tomato paste
1	bay leaf
2½	teaspoons salt
4	chicken thighs
¼	cup cooking oil
1	tablespoon curry powder
2	teaspoons grated fresh ginger
¼	teaspoon cayenne
¼	cup heavy cream

WINE RECOMMENDATION:
PAIR THIS CURRIED SOUP WITH A RICH, HIGHLY FLAVORED PINOT GRIS FROM ALSACE IN FRANCE OR A KABINETT RIESLING FROM THE MOSEL-SAAR-RUWER REGION IN GERMANY.

1. In a large pot, melt the butter over moderate heat. Add the carrots, celery, garlic and two-thirds of the onions. Cook, stirring frequently, until the vegetables are light brown, about 7 minutes. Add the stock, lentils, tomato paste, bay leaf and salt. Bring to a simmer. Add the chicken thighs. Simmer, partially covered, until the vegetables and lentils are very tender and the chicken is cooked through, about 30 minutes. Remove the chicken and set aside. Discard the bay leaf.

2. Puree the soup in a blender or food processor. Return to the pot. When the chicken is cool enough to handle, remove the meat from the skin and bones and cut it into bite-size pieces. Add the meat to the soup.

3. In a small frying pan, heat the oil over moderate heat. Add the remaining onion and cook, stirring frequently, until golden brown, about 7 minutes. Add the curry powder, ginger and cayenne. Cook another 30 seconds. Add this mixture to the soup. Stir in the cream and serve.

135

Cock-a-Leekie

Prunes add a pleasant sweetness to this Scottish soup, thick with barley and full of rich chicken flavor. Though prunes are traditional, white wine is a new element in the version here. We think the wine makes a great soup even better, but you can substitute stock or water if you prefer. The barley tends to soak up the liquid on standing. If too much liquid is absorbed so that the dish becomes more like porridge than soup, just add some water, or more stock if you like.

SERVES 6

1	3-pound chicken
2	onions
1	carrot
2	ribs celery
2	cloves garlic
1¾	teaspoons salt
7	cups Chicken Stock, page 299, or canned low-sodium chicken broth
2	cups dry white wine
1	quart water
1	bouquet garni: 12 parsley stems, 6 sprigs fresh thyme or 1 teaspoon dried, and 2 bay leaves
5	leeks, white and light-green parts only, split lengthwise, cut crosswise into thin slices and washed well
½	cup barley
12	pitted prunes, quartered
¼	teaspoon fresh-ground black pepper
2	tablespoons chopped fresh flat-leaf parsley

WINE RECOMMENDATION:
THIS DOWN-HOME DISH, WITH ITS SWEET PRUNE FLAVOR, BARLEY AND OVERALL RUSTIC FEEL, WOULD BE PERFECT WITH A YOUNG OREGON PINOT NOIR OR A BOTTLE OF VILLAGES-LEVEL RED WINE FROM THE CÔTE DE BEAUNE REGION OF BURGUNDY IN FRANCE.

1. Remove any excess fat from the chicken. Put the chicken in a large pot. Add the onions, carrot, celery, garlic, salt, stock, wine, water and bouquet garni and bring to a boil. Reduce the heat and cook at a bare simmer, partially covered, skimming occasionally, until the chicken is done, about 1 hour. Remove the chicken.

2. Add the leeks, the barley and the quartered prunes to the pot and continue cooking until the barley is tender, about 1 hour longer.

3. When the chicken is cool enough to handle, remove the meat from the skin and bones and tear the meat into shreds.

4. Remove the onions, carrot, celery, garlic and bouquet garni and put them into a strainer held over the pot. Press firmly to get all the liquid before discarding the vegetables and herbs.

5. Skim any fat from the soup. Add the chicken and pepper and simmer until the chicken is heated through. Serve the soup sprinkled with the parsley.

—Bob Chambers

Turkey Soup with Mushrooms and Wild Rice

The bonus to your Thanksgiving bird is that you can make this wonderful soup with the carcass and some of the leftover meat. Herbs, wild rice and mushrooms give it a special flavor, and the addition of chopped turkey makes it substantial enough to be a meal in itself.

SERVES 6

⅔ cup wild rice
2¼ teaspoons salt
5 cups water
2 tablespoons cooking oil
1 onion, cut into ¼-inch dice
2 carrots, cut into ¼-inch dice
2 ribs celery, cut into ¼-inch dice
2 cloves garlic, minced
9 cups Turkey Stock, page 300
4 teaspoons chopped fresh thyme, or 1½ teaspoons dried
½ teaspoon dried sage
2 cups cooked turkey, cut into ¼-inch cubes
6 ounces mushrooms, cut into thin slices
¼ teaspoon fresh-ground black pepper
2 tablespoons chopped fresh chives or scallion tops
2 tablespoons chopped fresh celery leaves, optional

WINE RECOMMENDATION: THIS SIMPLE, HOMEY DISH NEEDS AN EQUALLY ROUGH-HEWN WINE. A GOOD BET IS A YOUNG ZINFANDEL FROM ONE OF THE BETTER PRODUCERS IN California.

1. In a medium saucepan, combine the rice, ¼ teaspoon of the salt and the water. Bring to a boil over moderate heat. Reduce the heat and simmer, covered, until the rice is tender but still firm, about 40 minutes. Drain.

2. In a large pot, heat the oil over moderately low heat. Add the onion, carrots, celery and garlic and cook, stirring occasionally, until the onion is translucent, about 5 minutes. Add the stock, thyme, sage and the remaining 2 teaspoons salt and bring to a boil. Reduce the heat and simmer 5 minutes. Add the cooked rice, turkey, mushrooms and pepper and simmer until the vegetables are just done, about 5 minutes. Serve topped with the chives and celery leaves.

Turkey, Artichoke-Heart and Mushroom Soup

Transform turkey stock into this quick soup. If you have leftover turkey, cut some into bite-size pieces and throw them in just before serving.

SERVES 6

9   cups Turkey Stock, page 300
1   10-ounce package frozen artichoke
      hearts, thawed and cut into ½-inch
      pieces
¾   pound mushrooms, cut into thin
      slices
1   red bell pepper, cut into tiny dice, or
      ¼ cup diced pimiento
1   teaspoon salt
¼   teaspoon fresh-ground black pepper

WINE RECOMMENDATION:
THE RICH FLAVOR THIS SOUP GETS FROM THE TURKEY AND ARTICHOKES SHOULD BE BALANCED WITH A WHITE WINE THAT HAS A NOTICEABLE ACID BITE. TRY A RIESLING FROM ALSACE OR A SAUVIGNON BLANC FROM SANCERRE.

1. Put the stock in a large pot and bring to a boil.

2. Add the artichoke hearts, mushrooms, bell pepper and salt. Simmer until the vegetables are tender, about 15 minutes. Add the black pepper.

—Charles Pierce

140

CHAPTER 5 · MEAT SOUPS

Goulash Soup

Both mild and hot paprika flavor this robust beef soup. If you like spicier fare, juggle the ratio of hot to mild paprika to suit your taste.

SERVES 6

2 tablespoons cooking oil, more if needed

1½ pounds boneless beef chuck, cut into ½-inch cubes

3 onions, chopped

3 cloves garlic, minced

1 rib celery, chopped

1 carrot, chopped

4½ teaspoons mild paprika

1½ teaspoons hot paprika

¼ cup flour

1½ quarts Beef Stock, page 302, or canned low-sodium beef broth

1½ cups water

1½ cups canned crushed tomatoes

1½ teaspoons dried marjoram

1¾ teaspoons salt

3 tablespoons chopped fresh parsley

¼ teaspoon fresh-ground black pepper

WINE RECOMMENDATION:
PAIR THIS HUNGARIAN CLASSIC WITH A FRUITY YOUNG RED WINE FROM HUNGARY, SUCH AS A MERLOT OR AN EGRI BIKAVÉR.

1. In a large pot, heat the oil over moderately high heat. Add about half the beef. Brown well, about 8 minutes, and remove. Brown the remaining beef, adding more oil if needed. Remove.

2. Reduce the heat to moderately low. Add the onions, garlic, celery and carrot and cook, stirring occasionally, until the vegetables are soft, about 10 minutes. Add the paprika and flour and cook, stirring, 2 minutes.

3. Return the beef to the pot with any juice that has accumulated. Stir in the stock, water, tomatoes, marjoram and salt. Scrape the bottom of the pot to dislodge any brown bits. Bring to a simmer over moderately high heat. Reduce the heat and simmer, partially covered, until the meat is tender, about 1½ hours. Stir in the parsley and pepper.

Beef Consommé

Making Beef Stock, page 302, with extra meat and then clarifying it with egg whites produces a beautifully clear broth that's packed with intense flavor. The classic method of clarification combines ground beef and chopped vegetables with the egg whites, but our shortcut method using a concentrated stock works equally well.

SERVES 6 AS A FIRST COURSE

1½ quarts chilled Beef Stock, page 302, made with 4 pounds of beef bones rather than 3 and an additional 2 pounds beef chuck cut into cubes
1¼ teaspoons salt
3 egg whites

WINE RECOMMENDATION:
THE RICH, PURE BEEF FLAVOR OF THE CONSOMMÉ IS THE PERFECT BACKDROP FOR A COMPLEX PINOT NOIR FROM THE BURGUNDY REGION OF FRANCE. TRY A VILLAGES- OR PREMIER-CRU-LEVEL WINE FROM THE CÔTE DE BEAUNE, SUCH AS POMMARD, VOLNAY OR BEAUNE.

1. Scrape all of the fat from the top of the chilled stock. In a large pot, bring the stock to a boil over moderately high heat. Add the salt. If there is any sign of fat floating on top of the soup, remove it. The best way is to drag a clean, dry paper towel over the surface of the soup. Repeat with additional towels until no fat remains.

2. In a medium bowl, whisk the egg whites until frothy. Whisk them into the soup. Bring the soup back to a boil, still whisking. Turn off the heat and allow the soup to stand undisturbed for 10 minutes.

3. Rinse a dish towel several times in water to remove any residual soap. Set a sieve over a large bowl and line it with the rinsed dish towel. Pour the soup through the lined sieve and leave to

strain undisturbed. Gently lift the towel away, being careful not to squeeze any of its contents into the soup.

4. Serve the soup alone or with any of the garnishes at right.

GARNISHES FOR CONSOMMÉ

Chopped herbs, tiny dice of cooked vegetables, such as carrots or zucchini, or small pasta, such as stars (stelline), all make good garnishes for consommé. Whatever you choose should be cooked separately and added just before serving so as not to cloud the soup.

Beef and Barley Soup with Mushrooms

This variation of Lamb and Barley Soup with Mushrooms, page 167, is as good as the original, but the method is streamlined.

SERVES 6

2 tablespoons cooking oil, more if needed

1½ pounds boneless beef chuck, cut into ½-inch cubes

2 large onions, chopped

2 ribs celery, chopped

2 cloves garlic, minced

½ pound shiitake mushrooms, stems removed, caps diced

½ pound cremini mushrooms, chopped

⅔ cup red wine

9 cups water

2 teaspoons salt

½ cup barley

1 teaspoon chopped fresh rosemary, or ¼ teaspoon dried, crumbled

¼ teaspoon fresh-ground black pepper

6 tablespoons sour cream or yogurt

WINE RECOMMENDATION:
A BRAWNY RED WINE, SUCH AS A YOUNG CÔTES-DU-RHÔNE FROM FRANCE'S RHÔNE VALLEY, IS DELIGHTFUL WITH THIS DISH.

1. In a large pot, heat the oil over moderately high heat. Add about half of the meat. Brown well, about 8 minutes, and remove. Brown the remaining beef, adding more oil if needed. Remove.

2. Reduce the heat to moderately low, add the onions, celery and garlic and cook, stirring occasionally, until the onions are translucent, about 5 minutes. Increase the heat to moderate, add the mushrooms and sauté until soft, about 5 minutes. Add the wine and simmer 2 minutes, scraping the bottom of the pot to dislodge any brown bits.

3. Return the meat to the pot with any juice that has accumulated. Add the water and salt and bring to a simmer over moderately high heat. Reduce the heat and cook at a bare simmer for 30 minutes. Add the barley and rosemary and cook until the barley is tender, about 1 hour longer. Stir in the pepper. Serve topped with the sour cream or yogurt. If the soup thickens too much on standing, stir in more water.

Philadelphia Pepper Pot

Still popular in restaurants throughout the Philadelphia area, this soup is said to have been invented for Washington's troops at Valley Forge. Have the butcher chop the soup bones into pieces so that you can get all the flavor from them.

SERVES 6

1	pound honeycomb tripe, cut into ¼-inch pieces
1	tablespoon cooking oil
3	onions, chopped
2	ribs celery, chopped
1	green bell pepper, chopped
2	cloves garlic, minced
2	pounds veal or beef bones, cut into 1½-inch pieces
1	pound boiling potatoes (about 3), peeled and cut into ¼-inch dice
2	quarts Chicken Stock, page 299, or canned low-sodium chicken broth
1	bay leaf
2	teaspoons salt
1	teaspoon fresh-ground black pepper

WINE RECOMMENDATION:
FOR AN UNUSUAL BUT AUTHENTIC AC-COMPANIMENT TO THIS PEPPERY DISH, TRY HARD CIDER. A COLD BEER WILL ALSO DO JUST FINE.

1. Bring a large pot of water to a boil. Add the tripe and simmer 5 minutes. Drain the tripe and rinse with cold water. Return to the pot. Cover the tripe with cold, salted water and bring to a simmer over moderate heat. Cover, reduce the heat and cook at a bare simmer for 1½ hours. Drain.

2. In a large pot, heat the oil over moderately low heat. Add the onions, celery, bell pepper and garlic. Cook, stirring occasionally, until the onions are translucent, about 5 minutes. Add the tripe, bones, potatoes, stock, bay leaf and salt. Bring to a simmer over moderately high heat. Reduce the heat and cook at a bare simmer until the tripe is very tender, 1 to 1½ hours.

3. Skim any fat from the surface of the soup. Remove the bones and bay leaf and stir in the pepper.

Roasted-Beet Borscht

While there's no shame in using canned beets (substitute one sixteen-ounce can shoestring or sliced beets with their liquid), roasted beets keep their color better and turn the soup a glorious crimson. If you've never been fond of borscht, this old family recipe is the one to change your mind.

SERVES 6

1¾ pounds fresh beets with tops

1½ pounds flanken beef short ribs, trimmed and cut between the bones, or ½ pound boneless beef chuck, cut into 1-inch pieces

1 pound green cabbage (about ⅓ head), shredded

1 pound tomatoes (about 2), chopped, or 1¾ cups canned tomatoes with their juice (14½-ounce can), chopped

1 large onion, quartered and cut into thin slices

2 teaspoons salt

1 quart water

2 tablespoons lemon juice

2 tablespoons sugar

1 pound boiling potatoes (about 3), quartered

¼ teaspoon fresh-ground black pepper

WINE RECOMMENDATION: LOOK FOR A FULL BUT NOT OVERWHELMING WHITE WINE TO COMPLEMENT THIS DISH, SUCH AS A PINOT BLANC FROM ALSACE IN FRANCE OR A PINOT BIANCO FROM THE ALTO ADIGE REGION OF ITALY.

1. Heat the oven to 325°. Cut the leaves off the beets, leaving one inch of stem. Save the leaves for another dish or discard.

2. Wrap the beets in a double sheet of aluminum foil. Set the package on a baking sheet, seam-side up, and bake until the beets are tender when pierced with a knife, 1 to 2 hours, depending on size. When the beets are cool enough to handle, peel them and cut them into ½-inch dice.

3. In a large pot, combine the beets, beef, cabbage, the tomatoes and their juice, the onion, salt and water. Bring to a simmer over moderately high heat. Reduce the heat and cook at a bare simmer, covered, for 1½ hours.

4. Add the lemon juice and sugar and cook until the meat is tender, about 30 minutes longer. ➤

5. Meanwhile, put the potatoes in a medium saucepan of salted water. Bring to a boil and simmer until tender, about 20 minutes. Drain the potatoes. When cool enough to handle, peel them and cut them into ½-inch dice.

6. To serve, remove the bones, if any, from the soup. Add the pepper. Divide the diced potatoes among bowls and ladle the soup over them.

—Jane Sigal

MAKE IT AHEAD

You can make this borscht in advance, but to keep the potatoes white, wait to cook them until an hour or so before you plan to serve the soup. Combine the soup and potatoes at the last minute. If you don't mind pink potatoes, just add them to the soup during the last hour of cooking.

VEGETARIAN VARIATION ON VEGETABLE BEEF SOUP

You can make a delicious vegetarian version of our Vegetable Beef Soup, opposite page, by making the following changes:
◆ Omit the beef roast.
◆ Replace the Beef Stock with Vegetable Stock, page 303.
◆ Increase the tomato paste to two tablespoons.
◆ Blanch a half-pound of shredded cabbage in boiling water for one minute and drain. Add the cabbage to the soup with the tomatoes, corn and beans.

Vegetable Beef Soup

Brimming with vegetables and tender chunks of beef, this old-fashioned, thick and hearty soup is the real McCoy. A long-simmered beef broth produces an intensely flavored soup, well worth the effort.

SERVES 6

Ingredients for 1½ quarts Beef Stock, page 302

1	2-pound beef rump roast
2	tablespoons cooking oil
2	onions, chopped
2	carrots, chopped
2	ribs celery, chopped
2	cloves garlic, minced
1	large baking potato, peeled and cut into ½-inch cubes
1¾	cups canned tomatoes (14½-ounce can), drained and chopped
1	tablespoon tomato paste
¾	cup fresh (cut from about 1 ear) or frozen corn kernels
¼	pound green beans, cut into 1-inch lengths
2½	teaspoons salt
¼	teaspoon fresh-ground black pepper
3	tablespoons chopped mixed fresh herbs, such as dill, parsley and chives, optional

WINE RECOMMENDATION:
With its chunky fresh vegetables and broth infused with the flavor of beef, this soup benefits from a red wine that's full of fruit. Try either a merlot from California or a cabernet/shiraz blend from Australia.

1. Prepare the stock, adding the beef to the pot with the browned bones, vegetables and water. Simmer for 4 hours. Remove the beef. When it is cool enough to handle, cut it into bite-size pieces. Strain the stock. Press the vegetables firmly to get all the liquid. Skim the fat from the stock. You should have 1½ quarts of stock.

2. In a large pot, heat the oil over moderately low heat. Add the onions, carrots, celery and garlic and cook, stirring occasionally, until the onions are translucent, about 5 minutes.

3. Add the stock and potato and bring to a boil. Reduce the heat to low and simmer 10 minutes. Add the tomatoes, tomato paste, corn, beans and salt and simmer until all the vegetables are tender, about 10 minutes longer. Add the reserved meat, the pepper and herbs and heat through.

Oxtail and Lentil Soup

Thick, meaty and packed with rich flavor, this delicious dish is one of the best lentil soups we know. The oxtails marinate in balsamic vinegar and black pepper, which adds a hint of sweetness and spice. Though this soup does take a while to prepare, you can make it in advance; it just gets better with time.

Serves 6

4   pounds oxtails, cut into 2-inch pieces
6   tablespoons cooking oil, more if needed
½   cup balsamic vinegar
2   bay leaves
2¾   teaspoons salt
1   tablespoon fresh-ground black pepper
4   carrots, chopped
2   onions, chopped
2   cups lentils
12   cloves garlic
2   teaspoons dried thyme
3½   cups canned tomatoes (28-ounce can), drained and chopped
¼   cup chopped fresh flat-leaf parsley
1   teaspoon lemon juice
     Tabasco sauce, for serving

Wine recommendation: This thick, flavorful soup is perfect with a young, slightly sweet pinot noir from the Carneros region of California or a five-year-old Rioja from Spain.

1. In a large glass or stainless-steel bowl, toss the oxtails with 2 tablespoons of the oil, the vinegar, bay leaves, 1 teaspoon of the salt and 2 teaspoons of the pepper. Marinate for 1 hour or longer, tossing occasionally.

2. Drain the oxtails, reserving the marinade. Pat the meat dry with paper towels. In a large pot, heat 2 tablespoons of the oil over moderately high heat. Add about a third of the oxtails. Brown on all sides, about 8 minutes, and remove. Brown the remaining oxtails in 2 more batches, adding more oil if needed.

3. Return all the meat to the pot with any juice that has accumulated. Add the carrots, half the onions, the marinade and enough water to cover the oxtails by 1 inch. Bring to a boil and remove the foam that rises to the surface. Reduce the heat and simmer, covered, until the meat is very tender, about 2½ hours.

4. Remove the oxtails and strain the cooking liquid. Press the vegetables firmly to get all the liquid. When the oxtails are cool enough to handle, remove the meat from the bones, cutting off any cartilage and fat as you go. Cut the meat into ½-inch pieces and set aside. Skim the fat from the surface of the cooking liquid. If necessary, add enough water to the cooking liquid to measure 2 quarts.

5. In a large pot, heat the remaining 2 tablespoons oil over moderately low heat. Add the remaining onion and cook, stirring occasionally, until the onion is translucent, about 5 minutes.

6. Stir in the cooking liquid, lentils, garlic cloves, thyme, the remaining 1¾ teaspoons salt and 1 teaspoon pepper and bring to a simmer. Reduce the heat and simmer, covered, until the lentils are very soft, about 45 minutes.

7. In a food processor or blender, puree half the soup, making sure to include all the garlic cloves.

8. Return the puree to the pot and stir in the tomatoes, parsley and oxtail meat. Bring to a simmer and heat through. Add the lemon juice and serve with the Tabasco.

—Ann Chantal Altman

Spiced Beef Soup with Rice Noodles

The Vietnamese enjoy soups like this as a meal at any time of day—especially for breakfast. Such soups are easiest to eat with both chopsticks for the noodles and beef and a spoon for the rest of the soup. Be sure the stock is hot when you pour it into the bowls so that it will cook the beef slices. A squeeze of lime at the table gives just the right balance to the soup.

SERVES 6

5	pounds beef bones, preferably oxtail or a mixture of oxtail and shank bones, cut into 1½-inch pieces
3½	quarts water
6	star anise
1	2-inch piece fresh ginger, quartered
1	cinnamon stick
2	bay leaves
1	large onion, quartered
2½	teaspoons salt
1	tablespoon sugar
1	pound medium-width rice noodles*
1	pound beef eye of round
3	cups bean sprouts
1	tablespoon soy sauce
1½	teaspoons Asian sesame oil
1	tomato, cut into thin wedges
3	scallions including green tops, cut into thin slices
¼	cup shredded fresh basil
¼	cup whole fresh cilantro leaves
1	lime, cut into 6 wedges

*Available at Asian markets

WINE RECOMMENDATION:
EITHER A BEER OR A GEWÜRZTRAMINER FROM THE ALSACE REGION IN FRANCE IS IDEAL WITH THIS HIGHLY FLAVORED SOUP.

1. Put the bones in a large pot with enough water to cover. Bring to a boil and drain. Return the bones to the pot. Add the water, star anise, ginger, cinnamon stick, bay leaves, onion, salt and sugar. Bring to a boil, reduce the heat and simmer, partially covered, for 2 hours.

2. Meanwhile, in a large bowl, cover the rice noodles with cold water and leave to soften for 20 to 30 minutes. Drain and set aside.

3. Strain the stock. Press the bones and onion to get all the liquid. Skim off the fat. You should have 2 quarts of stock. Put the stock in a large saucepan and bring to a simmer over moderately high heat.

4. With a very sharp knife, cut the meat in half lengthwise and then cross-

wise into the thinnest possible slices. Divide the beef slices and bean sprouts among 6 large soup bowls.

5. In a large pot of boiling, salted water, cook half the noodles, stirring, until translucent but still slightly chewy, about 2 minutes. Lift the noodles from the water with tongs and drain. Cook the remaining noodles in the same way. Divide the noodles among the bowls.

6. Add the soy sauce and sesame oil to the simmering stock and ladle it over the noodles. Top with the tomato wedges, scallions, basil and cilantro and serve with lime wedges.

—Tracey Seaman

CUTTING EDGE

To cut raw meat into very thin slices easily, stick it in the freezer for about an hour. Then you can shave off nice even slices of the semi-frozen meat. Or, of course, you can ask the butcher to do the slicing for you.

Sweet and Sour Cabbage Soup

Cabbage, ground beef and tomatoes combine in a soup reminiscent of sweet and sour stuffed cabbage. The tangy broth is just slightly mellowed with brown sugar. Adjust the balance of sweet and sour by adding more or less sugar and vinegar to please your own taste.

SERVES 6

1	tablespoon cooking oil
½	pound ground beef
2	onions, chopped
2	cloves garlic, minced
1½	pounds green cabbage (about ½ head), shredded
3½	cups canned tomatoes with their juice (28-ounce can), chopped
2	quarts Chicken Stock, page 299, or canned low-sodium chicken broth
1	tart apple, such as Granny Smith, peeled, cored and grated
1 to 2	tablespoons wine vinegar or cider vinegar
1½	tablespoons brown sugar
2	teaspoons dry mustard
1	teaspoon ground ginger
1½	teaspoons salt
¼	teaspoon fresh-ground black pepper

WINE RECOMMENDATION: DESPITE THE GROUND BEEF, WITH ALL THE SPICES AND SWEETNESS THIS IS REALLY A WHITE-WINE DISH. LOOK FOR AN OFF-DRY KABINETT RIESLING FROM THE MOSEL-SAAR-RUWER REGION OF GERMANY, WHICH WILL HOLD ITS OWN AGAINST THE STRONG PERSONALITY OF THE SOUP.

1. In a large pot, heat the oil over moderate heat. Add the ground beef, onions and garlic and cook, breaking up the meat, until the beef is brown, about 5 minutes.

2. Add the cabbage, the tomatoes with their juice and the stock. Bring to a boil. Reduce the heat, cover and simmer for 30 minutes.

3. Stir in the apple, vinegar, brown sugar, mustard, ginger and salt. Continue simmering, uncovered, until the cabbage is very soft, about 30 minutes longer. Add the pepper.

Polish Sour-Rye Soup with Kielbasa

Kwas, a fermented liquid made from rye or oat flour, garlic and water, flavors this old-style Polish soup. You will need to start the *kwas* four to five days before you make the soup, but putting it together is simple and the result is well worth the trouble of advance planning. Be warned: The *kwas* will look bad and smell worse. Add the murky liquid courageously. We guarantee that the finished soup is exceptional.

SERVES 6

1 cup whole-grain rye or oat flour*

3 cups boiled water, cooled to lukewarm

2 cloves garlic, 1 crushed, 1 minced

¼ pound thick-sliced bacon, chopped

1 onion, chopped

½ pound cremini or white mushrooms, cut into thick slices

2 tablespoons all-purpose flour

1½ quarts Veal Stock or Chicken Stock, page 302 or 299, or canned low-sodium chicken broth

2 teaspoons salt

¾ pound boiling potatoes (about 2), peeled and cut into ¾-inch dice

1 tablespoon fresh marjoram, or 1 teaspoon dried

½ pound kielbasa, halved lengthwise and then cut crosswise into thin slices

½ cup heavy cream

¼ teaspoon fresh-ground black pepper

3 hard-cooked eggs, quartered, optional

¼ cup chopped fresh chives or scallion tops

* Available at health-food stores

WINE RECOMMENDATION: HEARTY AND FULL OF SMOKED SAUSAGE AND BACON, THIS SOUP IS PERFECTLY PAIRED WITH A RICH, SMOKY PINOT GRIS FROM ALSACE IN FRANCE. A GEWÜRZTRAMINER FROM THE SAME REGION WILL ALSO WORK NICELY.

1. With boiling water, sterilize a spoon and a 2-quart glass jar, measuring cup or crock. In the container, stir the whole-grain flour and 1½ cups of the lukewarm water until smooth. Add the crushed garlic clove and pour the remaining 1½ cups lukewarm water on top but don't stir it in. Cover the container with plastic wrap and pierce with a knife tip. Set aside in a warm place for 4 to 5 days. When the *kwas* has fermented sufficiently, it will have a sour aroma and there will be a clear separation of flour and liquid. Skim off any foam floating on the surface. Strain the liquid portion of the *kwas* and discard the settled flour. Refrigerate until ready to use.

2. In a large pot, cook the bacon until crisp. Pour off all but 2 tablespoons of

158

the fat. Add the onion and the minced garlic. Cook over moderately low heat, stirring occasionally, until translucent, about 5 minutes. Add the mushrooms and cook 5 minutes longer.

3. Stir in the all-purpose flour and cook, stirring, for 2 minutes. Gradually add the stock, stirring. Add the salt. Bring to a simmer and continue to simmer, uncovered, for 15 minutes.

4. Meanwhile, put the potatoes in a saucepan of salted water, bring to a boil and continue cooking until almost tender, about 7 minutes. Drain and set aside.

5. Add 1½ cups of the *kwas* to the soup, bring to a simmer and skim. Add the marjoram, potatoes and kielbasa. Simmer until the potatoes are tender, about 5 minutes.

6. Add the cream and pepper. Serve topped with the hard-cooked eggs, if using, and chives.

—Andrew Ziobro

Pork and Cabbage Soup with Cider

Apple cider and caraway seeds contribute their distinctive flavors to this soup. Serve it as a first course for eight followed by a light main course or as a one-dish meal with salad, good bread and a satisfying dessert.

SERVES 6

3   tablespoons butter, more if needed
1½   pounds boneless pork shoulder or loin, cut into ¾ -inch cubes
1   onion, chopped
¾   pound green cabbage (about ¼ head), shredded
1   teaspoon caraway seeds
2   teaspoons salt
1   quart Chicken Stock, page 299, or canned low-sodium chicken broth
2   cups apple cider
2   carrots, chopped
¼   teaspoon fresh-ground black pepper
1   tablespoon chopped fresh parsley

1. In a large pot, melt 2 tablespoons of the butter over moderately high heat. Add about half of the pork. Brown well on all sides, about 8 minutes, and remove. Brown the remaining pork, adding more butter if needed. Remove.

2. Reduce the heat to moderately low. Melt the remaining tablespoon butter in the pot. Add the onion and cook, stirring occasionally, until translucent, about 5 minutes. Add the cabbage, caraway seeds and salt. Cover and cook, stirring occasionally, until the cabbage wilts, about 5 minutes.

3. Return the pork to the pot with any juice that has accumulated. Add the stock, cider and carrots. Bring to a sim-

mer over moderately high heat. Reduce the heat and simmer, partially covered, until the pork is tender, about 45 min-

utes. Add the pepper. Just before serving, stir in the parsley.

—Charles Pierce

CABBAGE VARIETIES

Green cabbage is the one that everyone knows—a round, tight head of waxy leaves that comes in a range of colors from pale to dark green. **Red cabbage** is the same thing, just a different color. A little less common is **Savoy cabbage** with its round head of crinkled leaves varying from light to dark green. These three are similar in taste. Chinese cabbages, of which there are two types, **bok choy** and **napa**, have elongated heads. Their thick-ribbed leaves are milder in flavor than those of green, red and Savoy cabbage. Bok choy is pale green, almost white. The tips of the napa leaves are greener and more crinkled.

Vietnamese Pork and Cabbage-Roll Soup

Little cabbage packages filled with a zesty pork mixture and tied with scallion greens are the main attraction in this traditional Vietnamese soup, adapted from *Simple Art of Vietnamese Cooking* by Binh Duong and Marcia Kiesel. Dramatically presented, a pair of cabbage rolls are nestled in a mound of rice and a ginger-cilantro-pork broth is poured on top. Because the stock is such an important element, we don't advise using canned broth in this recipe, though you can substitute chicken stock for the pork. For a less substantial dish, omit the rice.

SERVES 6

¼ ounce dried Chinese black mushrooms or dried shiitake mushrooms* (about 3 medium mushrooms)

5 ounces ground pork

1 clove garlic, minced

2 tablespoons plus 2 teaspoons Asian fish sauce (nam pla or nuoc mam)*

¼ teaspoon salt

¼ teaspoon fresh-ground black pepper

1 head green cabbage, cored

3 scallions, white parts cut into thin slices, green tops left whole

1½ quarts water

3 cups rice

1½ quarts Asian Pork Stock or Chicken Stock, page 301 or 299

2 tablespoons chopped fresh cilantro

1 lime, cut into 6 wedges

*Available at Asian markets

1. In a medium bowl, soak the mushrooms in hot water to cover until softened, about 20 minutes. Drain and rinse the mushrooms well to remove any remaining grit. Squeeze to extract as much water as possible. Discard the stems and mince the caps. Put them in a bowl and stir in the pork, garlic, 2 teaspoons of the fish sauce, ⅛ teaspoon of the salt and ⅛ teaspoon of the pepper.

2. Bring a large pot of water to a boil. Remove any broken outer leaves from the cabbage. Gently remove 6 nice leaves. Put them in the pot of water and boil gently until wilted but still light green, about 2 minutes. Carefully remove the cabbage leaves and rinse with cold water. Drain thoroughly. Add the

scallion tops to the boiling water and cook for 10 seconds. Drain. Rinse with cold water and drain thoroughly. Cut out the tough stems from the cabbage and cut each leaf in half. Cut each scallion top lengthwise into 4 strips.

3. Put one-twelfth of the pork filling near the bottom of a cabbage-leaf half. Fold the two sides in and then roll up. Tie with a scallion strip. Repeat with the remaining cabbage leaves.

4. In a medium pot, bring the water to a boil. Add the rice. Reduce the heat, cover and simmer until the rice is tender and all the water is absorbed, about 25 minutes.

5. In a large pot, bring the stock to a boil over moderately high heat. Reduce the heat to low and add the remaining 2 tablespoons fish sauce and ⅛ teaspoon salt, the sliced scallions and the cabbage rolls. Simmer, partially covered, until the cabbage rolls are tender, 12 to 14 minutes. Add the remaining ⅛ teaspoon pepper and the cilantro.

6. Put the rice in individual serving bowls and top with the cabbage rolls. Ladle the hot soup into the bowls and serve with the lime wedges.

BLANCHING CABBAGE

Blanching the cabbage leaves makes them pliable enough to roll up around stuffing. Usually you can peel off the outside leaves from the raw cabbage and blanch just the number you need, but sometimes they cling so tightly to the head that getting them off without tearing is difficult. To loosen the leaves, blanch the whole head. Immerse it in boiling water, and then cook for about eight minutes. Rinse with cold water until completely cool and drain. The leaves will peel off easily. This method also saves time if you plan to make a lot of rolls, using most of the cabbage.

MAKE IT AHEAD

While this soup takes a little time to make, you can prepare all of the components, except the rice, ahead and cook them together just before serving.

Chinese Hot and Sour Soup

Both China and Thailand boast their own interpretation of hot and sour soup. This Chinese version is filled with slivered pork, tofu, dried mushrooms and scallions.

SERVES 6

½   pound pork loin
1   1-inch piece fresh ginger
3   tablespoons dry sherry
¼   cup soy sauce
1   teaspoon fresh-ground black pepper
½   ounce dried Chinese black mushrooms or dried shiitake mushrooms* (about 6 medium mushrooms)
½   ounce dried tree-ear mushrooms*
6   dried lily buds,* optional
6   tablespoons cornstarch
2   quarts Chicken Stock, page 299, or canned low-sodium chicken broth
¾   pound firm tofu
2½   teaspoons salt
    Large pinch cayenne
5   scallions including green tops, chopped
¼   cup red-wine vinegar
¾   teaspoon Asian sesame oil
1   teaspoon sugar
2   eggs, beaten

*Available at Asian markets

WINE RECOMMENDATION:
SERVE THIS CLASSIC WITH A COLD BEER OR A YOUNG GEWÜRZTRAMINER OR CHENIN BLANC FROM CALIFORNIA.

1. Cut the pork into the thinnest possible slices. Stack the slices and cut them into ¼-inch-wide strips. Peel the ginger and cut it into the thinnest possible slices. Stack the slices and cut them into thin slivers. Put the pork and ginger in a bowl. Stir in the sherry, soy sauce and black pepper. Set aside to marinate for at least 30 minutes.

2. In a bowl, soak the mushrooms and lily buds, if using, in hot water to cover until softened, about 20 minutes. Remove the mushrooms and strain their liquid through a sieve lined with cheesecloth or a paper towel into a bowl. Reserve 6 tablespoons of the soaking liquid. Drain and rinse the mushrooms well to remove any remaining grit. Squeeze the mushrooms and lily buds to remove as much water as possible.

3. Discard the stems from the black mushrooms and cut the caps into thin slices. Chop the tree-ear mushrooms into ¼-inch pieces. Cut the lily buds

into thin slices. In a small bowl, combine the reserved mushroom-soaking liquid with the cornstarch and set aside.

4. In a large pot, bring the stock to a simmer. Cut the tofu into ⅛-inch slices. Stack the slices and cut them into ¼-inch-wide strips. Add the tofu, mushrooms and lily buds to the simmering stock with the salt and cayenne. Simmer 5 minutes. Add the pork mixture, scallions, vinegar, sesame oil and sugar and simmer 3 minutes longer.

5. Stir the reserved cornstarch mixture and add it to the soup. Simmer until slightly thickened, about 1 minute. Pour the eggs into the soup in a thin stream, stirring, and simmer for 2 minutes.

LOW-SALT STOCK

While nothing beats homemade meat or poultry stock for flavor, in most cases canned broth is a good alternative. Stock is usually made with very little or no salt for a couple of reasons: the cook can then control the seasoning according to the needs of the dish and the stock can be reduced for more intense flavor, if needed, without getting too salty. Therefore, low-sodium broth, which our recipes specify, more closely resembles the real thing than does standard broth. If you use regular canned broth, simply reduce the amount of salt in the recipe and, as always, taste carefully for seasoning before serving the dish.

Lamb and Barley Soup with Mushrooms

Red wine, mushrooms, rosemary and sour cream embellish what would otherwise be plain old Scotch Broth. If you'd like to make the traditional soup, just leave out the extra ingredients. Be sure to ask your butcher to cut the shanks into pieces for you.

SERVES 6

6	pounds lamb shanks, cut into 1½-inch pieces
3	large onions, 1 quartered, 2 chopped
6	cloves garlic, 4 left whole, 2 minced
2	carrots, cut into 2-inch pieces
2½	teaspoons salt
	Fresh-ground black pepper
⅔	cup red wine
3	quarts water
1½	tablespoons cooking oil
2	ribs celery, chopped
½	pound shiitake mushrooms, stems removed, caps diced
½	pound cremini mushrooms, chopped
½	cup barley
1	teaspoon chopped fresh rosemary, or ¼ teaspoon dried, crumbled
6	tablespoons sour cream or yogurt

WINE RECOMMENDATION:
MATCH THIS RICH, RUSTIC SOUP WITH AN AGGRESSIVE, HIGH-ALCOHOL RED WINE. TRY A YOUNG ZINFANDEL FROM CALIFORNIA OR A CHÂTEAUNEUF-DU-PAPE FROM FRANCE.

1. Heat the oven to 450°. Put the lamb shanks, the quartered onion, the whole garlic cloves and the carrots in a large roasting pan and sprinkle with ½ teaspoon of the salt and a pinch of pepper. Roast in the oven, stirring occasionally, until the meat and vegetables are well browned, about 1 hour.

2. Transfer the contents of the pan to a large pot. Discard any fat from the pan. Pour the wine into the roasting pan and scrape to dislodge any brown bits. Add this mixture to the meat and vegetables. Add the water and the remaining 2 teaspoons salt. Bring to a simmer over moderately high heat. Reduce the heat and cook at a bare simmer, partially covered, until the meat is tender, about 1½ hours. Strain into a large bowl. Reserve the shanks. Press the vegetables firmly to get all the liquid. Skim the fat from the stock. If necessary, add enough water to the stock to measure 2 quarts. ➤

3. When the lamb is cool enough to handle, remove the meat from the bones and trim away all the gristle and fat. Cut the meat into small pieces.

4. In a large pot, heat the oil over moderately low heat. Add the chopped onions, the minced garlic and the celery and cook, stirring occasionally, until the onions are translucent, about 5 minutes. Add the mushrooms and sauté over moderately high heat until soft, about 5 minutes. Add the stock and bring to a boil. Add the barley and rosemary. Simmer until the barley is cooked, about 1 hour.

5. Return the meat to the soup and heat through. Serve topped with the sour cream or yogurt. If the soup thickens too much on standing, stir in some water.

COOKING OIL

In our recipes, cooking oil refers to any readily available, reasonably priced nut, seed or vegetable oil with a high smoking point. Peanut, sunflower, canola, safflower, corn or generic vegetable oil will all fill the bill. You can heat these oils to about 400° before they begin to smoke and develop an unpleasant flavor.

CHAPTER 6 · COLD SOUPS

Cold Curried Zucchini Soup with Cilantro

Cool, spicy, tangy and vibrant green, this refreshing soup looks as good as it tastes. It's the most delicious way we know to use up an abundance of summer zucchini. For the best color and flavor, make the soup the day you plan to serve it.

SERVES 6

3 tablespoons butter

3 onions, chopped

3 pounds zucchini (about 5 large), quartered lengthwise, seeded and cut crosswise into ½-inch slices

1½ teaspoons curry powder

1½ teaspoons sugar

1½ quarts Chicken Stock, page 299, or canned low-sodium chicken broth

1½ teaspoons salt

3 tablespoons chopped fresh cilantro, plus whole leaves for garnish

1½ cups plain yogurt

¼ teaspoon fresh-ground black pepper

WINE RECOMMENDATION:
THIS LIVELY SOUP WORKS BEST WITH A WINE THAT HAS A BIT OF ACIDITY (FOR THE VEGETABLES) AND A TOUCH OF SWEETNESS (FOR THE SPICES). A GOOD SELECTION WOULD BE A RECENT VINTAGE OF KABINETT RIESLING FROM THE MOSEL-SAAR-RUWER REGION OF GERMANY.

1. In a large pot, melt the butter over moderately low heat. Add the onions. Cook, stirring occasionally, until the onions are translucent, about 5 minutes. Add the zucchini, curry powder and sugar and cook, stirring, for 1 minute.

2. Add the stock and salt and bring the mixture to a boil. Reduce the heat and simmer, partially covered, until the zucchini is tender, about 10 minutes. Let cool.

3. In a blender or food processor, puree the zucchini mixture and chopped cilantro with the yogurt and pepper. Refrigerate to chill, at least 2 hours. Serve topped with the whole cilantro leaves.

Gazpacho

Here's our favorite recipe for this cold classic. The soup is especially good for summer entertaining since it can be made a day ahead. It looks appealing garnished with small cubes of the main ingredients—tomato, cucumber and green pepper.

SERVES 6

2	pounds tomatoes (about 4), peeled and seeded
2	medium cucumbers, peeled, halved lengthwise and seeded
2	green bell peppers
2	onions, chopped
2	ribs celery, chopped
1	quart tomato or V-8 juice
¼	cup olive oil
⅓	cup red-wine vinegar
2	tablespoons lemon juice
2	teaspoons Worcestershire sauce
4	cloves garlic, minced
2	tablespoons chopped fresh flat-leaf parsley
1	tablespoon chopped fresh chives or scallion tops
1	teaspoon sugar
2	teaspoons salt
½	teaspoon fresh-ground black pepper Cheese and Herb Croutons, page 306

WINE RECOMMENDATION:
WITH ITS PROFUSION OF FRESH TOMATO AND VEGETABLE TASTES, THIS SOUP IS BEST PAIRED WITH A SIMPLE, STRAIGHTFORWARD WHITE WINE WITH DECENT ACIDITY. A GOOD CHOICE FROM SPAIN WOULD BE A RECENT VINTAGE OF ONE OF THE NEW-STYLE WHITE WINES MADE FROM THE ALVARIÑO GRAPE.

1. Chop three-quarters of the tomatoes and one and a half of the cucumbers and bell peppers.

2. Put the chopped tomatoes, cucumber and bell pepper in a food processor or blender and add the onions, celery, tomato juice, oil, vinegar, lemon juice, Worcestershire sauce, garlic, 1 tablespoon of the parsley, the chives, sugar, salt and black pepper. Process or blend until almost smooth. Refrigerate to chill, at least 2 hours.

3. Cut the remaining tomato, cucumber and bell pepper into small dice. Serve the soup topped with the diced vegetables, the remaining 1 tablespoon parsley and the croutons.

Carrot and Cumin Soup

Ground almonds give an extra dimension to this carrot soup with an Indian accent. We found that we liked the soup warm, too, so serve it cold in the summer and warm in the colder months.

SERVES 6

¾	cup sliced almonds
2	tablespoons cooking oil
2	pounds carrots, chopped
4	onions, chopped
4	ribs celery, chopped
2	cloves garlic, minced
2½	teaspoons ground cumin
1	teaspoon ground coriander
2	quarts water
2¼	teaspoons salt
½	teaspoon honey
½	teaspoon fresh-ground black pepper
¼	cup chopped fresh cilantro
½	cup sour cream or yogurt

 SWEET CARROTS

Apart from sugar beets, carrots have more natural sugar than any other vegetable and should have a delicious sweetness to them. However, carrots vary widely depending on where they're grown, their age and variety. They may not always be as sweet as you'd like. Taste the soup and, if necessary, add extra honey.

WINE RECOMMENDATION: THIS MILDLY SPICY SOUP WILL PAIR BEST WITH A RECENT VINTAGE KABINETT RIESLING FROM THE MOSEL-SAAR-RUWER REGION OF GERMANY OR A GEWÜRZTRAMINER FROM ALSACE IN FRANCE.

1. In a small, heavy frying pan, toast the almonds over moderately low heat, stirring frequently, until light brown, about 5 minutes. When cool, reduce ½ cup of the almonds to a powder in a food processor, blender or rotary grater.

2. In a large pot, heat the oil over moderately low heat. Add the carrots, onions, celery and garlic. Cover and cook, stirring occasionally, until the vegetables are soft, about 10 minutes. Add the ground almonds, cumin and coriander and cook another 30 seconds. Add the water and salt. Bring to a boil. Reduce the heat and simmer, partially covered, until the vegetables are very soft, about 15 minutes. Add the honey and pepper.

3. Puree the soup in a blender or food processor. Refrigerate to chill, at least 2 hours. Stir in the cilantro. Top each serving with a dollop of sour cream and the remaining toasted almonds.

Yellow-Pepper and Mascarpone Soup

Yellow peppers give both sweetness and beautiful color to this smooth soup. It's delicious chilled, but, like Carrot and Cumin Soup, page 173, you can serve it warm as well.

SERVES 6

3   tablespoons olive oil
5   yellow bell peppers, chopped
1   onion, chopped
1   carrot, chopped
1   pound baking potatoes (about 2), peeled and chopped
1   quart Chicken Stock, page 299, or canned low-sodium chicken broth
1   quart water
1½ teaspoons salt
¼   cup mascarpone cheese or heavy cream
¼   teaspoon fresh-ground black pepper
8   fresh basil leaves, shredded

WINE RECOMMENDATION:
THE MILD, VEGETAL TASTE OF THIS SOUP OFFERS WIDE LATITUDE IN WINE SELECTION. TRY A RELATIVELY LIGHT AND REFRESHING CHARDONNAY OR PINOT GRIGIO FROM THE ALTO ADIGE REGION IN ITALY.

1. In a large pot, heat the oil over moderate heat. Add the peppers, onion, carrot and potatoes and cook, stirring occasionally, until they begin to soften, about 8 minutes.

2. Add the stock, water and salt and bring to a boil. Reduce the heat to low and simmer, partially covered, until the vegetables are very soft, about 30 minutes.

3. Puree the soup in a food processor or blender. Stir in the mascarpone until it melts. Add the black pepper. Refrigerate the soup to chill, at least 2 hours. Serve topped with the basil.

—Erica De Mane

PICKING PEPPERS

You can change the color and flavor of this soup by substituting other bell peppers for the yellow ones. The red and orange varieties are especially good and colorful and have the same pleasant sweetness. Green peppers also work well, though, of course, give an entirely different taste.

Avocado and Tomatillo Soup

Tangy lime juice and tomatillos set off the richness of the avocados in this inventive soup.

SERVES 6 AS A FIRST COURSE

3   poblano chiles
3   avocados, preferably Hass, cut into pieces
1   pound tomatillos, husked, rinsed, cored and quartered
3½   cups cold water
3   tablespoons lime juice, from about 2 limes
1½   teaspoons salt
¾   teaspoon fresh-ground black pepper
3   scallions including green tops, cut into thin slices

WINE RECOMMENDATION: EVERY INGREDIENT IN THIS SPICY SOUP ARGUES FOR BEER, PREFERABLY ONE OF THE LIGHTER MEXICAN VARIETIES, AS THE BEVERAGE OF CHOICE. IF WINE IS A MUST, TRY A WHITE WINE FROM CALIFORNIA WITH ENOUGH SWEETNESS TO STAND UP TO THE HEAT, SUCH AS A CHENIN BLANC OR GEWÜRZTRAMINER.

1. Roast the poblanos over an open flame or broil 4 inches from the heat, turning with tongs until charred all over, about 10 minutes. When the chiles are cool enough to handle, pull off their skin. Remove the stems, seeds and ribs. Cut the chiles into small dice.

2. Puree the poblanos, avocados and tomatillos with the water, lime juice, salt and pepper in a blender or food processor. Refrigerate to chill, at least 2 hours. Serve topped with the scallions.

—Susan Feniger and
Mary Sue Milliken
Border Grill

Lithuanian Borscht

At Square One in San Francisco, Chef Goldstein uses an array of garnishes to top off her refreshing borscht. Chopped eggs, cucumber, potatoes and scallions, along with a dollop of sour cream, give textural as well as color contrast.

SERVES 6

3	pounds beets (about 7), 1 peeled and coarsely grated, the rest unpeeled
¼	cup red wine
1	pound boiling potatoes (about 3)
2	tablespoons butter
2	red onions, chopped
1½	cups Chicken Stock, page 299, or canned low-sodium chicken broth
1	quart buttermilk
1½	teaspoons salt
¼	teaspoon fresh-ground black pepper
½	cup sour cream
3	hard-cooked eggs, chopped
1	large cucumber, peeled, halved lengthwise, seeded and chopped
3	scallions including green tops, minced

WINE RECOMMENDATION:
MATCHING A WINE WITH BORSCHT IS A REAL CHALLENGE. TRY EITHER A WHITE OR A RED, BUT KEEP IT SIMPLE. A RIESLING FROM THE MOSEL-SAAR-RUWER REGION IN GERMANY IS A GOOD CHOICE FOR THE WHITE; FOR THE RED, A CORBIÈRES FROM THE SOUTH OF FRANCE.

1. In a small bowl, combine the grated beet with the wine. Set aside.

2. In a large pot, cover the unpeeled beets with salted water and bring to a boil. Reduce the heat and simmer until the beets are tender, about 40 minutes. Drain. When the beets are cool enough to handle, peel and cut all but 1 of them into thick slices. Cut the remaining beet into matchstick strips.

3. Meanwhile, in a medium saucepan, cover the potatoes with salted water and bring to a boil. Cook until tender, about 20 minutes. Drain. When the potatoes are cool enough to handle, peel them and cut them into ½-inch dice.

4. In a medium saucepan, melt the butter over moderately low heat. Add the onions and cook, stirring occasionally, until the onions are soft, about 10 min-

utes. Add the stock and bring to a boil over high heat.

5. In a blender or food processor, puree the onion mixture, beet slices and grated beet with the wine. Transfer to a large bowl and stir in the buttermilk. Add the beet strips, salt and pepper. Refrigerate to chill, at least 2 hours.

6. Top each serving with a dollop of sour cream and some of the potatoes, eggs, cucumber and scallions.

—Joyce Goldstein
Square One

 ## TO SAVE TIME

While fresh beets make the best borscht, cooked, jarred beets are a close second for this soup, and they'll save you the forty minutes it takes to cook fresh. You'll need four one-pound jars of beets in place of the three pounds of fresh ones called for in the recipe. Don't worry about the grated raw beet; just add the wine when pureeing the soup. Since jarred beets are small, replace the one cut into matchstick strips with about three.

Vichyssoise

A French chef working in America invented this cold version of the traditional leek and potato soup. Of course, you can serve it warm, too.

SERVES 6

4	tablespoons butter
2½	pounds leeks (about 7), white and light-green parts only, split lengthwise, cut crosswise into slices and washed well
2½	pounds baking potatoes (about 5), peeled and sliced
1½	quarts Chicken Stock, page 299, or canned low-sodium chicken broth
1½	teaspoons salt
¼	teaspoon fresh-ground black pepper
1¾	cups heavy cream
1	tablespoon chopped fresh chives or scallion tops

WINE RECOMMENDATION:
CONTRAST THE SWEET TASTE AND LUSCIOUS TEXTURE OF THIS CLASSIC WITH A GLASS OF DRY, NUTTY SHERRY. LOOK FOR EITHER A FINO OR A MANZANILLA FROM A GOOD PRODUCER.

1. In a large pot, melt the butter over moderately low heat. Add the leeks. Cover and cook, stirring occasionally, until soft, about 10 minutes.

2. Add the potatoes, stock and salt. Cover and cook until the vegetables are very soft, about 40 minutes.

3. In a food processor or blender, puree the soup in batches. Stir in the pepper and heavy cream and refrigerate to chill, at least 2 hours. Serve sprinkled with the chives.

Chilled Fresh-Tomato Soup with Summer Relish

A soup this simple (no cooking involved) requires perfectly ripe, flavorful tomatoes. Enjoy it during the height of summer.

SERVES 6

6   pounds tomatoes (about 12)
¼   cup balsamic vinegar
2¼   teaspoons salt
     Fresh-ground black pepper
¾   cup plain yogurt
¼   cup finely chopped red onion
6   tablespoons finely chopped red bell pepper
6   tablespoons seeded, peeled and finely chopped cucumber
3   tablespoons minced fresh basil
2   tablespoons minced fresh mint
½   avocado, preferably Hass

WINE RECOMMENDATION: CHOOSE A STRAIGHTFORWARD, QUAFFABLE WHITE WINE TO REFRESH THE PALATE AND COMPLEMENT THE FRESH GARDEN FLAVORS OF THIS SOUP. ONE OF THE NEW-STYLE WHITE WINES FROM THE CÔTES DE PROVENCE OR THE CÔTES DE GASCOGNE REGION OF FRANCE WOULD BE A GOOD CHOICE.

1. Chop the tomatoes and work them through a food mill to remove the skin and seeds. Or peel and seed them and puree in a food processor or blender. Stir in the vinegar, 1¾ teaspoons of the salt and ¼ teaspoon black pepper. Refrigerate to chill, at least 2 hours.

2. In a small bowl, combine the yogurt, onion, bell pepper, cucumber, basil, mint, the remaining ½ teaspoon salt and ⅛ teaspoon black pepper. Just before serving, cut the avocado into small dice and stir it into the relish. Serve the soup topped with the relish.

—John Ash
Fetzer Vineyard

Chilled Tomato and Red-Pepper Soup

At Fleur de Lys, Chef Keller serves this refreshing soup with a spoonful of caviar. Though we'd certainly never turn down caviar, the luscious summer combination of tomatoes and red peppers stands perfectly well on its own.

SERVES 6

6   red bell peppers
3   tablespoons olive oil
1   onion, chopped
2   pounds tomatoes (about 4), peeled, seeded and chopped
3   cloves garlic, minced
2   tablespoons chopped fresh basil
¼   teaspoon dried thyme
1½ teaspoons sugar
2   teaspoons salt
7   cups Chicken Stock, page 299, or canned low-sodium chicken broth
½   teaspoon fresh-ground black pepper
1¼ cups light cream, plus more if needed
1   tablespoon sherry vinegar or wine vinegar
30 watercress leaves
2   tablespoons beluga or golden caviar, optional

WINE RECOMMENDATION:
THE DEEP, ROASTED FLAVOR OF THE RED BELL PEPPERS IS PERFECT WITH A FULL-BODIED WHITE WINE, SUCH AS A PINOT GRIS FROM THE ALSACE REGION IN FRANCE.

1. Roast the peppers over an open flame or broil 4 inches from the heat, turning with tongs until charred all over, about 10 minutes. When the peppers are cool enough to handle, pull off their skin. Remove the stems, seeds and ribs. Cut the peppers into small dice.

2. In a large pot, heat the oil over moderately low heat. Add the onion and cook, stirring occasionally, until translucent, about 5 minutes. Add the roasted peppers, tomatoes, garlic, basil, thyme, sugar and salt. Cook, stirring occasionally, for 5 minutes.

3. Add the stock, bring to a boil and simmer, partially covered, until the peppers are soft, about 20 minutes.

4. Puree the soup in a blender or food processor until smooth. Add the black pepper and refrigerate to chill, at least 2 hours.

5. Stir in the cream and vinegar. If the soup seems too thick, stir in a few more tablespoons cream. Top each serving with watercress leaves and a teaspoon of caviar, if using.

—Hubert Keller
Fleur de Lys

HOW TO PEEL, SEED AND CHOP A TOMATO

Tomato skin is sometimes papery or tough, and the seeds can have an unpleasant texture; so you may want to discard them. For easy peeling, cut out the core and slash an "X" on the base of the tomato. Then drop the tomato into boiling water and leave just until the skin begins to curl away from the "X," ten to fifteen seconds. Transfer the tomato to a bowl of cold water and, when cool enough to handle, strip away the skin. Cut the tomato in half crosswise and squeeze out the seeds, or scoop them out with your fingertips. Don't waste your time peeling and seeding, however, if you plan to strain a soup or stew.

Cold Cucumber Soup with Crab, Dill and Toasted Fennel Seeds

A moat of pale-green cream of cucumber soup surrounds a small mound of crab in this delicate summertime dish. A shower of mixed chopped herbs and toasted fennel seeds adds subtle flavor without overwhelming the soup. For the full effect, choose wide, shallow bowls for serving.

SERVES 6

6 pounds European cucumbers, 5¼ pounds halved, seeded and cut into chunks, ¾ pound seeded and cut into ⅛-inch dice, for garnish

8 teaspoons lemon juice

2 tablespoons sugar

¾ cup heavy cream

1¾ teaspoons salt
Fresh-ground black pepper
Large pinch cayenne

1½ teaspoons fennel seeds

9 ounces lump crabmeat (about ¾ cup), picked free of shell

½ pound plum tomatoes (about 3), peeled, seeded and cut into ¼-inch dice

1 tablespoon minced fresh chives or scallion tops

¾ teaspoon grated lemon zest

1 tablespoon shredded celery leaves

8 fresh basil leaves, shredded

1 tablespoon chopped fresh dill

WINE RECOMMENDATION:
THE SWEETNESS OF THE CRABMEAT AND THE DISTINCTIVE FLAVORS OF THE DILL AND TOASTED FENNEL SEEDS WILL BOTH PAIR WELL WITH A CRISP, AGGRESSIVE BOTTLE OF SAUVIGNON BLANC FROM EITHER CALIFORNIA OR WASHINGTON STATE.

1. In a food processor or blender, puree the cucumber chunks with 4 teaspoons of the lemon juice and the sugar until smooth. Strain into a large bowl and add the cream, 1 teaspoon of the salt, ¼ teaspoon black pepper and the cayenne. Refrigerate to chill, at least 2 hours.

2. In a small frying pan, toast the fennel seeds over moderately high heat, shaking the pan, until fragrant, about 30 seconds. Grind the seeds in a mortar with a pestle or in a spice grinder.

3. In a small bowl, combine the crabmeat, tomatoes, chives, lemon zest, the remaining 4 teaspoons lemon juice and ¾ teaspoon salt and a pinch of black pepper.

4. To serve, press 3 tablespoons of the crab mixture into a ¼-cup dry measuring cup and unmold in the center of a soup bowl. Sprinkle the diced cucumber on top. Ladle the soup around the crab and sprinkle with the ground fennel seeds, celery leaves, basil and dill.

—Gray Kunz
Lespinasse

TOASTING SPICES

You'll get more flavor from your spices if you toast them briefly before adding them to a dish. This is particularly important when the spice is not put in until the end of cooking, or is used in a dish that requires no cooking at all, such as the cold soup on this page. Heat the spices in a pan over moderately high heat, just until fragrant, about 30 seconds. Be sure not to let the pan get too hot, or the spices may scorch.

Cold Cantaloupe and Grappa Soup

Simply beautiful with its pastel hue speckled with mint, this frothy, refreshing dessert soup makes a perfect finale to a light summer meal. Italian grappa lends a wonderful perfume and flavor, but, if you can't find grappa, any good brandy will do.

SERVES 6

7   pounds cantaloupe (about 3), peeled, seeded and chopped
½   cup plus 1 tablespoon lemon juice (from about 4 lemons)
6   tablespoons honey
6   tablespoons sugar
3   tablespoons grappa
20   fresh mint leaves, chopped
3   cups heavy cream
6   tablespoons pine nuts

1. In a food processor or blender, puree the cantaloupe with the lemon juice, honey and sugar until smooth and frothy, about 1 minute. Pour into a large bowl and stir in the grappa and mint.

2. In a large bowl, with a whisk, whip the cream just until frothy, about 2 minutes. Stir into the cantaloupe puree and refrigerate to chill, at least 2 hours.

3. In a small, heavy frying pan over moderate heat, toast the pine nuts, stirring, until lightly browned, about 5 minutes. Remove and let cool. Serve the soup sprinkled with the pine nuts.

—Michael Chiarello
Tra Vigne

WHAT IS GRAPPA?

After grapes are pressed to extract the juice for wine, the mixture of skin, stems and seeds that remains is left to ferment. Grappa is the clear, fiery alcohol distilled from this fermented residue. Unlike brandy, grappa is neither aged nor graded. Your best chance of getting a grappa you'll like is to choose one from an Italian producer whose wines you enjoy.

Cold Peach
and Ginger Soup with
Peach Sorbet

Peaches, small scoops of peach sorbet and fresh mint in an ice-cold wine and ginger syrup make this pretty soup an ideal dessert for hot summer evenings. The sorbet is easy because it's made from part of the soup, but, if you prefer, simply buy the flavor of your choice—strawberry, raspberry, lemon or coconut all work well here. In that case, the soup will serve one or two more people. For an elegant presentation, use wide, shallow bowls and serve the soup with cookies, such as brandy snaps or coconut macaroons.

SERVES 6

1   quart dry white wine

2⅓ cups water

1   cup sugar

2   tablespoons chopped fresh ginger

4   3-inch-long strips lemon zest

4   pounds peaches (about 12), peeled and cut into approximately ½-inch pieces

4   teaspoons lemon juice

2   tablespoons cognac or other brandy

2   tablespoons shredded fresh mint leaves

1. In a large pot, combine the wine, water, sugar, ginger and lemon zest and bring to a boil over moderately high heat. Remove from the heat and let infuse for 5 minutes. Strain and return to the pot.

2. Add the peaches and lemon juice to the ginger syrup and bring to a simmer over moderate heat. Reduce the heat and simmer 1 minute.

3. Pour into a bowl and let cool. Add the brandy. Refrigerate to chill, at least 2 hours.

4. If making the sorbet, remove 2 cups of the peaches and syrup and puree in a blender or food processor. Pour the mixture into an ice-cream maker and freeze according to the manufacturer's instructions. Transfer the sorbet to a chilled container and freeze until firm, about 1 hour.

5. Ladle the soup into chilled bowls, top with the mint and small scoops of the sorbet and serve.

VARIATION

For a thicker, soupier soup, save a few pieces of peach for garnish and puree the rest of the mixture in a food processor. Serve topped with the reserved peaches and mint.

LEFTOVERS?

You can make an ideal summer aperitif from leftover peach soup. Puree the soup and stir a couple of tablespoons into a glass of not-too-expensive champagne or still white wine.

WINE WITH FRUIT SOUPS

A sweet white wine is a classic accompaniment to a fruit dessert course. It stands up to and nicely mirrors the sweetness of the fruit. To keep the sweetness from being cloying, look for a dessert wine with plenty of acidity, such as a spätlese or auslese riesling from Germany or a sweet chenin blanc from the Loire Valley, such as a Vouvray. Loire Valley wines are sold in a range from dry to sweet. Check at a helpful wineshop before buying. With any of the fruit soups here, you might also try Asti Spumante, a sweet sparkling wine from the Piedmont region of Italy.

Cold Red-Fruit Soup with Beaujolais

Ruby red with raspberries, strawberries and cherries, all poached in Beaujolais, this soup celebrates the abundance of summer. Cinnamon and black pepper are spicy complements to the sweet fruit. You can change the ingredients as the season progresses. Blackberries or blueberries could stand in for the cherries when they're no longer available. Cook the berries just a couple of minutes rather than the ten needed to soften the cherries. Gingersnaps make an excellent accompaniment to this light and refreshing dessert.

SERVES 6

3   cups Beaujolais or another light, fruity red wine
3   cups water
1¼   cups sugar
3   3-inch-long strips lemon zest
1   cinnamon stick
12   peppercorns
3   pounds black cherries, halved and pitted
1½   pints strawberries, sliced
1½   pints raspberries
4½   teaspoons kirsch
¾   cup heavy cream and 2 teaspoons sugar, optional

1. In a large pot, combine the wine, water, sugar, zest, cinnamon stick and peppercorns. Bring to a boil over moderately high heat, reduce the heat and simmer for 5 minutes.

2. Add the cherries, bring back to a simmer and poach for 10 minutes. Strain the liquid, discard the seasonings and set the cherries aside. Return the liquid to the pot.

3. Add the strawberries and raspberries to the pot. Bring back to a simmer and poach for 2 minutes. Puree the soup in a blender or food processor. Strain, pressing the pureed fruit through the sieve. Add the reserved cherries and the kirsch and refrigerate to chill, at least 2 hours.

4. Whip the cream, if using, with the 2 teaspoons sugar until the cream holds soft peaks. Ladle the soup into bowls and top each serving with a dollop of cream.

CHAPTER 7 · FISH & SHELLFISH STEWS

Cioppino

A combination seafood and tomato broth brimming with crab or lobster, shrimp, mussels, clams and chunks of fish fillets, this dish originated in San Francisco as a fisherman's stew. Dungeness crab, native to the West Coast, is commonly used in California cioppino, but lobster works equally well. In fact, you can vary all the fish choices according to what's available—and how much you want to spend. Served with a salad and sourdough bread, this stew makes a generous meal.

SERVES 6

¼	cup olive oil
2	onions, chopped
1	green bell pepper, chopped
4	cloves garlic, minced
½	teaspoon chopped fresh thyme, or ¼ teaspoon dried
2	cups dry white wine
18	littleneck or cherrystone clams, scrubbed
18	mussels, scrubbed and debearded
2	live Dungeness crabs (2 pounds each), or 3 live lobsters (1¼ pounds each)
1½	pounds large shrimp, shells removed and reserved
1	quart water
1	bay leaf
1½	quarts canned tomatoes, drained and chopped
1½ to 2¼ teaspoons salt	
2	pounds firm white fish fillets, such as sea bass, red snapper, halibut or monkfish, cut into 2-inch chunks
½	cup chopped fresh flat-leaf parsley
½	teaspoon Tabasco sauce
¼	teaspoon fresh-ground black pepper

WINE RECOMMENDATION:

THIS SAN FRANCISCO CLASSIC SHOULD BE PAIRED WITH A SIMPLE, STRAIGHTFORWARD WHITE WINE FROM CALIFORNIA. TRY A BLEND FROM ONE OF THE BETTER PRODUCERS, SUCH AS ROBERT MONDAVI OR MONTEREY VINEYARDS. DESPITE THEIR LARGE BOTTLES AND MODEST PRICES, THESE WINES CAN BE QUITE GOOD.

1. In a large pot, heat the oil over moderately low heat. Add the onions, bell pepper, garlic and thyme. Cook, stirring occasionally, until the onions are translucent, about 5 minutes. Add the wine.

2. Discard any clams and mussels that are broken or do not clamp shut when tapped. Add the clams to the pot. Cover, raise the heat to high and bring to a boil. Cook, shaking the pot occasionally, just until the clams open, about 3 minutes. Remove the open clams and continue to cook, uncovering the pot as necessary to remove the clams as soon as their shells open. Discard any that do not open. Add the mussels and cook in the same way as the clams, removing

them as soon as their shells open, about 3 minutes. Reserve the cooking liquid.

3. If using crabs, put them in a pan of ice for 15 minutes. Remove. Steam over boiling water until just done, about 15 minutes. If using lobsters, cook them in a large pot of boiling, salted water until just done, about 8 minutes.

4. If using crabs: When cool enough to handle, remove the flap (apron) on the underside. Remove the back shell and break the crab in half down the middle. Discard the viscera and gills and rinse the inside of the body. Separate the legs and claws from the body section. Crack the legs and claws and remove the meat from the shells. Cut the body into 4 pieces and remove the meat. If using lobsters: When cool enough to handle, twist to separate the tail section and the large front legs with the claws from the body. Remove the tail meat from the shell and cut into ¾-inch slices. Crack the large legs and claws and

remove the meat, keeping the claws whole if possible.

5. Add the crab or lobster shells, the shrimp shells, water and bay leaf to the pot containing the cooking liquid. Bring to a boil, reduce the heat and simmer for 30 minutes. Strain through a sieve lined with a paper towel into a large pot.

6. Add the tomatoes and 1½ teaspoons of the salt to the pot. Simmer until reduced to 7 cups, about 15 minutes. Taste for seasoning and, if necessary, add ½ to ¾ teaspoon salt. The amount needed can vary considerably depending on the saltiness of the clams and mussels.

7. Add the shrimp and fish fillets. Bring to a simmer and cook until almost done, about 2 minutes. Add the crab or lobster meat, the mussels, clams, parsley, Tabasco and pepper and simmer, covered, until hot, about 1 minute.

 MAKE IT AHEAD

Crab and lobster, clams and mussels all get tough when overcooked, and fish fillets get flabby. So this is not a soup to keep simmering on the stove until guests are ready to eat. You can, however, do almost all the cooking (through step six) ahead of time. At the last minute, simmer the shrimp and fish fillets for two minutes, add the rest of the seafood, reheat for one more minute and you're ready.

Romesco Seafood Stew

Mildly spiced with chiles and thickened with hazelnuts, almonds and bread, the Spanish sauce called *romesco* can top grilled meats or fish, or, as here, constitute the base of a delicious stew. Use a mixture of any firm white fish you like.

SERVES 6

¼   cup hazelnuts

¼   cup blanched almonds

1   dried ancho chile

6   tablespoons olive oil

1   slice bread, crusts removed

3   cloves garlic, chopped

1   small, dried red chile pepper, seeds removed, minced, or ½ teaspoon dried red-pepper flakes

½   cup chopped fresh flat-leaf parsley

1   pound tomatoes (about 2), peeled, seeded and chopped, or 1¾ cups canned tomatoes (14½-ounce can), drained and chopped

2   tablespoons plus 1 teaspoon lemon juice

¾ to 1¼   teaspoons salt

½   teaspoon fresh-ground black pepper

3   cups Fish Stock, page 303, or bottled clam juice

½   pound medium shrimp, shells removed and reserved

3   pounds firm white fish fillets, such as sea bass, red snapper, halibut or monkfish, cut into 2-by-3-inch chunks

¼   cup flour

½   cup dry white wine

1   teaspoon dried thyme

1   dozen littleneck or cherrystone clams, scrubbed

WINE RECOMMENDATION:
MATCH THE BOLD FLAVORS OF THIS DISH WITH A RICH SÉMILLON EITHER FROM WASHINGTON STATE OR FROM AUSTRALIA, WHERE IT IS SOMETIMES BLENDED WITH CHARDONNAY.

1. Heat the oven to 350°. Put the nuts on a baking sheet, keeping them separate, and roast in the oven until the hazelnut skins crack and loosen and the nuts are golden brown, about 10 minutes. Wrap the hot hazelnuts in a kitchen towel and firmly rub them together to loosen most of the skin. Discard the skin. Let the nuts cool.

2. Soak the ancho chile in boiling water to cover until softened, about 20 minutes. Drain. Stem, seed and chop the chile.

3. In a large pot, heat 4 tablespoons of the oil over moderate heat. Add the bread. Fry, turning once, until golden brown, about 5 minutes. Put the bread and oil in a bowl and let cool. ➤

4. In a blender, pulverize the nuts. Add the ancho chile, the fried bread and oil from frying, the garlic, red chile, 2 tablespoons of the parsley, half the tomatoes, 2 tablespoons of the lemon juice, ½ teaspoon of the salt and ¼ teaspoon of the black pepper and puree until smooth.

5. In a medium saucepan, bring the stock to a boil. Add the shrimp shells. Reduce the heat and simmer, partially covered, for 10 minutes. Strain. Press the shells firmly to get all the liquid.

6. Heat the remaining 2 tablespoons oil in a large pot over moderately high heat. Season the fish with ¼ teaspoon of the salt and the remaining ¼ teaspoon pepper. Toss with the flour and shake off the excess. Brown half of the fish, about 2 minutes a side, and remove. Brown the remaining fish. Remove.

7. Reduce the heat to moderately low. Add the chile puree and cook, stirring, 1 minute. Add the stock, wine and thyme. Bring to a boil over moderately high heat. Discard any clams that have broken shells or that do not clamp shut when tapped. Add the clams and simmer until they begin to open, about 5 minutes, removing the clams as they open.

Reduce the heat to moderately low. Add the fish, shrimp and the remaining tomato. Bring back to a simmer and simmer until the fish and shrimp are just done, about 3 minutes longer.

8. Remove all the seafood. Boil the liquid until reduced to 4 cups, about 5 minutes. Stir in ¼ to ½ teaspoon salt, if needed, the remaining 1 teaspoon lemon juice and 6 tablespoons parsley. Return all the seafood to the pot. Heat through.

SALTY BIVALVES

As with seawater, the saltiness of bivalves (the shellfish category that includes clams, oysters and mussels) can vary from day to day and place to place. You may cook mussels and find the cooking liquid flat and insipid one day only to find the next batch intensely salty. Therefore, in all of our recipes that include the liquid used to cook clams or mussels or the liquor from oysters, we give a range of salt. As with anything you cook, taste and adjust the seasoning as needed.

Indian-Style Curried Fish Stew

Curry powder, ginger, coconut milk and cilantro combine to make a spicy, bright-yellow stew, thick with chunks of fish and vegetables. It's quick to prepare and is a meal in itself. Use one type of firm white fish, such as orange roughy, halibut or monkfish, or a combination.

SERVES 6

3	tablespoons curry powder
½	cup plus 2 tablespoons water
8	macadamia or cashew nuts, chopped
3	shallots, chopped
4	cloves garlic, chopped
1	tablespoon chopped fresh ginger
2	jalapeño peppers, seeds and ribs removed, chopped
1	15-ounce can unsweetened coconut milk
2	tablespoons cooking oil
1	pound boiling potatoes (about 3), peeled and cut into 1-inch dice
4	carrots, cut into ¼-inch slices
½	teaspoon grated lime zest
1	1-inch piece cinnamon stick
2	cloves
½	teaspoon sugar
1	teaspoon salt
3	pounds orange-roughy fillets or other firm white fish fillets, such as sea bass, red snapper, halibut or monkfish, cut into 2-by-1½-inch chunks
1	tablespoon lime juice
¼	cup chopped fresh cilantro

WINE RECOMMENDATION:
Pair this stew's sweetness and spice with a vigorous white wine that combines plenty of acidity and an off-dry taste—a demi-sec Vouvray from France or a trocken riesling from Germany.

1. In a small bowl, combine the curry powder and 2 tablespoons of the water to make a thick paste. In a blender, puree the nuts, shallots, garlic, ginger and jalapeños with 2 tablespoons of the coconut milk.

2. In a large pot, heat the oil over moderately low heat. Add the pureed nut mixture and cook, stirring, for 3 minutes. Add the curry paste and cook, stirring, 2 minutes longer. Add the remaining coconut milk and ½ cup water, the potatoes, carrots, zest, cinnamon stick, cloves, sugar and salt. Bring to a simmer over moderately high heat. Reduce the heat and simmer, partially covered, until the potatoes are tender, about 25 minutes.

3. Add the fish, return to a simmer and continue simmering, partially covered, until just done, about 3 minutes. Remove the cinnamon stick and cloves. Stir in the lime juice and cilantro.

Shellfish Stew with Red-Pepper Sauce

Full flavors and very little fat are hallmarks of this seafood stew. Accompanied with garlicky toasted croûtes and a dollop of red-pepper sauce, it makes an easy-to-prepare meal.

SERVES 6

1   cup canned tomatoes with their juice

¼   teaspoon fennel seeds

1   tablespoon olive oil

3   medium leeks, white and light-green parts only, split lengthwise, chopped and washed well

1   onion, chopped

4   cloves garlic, minced

3   cups Fish Stock, page 303, or 1½ cups bottled clam juice diluted with 1½ cups water

1   cup dry white wine

2½   teaspoons chopped fresh thyme or ¾ teaspoon dried

1   bay leaf

½ to 1 teaspoon salt

2   dozen medium mussels, scrubbed and debearded

1   pound sea scallops

1   pound large shrimp, shelled

¼   teaspoon fresh-ground black pepper
     Low-Fat Garlic Croûtes, page 309
     Red-Pepper Sauce, next page

WINE RECOMMENDATION: MATCH THE MEDITERRANEAN-INSPIRED FLAVORS OF THIS DISH WITH A WHITE OR ROSÉ WINE FROM THE SAME AREA, SUCH AS A CÔTES DE PROVENCE OR A CASSIS.

1. In a food processor, puree the tomatoes with their juice. Grind the fennel seeds in a mortar with a pestle or chop them with a large knife.

2. In a large pot, heat the oil over moderately low heat. Add the leeks, onion and garlic. Cover and cook, stirring occasionally, until soft, about 10 minutes. Add the tomatoes, fennel seeds, stock, wine, thyme, bay leaf and ½ teaspoon of the salt. Bring to a boil, reduce the heat and simmer, stirring occasionally, for 20 minutes.

3. Discard any mussels that have broken shells or do not clamp shut when tapped. Add the mussels to the pot. Cover, raise the heat to high and bring to a boil. Cook, shaking the pot occasionally, just until the mussels begin to open, about 3 minutes. Remove the open mussels. Continue to cook, uncovering the pot as necessary to remove the mussels as soon as their shells open. Discard any

that do not open. When the mussels are cool enough to handle, remove them from their shells, holding them over the pot to catch all the juices. Set aside.

4. Add the scallops and shrimp to the pot, bring to a simmer and continue simmering, stirring occasionally, until just done, about 3 minutes.

5. Discard the bay leaf and stir in the pepper. Return the mussels to the stew. Taste the stew for salt and, if necessary, add ¼ to ½ teaspoon salt. The amount of salt needed can vary considerably depending on the saltiness of the mussels.

6. Ladle the stew into shallow bowls. Serve with the croûtes, each one topped with a dollop of the red-pepper sauce. Serve the remaining red-pepper sauce alongside.

—Georgia Chan Downard

RED-PEPPER SAUCE

This sauce is wonderfully versatile. Try it with other soups and stews, too.

MAKES ABOUT ½ CUP

1	small red bell pepper
½	cup fresh basil leaves
1	clove garlic, chopped
2	teaspoons grated Parmesan cheese
1½	teaspoons olive oil
½	teaspoon balsamic vinegar
½	teaspoon salt
¼	teaspoon fresh-ground black pepper

1. Roast the bell pepper over an open flame or broil 4 inches from the heat, turning with tongs until charred all over, about 10 minutes. When the pepper is cool enough to handle, pull off the skin. Remove the stem, seeds and ribs.

2. In a food processor, combine the roasted pepper, basil, garlic, Parmesan, oil, vinegar, salt and pepper and blend until almost smooth.

Spanish Fish Stew with Garlic, Paprika and Red Peppers

Colorful with paprika, tomatoes, peppers and saffron, this dish is representative of the many wonderful fish stews from Spain. Paprika—dried and powdered red pepper—is an integral part of Spanish cuisine, as is garlic, both of which play important roles here. Served with Rustic Croûtes, page 309, and the strong, garlic-flavored mayonnaise from the Mediterranean called Aioli, page 304, this stew makes a festive meal.

SERVES 6

- 3 red bell peppers
- 6 tablespoons olive oil
- 10 cloves garlic, unpeeled
- 3 pounds firm white fish fillets, such as sea bass, red snapper, halibut or monkfish, cut into 2-by-3-inch chunks
- 1¼ teaspoons salt
- ½ teaspoon fresh-ground black pepper
- ½ cup dry white wine
- 1 pound tomatoes (about 2), peeled, seeded and chopped, or 1¾ cups canned tomatoes with their juice (14½-ounce can), chopped
- 1½ teaspoons paprika
- 5 cups Fish Stock, page 303
  Large pinch saffron
- 1½ pounds boiling potatoes (about 4), peeled and cut into ½-inch slices
- 1 tablespoon lemon juice
- 2 tablespoons chopped fresh parsley
  Rustic Croûtes, page 309
  Aioli, page 304

WINE RECOMMENDATION:
A SPANISH WINE, PARTICULARLY SOME OF THE FRESHER, MORE COMPLEX WINES BEING MADE FROM THE ALVARIÑO GRAPE, PAIRS NICELY WITH THIS STEW.

1. Roast the peppers over an open flame or broil 4 inches from the heat, turning with tongs until charred all over, about 10 minutes. When the peppers are cool enough to handle, pull off the skin. Remove the stems, seeds and ribs. Chop the peppers.

2. In a large pot, heat the oil over low heat. Add the garlic cloves and cook, covered, stirring occasionally, until soft and golden brown, about 15 minutes. Remove with a slotted spoon. When the garlic is cool enough to handle, peel the cloves. Raise the heat to moderately low. Add the roasted peppers and cook, stirring occasionally, until golden brown, about 10 minutes. Remove with a slotted spoon. ➤

3. Raise the heat to moderately high. Sprinkle the fish with ¼ teaspoon of the salt and ¼ teaspoon of the black pepper. Brown half the fish, about 2 minutes a side, and remove. Brown the remaining fish. Remove. Pour the wine into the hot pot. Simmer 2 minutes, scraping the bottom of the pot to dislodge any brown bits.

4. In a food processor or blender, puree the roasted peppers, the garlic and tomatoes with the wine from the pot, the paprika and the remaining 1 tea-spoon salt and ¼ teaspoon black pepper. Add the puree to the pot with the stock, saffron and potatoes. Bring to a boil, reduce the heat and simmer, partially covered, until the potatoes are tender, about 25 minutes.

5. Add the fish. Bring to a simmer and cook until the fish is just done, 2 to 3 minutes. Stir in the lemon juice and 1 tablespoon of the parsley. Sprinkle with the remaining parsley and serve with the croûtes and aioli.

Vegetable Stew with Steamed Red Snapper

Butternut squash, fennel, onions and fresh herbs make a full-flavored vegetable stew. Fillets of red snapper cook to perfection when they are arranged on top of the simmering stew and left to steam just until done.

SERVES 6

2 tablespoons butter
2½ pounds butternut squash (about 1), peeled and cut into 1½-inch chunks
2 fennel bulbs, cut into ½-inch slices
3 onions, cut into thick slices
4 scallions including green tops, cut into 1-inch lengths
6 cloves garlic, minced
1 pound tomatoes (about 2), peeled, seeded and chopped, or 1¾ cup canned tomatoes with their juice (14½-ounce can), chopped
¼ cup chopped fresh parsley
6 tablespoons chopped fresh dill
1 cup water
2 tablespoons white wine
2¼ teaspoons salt
Fresh-ground black pepper
3 pounds red-snapper fillets, skin left on, or other firm white fish fillets, such as sea bass or halibut

1. In a large pot, melt the butter over moderately low heat. Add the squash, fennel, onions, scallions, garlic, tomatoes, parsley, 4 tablespoons of the dill, the water, wine and 2 teaspoons of the salt and stir to combine. Bring to a boil. Reduce the heat and cover. Simmer the stew, stirring occasionally, until the vegetables are tender, about 1 hour. Stir in ¼ teaspoon pepper.

2. Sprinkle the fish with the remaining ¼ teaspoon salt and a pinch of pepper. Arrange the fillets, skin-side up, on top of the vegetables. Increase the heat to high and cover. Cook the fish until just done, 8 to 10 minutes. Transfer the fish to individual plates or a platter. Spoon the vegetables and their liquid around the fish and sprinkle with the remaining 2 tablespoons dill.

Cod and Sweet-Pepper Stew with Tarragon Aioli

Chicken stock is used in place of fish stock to mellow the flavor of this stew. Serve it with plenty of crusty bread to soak up the fragrant sauce. If you can't get fresh tarragon, add two teaspoons dried with the wine and serve the stew with plain Aioli, page 304.

SERVES 6

¼ cup olive oil
2 red bell peppers, cut into thin strips
1 yellow bell pepper, cut into thin strips
1 large onion, cut into thin slices
3 anchovy fillets, chopped
3 cloves garlic, minced
2 bay leaves
½ cup dry white wine
1½ cups Chicken Stock, page 299, or canned low-sodium chicken broth
1 pound new potatoes, about 6, quartered
1 teaspoon salt
3 pounds cod fillets, cut into 2-inch chunks
1 tablespoon chopped fresh tarragon
¼ teaspoon fresh-ground black pepper
   Tarragon Aioli, below

TARRAGON AIOLI

Give Aioli, page 304, an added dimension by adding 2 tablespoons chopped fresh tarragon and 3 tablespoons lemon juice to the basic recipe.

WINE RECOMMENDATION:
THIS HEARTY STEW WILL GO WELL WITH A STRAIGHTFORWARD WHITE WINE, SUCH AS A CÔTES DE GASCOGNE FROM SOUTHWESTERN FRANCE OR AN ALVARIÑO FROM SPAIN.

1. In a deep frying pan, heat the oil over moderate heat. Add the peppers and onion and cook, stirring occasionally, until soft, about 10 minutes. Add the anchovies, garlic and bay leaves and cook, stirring, until the garlic is soft, about 1 minute.

2. Add the wine and simmer until reduced to about 1 tablespoon. Add the stock, potatoes and salt. Cover and simmer over low heat until the potatoes are tender, about 15 minutes.

3. Add the fish, tarragon and pepper. Cover and cook, stirring once or twice, until the fish is just done, about 3 minutes. Discard the bay leaves. Stir one-quarter of the aioli into the stew. Pass the rest separately.

—Erica De Mane

Three-Fish Stew
with Leeks and Carrots

Thick chunks of juicy fish and a flavorful sauce make this simple fisherman's stew a memorable one. A salad of assorted greens completes the meal.

SERVES 6

¾ pound boiling potatoes (about 2), peeled and cut into ½-inch dice

2 leeks, white and light-green parts only, cut into 2-inch-long matchstick strips and washed well

2 carrots, cut into 2-inch-long matchstick strips

4 tablespoons butter

3 shallots, minced

1 quart Fish Stock, page 303

2 teaspoons salt

1 tablespoon chopped fresh thyme, or 1 teaspoon dried

¾ pound monkfish fillet, cut into 1½-inch chunks

¾ pound swordfish steak, skinned, cut into 1½-inch chunks

1½ pounds firm white fish fillets, such as sea bass, red snapper or halibut, cut into 1½-inch chunks

¼ cup flour

¼ teaspoon fresh-ground black pepper

WINE RECOMMENDATION: THE DELICATE YET STRAIGHTFORWARD FLAVORS OF THIS STEW GO WELL WITH ANY NUMBER OF MEDIUM-BODIED WHITE WINES. TRY A YOUNG PINOT GRIS FROM OREGON OR A PINOT BLANC FROM THE ALSACE REGION IN FRANCE.

1. Put the potatoes in a medium saucepan of salted water. Bring to a boil and simmer until almost tender, about 8 minutes. Add the leeks and carrots and cook until all the vegetables are tender, about 5 minutes longer. Drain.

2. In a large pot, heat 1 tablespoon of the butter over moderately low heat. Add the shallots and cook, stirring occasionally, until translucent, about 5 minutes.

3. Add the stock, salt and thyme and bring to a boil. Add the fish, reduce the heat and simmer until the fish is just done, about 3 minutes. With a slotted spoon, transfer the fish to a bowl.

4. In a large pot, melt the remaining 3 tablespoons butter over moderate heat. Stir in the flour. Cook, stirring, for 2 minutes.

5. Whisk in the cooking liquid. Bring back to a boil, whisking constantly, and let boil for 2 minutes. Stir in the pepper. Add the vegetables and fish and heat until warmed through.

—Charles Pierce

WHEN IS FISH DONE?

An extra minute on the stove can transform a piece of fish from moist and flavorful to dry and unappetizing. So don't wait until you think the fish is completely cooked before checking it; you may be too late. Insert a knife or fork into a piece of fish and peek. The fish should be removed from the heat when the center looks almost opaque. The heat of the fish will continue to cook it, and it will arrive at the table just cooked and opaque throughout.

Salmon and Red-Wine Stew

Though salmon and red wine may seem an unlikely pair, the rich fish stands up beautifully to this hearty wine sauce.

SERVES 6

½	pound bacon, chopped
1	pound mushrooms, quartered
¾	pound small white onions, about 1-inch in diameter, peeled
1½	teaspoons salt
5	tablespoons butter
1	teaspoon sugar
¼	cup flour
2½	cups red wine
1¾	cups canned tomatoes (14½-ounce can), drained and chopped
3	pounds salmon fillet, skinned, cut into 1½-inch chunks
2	tablespoons chopped fresh parsley
¼	teaspoon fresh-ground black pepper Triangular Croûtes, page 309

WINE RECOMMENDATION:
PINOT NOIR, AND SPECIFICALLY PINOT NOIR FROM OREGON, IS A PERFECT CHOICE FOR THIS FISH STEW, BOTH FROM A GEOGRAPHICAL PERSPECTIVE AND IN TERMS OF TASTE. LOOK FOR A THREE- TO FIVE-YEAR-OLD BOTTLE FROM THE WILLAMETTE VALLEY.

1. In a medium frying pan, cook the bacon until crisp. Drain on paper towels. Pour off all but 1 tablespoon of the fat.

2. Add the mushrooms to the pan and cook over moderate heat, stirring occasionally, until brown, about 5 minutes. Remove the mushrooms.

3. Add the onions to the pan with ½ teaspoon of the salt, 1 tablespoon of the butter, the sugar and just barely enough water to cover. Bring to a boil, reduce the heat and simmer until the onions are tender and the water has evaporated, 10 to 15 minutes. Continue cooking, stirring, until the onions brown, about 7 minutes longer.

4. In a medium pot, heat the remaining 4 tablespoons butter. Add the flour and cook, stirring, until the flour browns, about 5 minutes. Whisk in the wine and ¾ cup water. Bring to a boil, whisking

constantly. Add the bacon, mushrooms, onions, tomatoes and the remaining 1 teaspoon salt and bring back to a simmer. Simmer, stirring occasionally, until the liquid reduces to about 3 cups, 10 to 15 minutes. Add the salmon to the stew and bring back to a simmer. Cover the pot and cook until the salmon is just done, 2 to 3 minutes.

5. Stir in the parsley and pepper and serve with the croûtes.

WINES FOR COOKING

Since the alcohol evaporates when heated, it's the flavor of the wine that's important for cooking. And because wines have very different flavors, a dish or sauce based on wine can vary tremendously depending on which you use. Avoid any that are overly fruity or tart because cooking will only emphasize these characteristics. When a recipe calls for red wine, you'll want one with good body and strong color and flavor. A merlot or a French Côtes-du-Rhône are excellent choices if you're using only a small amount, or if the sauce, such as this one, has few other ingredients. Recipes that call for a larger amount, usually reduced to concentrate flavor, or that cook for a long time, such as Boeuf Bourguignon, page 254, will be just fine with any moderately priced French, Italian or California blend. These usually come in 1.5 liter bottles. For recipes that call for dry white wine, a French, Italian or California blend is again your best bet. Avoid so-called *cooking* wines sold in supermarkets. If you ever taste one, you'll see why.

Spicy Catfish Stew

Chunks of catfish with corn, bell peppers and lima beans in a spicy tomato broth make a lively, Southern-style stew that's quick and easy to prepare. Once exclusively a Southern and Midwestern specialty, catfish is now farm-raised and widely available. With its firm flesh, it is ideal for a stew.

SERVES 6

4	strips bacon, chopped
2	onions, chopped
1	green bell pepper, chopped
1	red bell pepper, chopped
2	ribs celery, chopped
¾	cup dry white wine
2½	cups bottled clam juice
4½	cups tomato juice
1	pound boiling potatoes (about 3), peeled and cut into ½-inch dice
1	teaspoon Tabasco sauce
1½	teaspoons dried oregano
½	teaspoon dried marjoram
1	bay leaf
2½	teaspoons salt
½	teaspoon dry mustard
	Pinch sugar
2	cups frozen baby lima beans
2	cups fresh (cut from about 3 ears) or frozen corn kernels
3	pounds catfish fillets, cut into 1½-inch chunks
¾	teaspoon lemon juice
¼	teaspoon fresh-ground black pepper
2	tablespoons chopped fresh parsley

WINE RECOMMENDATION:
THIS DOWN-HOME DISH CALLS OUT FOR A SIMILAR DRINK. LOOK FOR A WHITE-WINE BLEND FROM A GOOD CALIFORNIA PRODUCER. OR FORGET THE WINE AND OPEN A COLD BEER.

1. In a large pot, cook the bacon until crisp. Drain on paper towels. Add the onions, bell peppers and celery to the pot and cook until the onions are translucent, about 5 minutes. Add the wine and cook until almost evaporated.

2. Add the clam juice, tomato juice, potatoes, Tabasco sauce, oregano, marjoram, bay leaf, salt, mustard and sugar. Bring to a boil, reduce the heat and simmer, partially covered, for 15 minutes. Discard the bay leaf.

3. Add the lima beans and simmer 3 minutes. Add the corn and simmer 8 minutes more. Add the catfish, bring back to a simmer and cook until just done, about 2 minutes. Stir in the lemon juice and pepper. Serve topped with the bacon and parsley.

Vietnamese Swordfish Stew with Scallions

Chunks of swordfish and tofu cooked with a Vietnamese blend of lime juice, fish sauce and hot peppers make this a unique and refreshing stew. A medium-firm tofu works best here.

SERVES 6

5	tablespoons lime juice, from about 4 limes
3	tablespoons Asian fish sauce (nam pla or nuoc mam)*
6	scallions including green tops, cut into thin slices
1½	teaspoons rice-wine or white-wine vinegar
¾	teaspoon turmeric
2½	teaspoons sugar
1	tablespoon anchovy paste
2	pounds swordfish steaks, 2 inches thick, skinned, cut into 2-inch chunks
2	tablespoons cooking oil
1	pound tofu, cut into 1-inch cubes
¾	cup macadamia or cashew nuts, chopped
4	cloves garlic, crushed
1	jalapeño pepper, seeds and ribs removed, chopped
2	cups water
4	carrots, cut into ¼-inch diagonal slices
2	tablespoons chopped fresh dill
5	radishes, shredded
2	tablespoons chopped fresh cilantro

* Available at Asian markets

WINE RECOMMENDATION: A FRESH, AGGRESSIVELY FLAVORED SAUVIGNON BLANC FROM SANCERRE IN FRANCE OR FROM NEW ZEALAND WILL COMPLEMENT THE PRONOUNCED FLAVORS OF THE DILL, ANCHOVIES, FISH SAUCE AND RADISHES IN THIS STEW WITHOUT BEING OVERWHELMED BY THEM.

1. In a glass or stainless-steel bowl, combine 2 tablespoons of the lime juice, 1 tablespoon of the fish sauce, half the scallions, ½ teaspoon of the vinegar, the turmeric, ½ teaspoon of the sugar and 1 teaspoon of the anchovy paste. Add the fish and stir to coat. Let sit for 1 hour, stirring once or twice.

2. In a large nonstick frying pan, heat 1 tablespoon of the oil over moderately high heat. Add the tofu. Brown on all sides, about 4 minutes in all, and remove. Drain the fish, reserving the marinade. Pat the fish dry with paper towels. Add half the fish to the pan. Brown on all sides, about 4 minutes in all, and remove. Heat the remaining tablespoon oil and brown the rest of the fish. Remove.

3. In a blender, puree ½ cup of the macadamia nuts with the remaining 3

FISH & SHELLFISH STEWS

tablespoons lime juice, 2 tablespoons fish sauce, 1 teaspoon vinegar, 2 teaspoons sugar and 2 teaspoons anchovy paste, the garlic and jalapeño.

4. In a medium saucepan, bring the 2 cups water and the carrots to a boil. Cook, partially covered, for 6 minutes. Stir in the reserved marinade and the pureed nut mixture. Add the tofu, fish, the remaining scallions and the dill. Bring to a simmer over moderate heat. Reduce the heat and simmer, covered, until the fish is just done, 2 to 3 minutes.

5. Serve topped with the remaining ¼ cup macadamia nuts, the radishes and cilantro.

Fresh-Tuna Stew with Potatoes and Rosemary

Cubes of tuna steak are simmered with potatoes and peppers in fragrant rosemary broth for a stew that's both unusual and delicious.

SERVES 6

3	tablespoons olive oil
2½	pounds tuna steaks, 1½-inch thick, skinned, cut into 1½-inch chunks
3	onions, chopped
4	cloves garlic, minced
3	green bell peppers, cut into thin strips
1	quart Chicken Stock, page 299, or canned low-sodium chicken broth
1½	pounds boiling potatoes (about 4), cut into 1½-inch chunks
1½	teaspoons dried rosemary, crumbled
1¼	teaspoons salt
¼	cup chopped fresh flat-leaf parsley
¼	teaspoon fresh-ground black pepper

WINE RECOMMENDATION:
THE RICHNESS OF THE TUNA AND THE FLAVOR OF ROSEMARY PAIR WELL WITH A MEDIUM-BODIED, MILDLY FLAVORED WHITE WINE. TRY A PINOT BLANC FROM ALSACE IN FRANCE.

1. In a large pot, heat 1 tablespoon of the oil over moderately high heat. Add half the tuna. Brown on all sides, about 4 minutes in all, and remove. Add another tablespoon of the oil to the pot and brown the remaining fish. Remove.

2. Add the remaining 1 tablespoon oil to the pot and reduce the heat to moderately low. Add the onions and garlic and cook, stirring occasionally, until translucent, about 5 minutes. Add the bell peppers and cook, stirring, until they begin to soften, about 5 minutes.

3. Add the stock, potatoes, rosemary and salt. Bring to a simmer. Cook until the potatoes are tender, about 20 minutes. Mash about 5 potato chunks with a fork to thicken the stew. Return the tuna to the pot. Increase the heat to moderate. Simmer, stirring occasionally, until the tuna is medium-rare, about 2 minutes longer. Stir in the parsley and pepper.

—Judith Sutton

CHAPTER 8 · POULTRY STEWS

Middle Eastern Chicken Stew

Eggplant, tomatoes, chickpeas and turmeric give this full-flavored chicken stew its Middle Eastern accent. Mint, another popular ingredient in that part of the world, adds a refreshing note.

SERVES 6

5	tablespoons olive oil
2	medium eggplants (about 1¼ pounds each), cut into 1½-inch cubes
5	pounds chicken parts
3	onions, chopped
2	cloves garlic, minced
1	teaspoon turmeric
7	cups canned tomatoes with their juice (two 28-ounce cans), chopped
1¾	cups canned chickpeas (16-ounce can), drained and rinsed
2¼	teaspoons salt
¼	teaspoon fresh-ground black pepper
2	tablespoons chopped fresh flat-leaf parsley
2	tablespoons chopped fresh mint

WINE RECOMMENDATION:
SERVE A LIGHT AND SIMPLE WHITE WINE WITH THIS STEW. TRY A YOUNG BOTTLE OF PINOT GRIGIO FROM ITALY.

1. In a large, nonstick frying pan, heat 1 tablespoon of the oil over moderately high heat until very hot. Add about a third of the eggplant and cook, stirring, until brown on all sides, about 5 minutes. Remove. Brown the remaining eggplant in 2 more batches, using 1 tablespoon of the oil per batch, and remove.

2. In a large pot, heat the remaining 2 tablespoons oil over moderately high heat. Add about a third of the chicken and brown well on both sides, about 8 minutes in all. Remove. Brown the remaining chicken in two batches and remove. Discard all but 2 tablespoons of the oil and reduce the heat to moderately low.

3. Add the onions and garlic and cook, stirring occasionally, until the onions are translucent, about 5 minutes. Add the turmeric and cook, stirring, for 30 seconds. Add the tomatoes with their juice and raise the heat to moder-

ately high. Bring to a boil and simmer until reduced to 4½ cups, about 15 minutes.

4. Add the eggplant, the chicken with any juice that has accumulated, the chickpeas and salt and bring to a simmer over moderate heat. Reduce the heat and cook at a bare simmer, partially covered, until the chicken is tender, 25 to 30 minutes. Stir in the pepper. Serve topped with the parsley and mint.

SLICK OIL TRICKS

Eggplant seems to soak up oil insatiably. As soon as you pour in more oil, the eggplant blots it up and sticks to the pan again so that you have to add even more, ad infinitum. To cut down on the amount of oil needed, use a nonstick pan and cook the eggplant quickly over moderately high heat. Another possibility is to toss eggplant cubes or brush slices with oil and bake rather than fry.

Provençal Chicken with Fennel and Olives

When fennel is out of season, try this easy stew with sliced red or green bell peppers instead.

SERVES 6

6   chicken thighs
6   chicken drumsticks
¾   cup flour
5   tablespoons olive oil
2   large fennel bulbs, cut into thin slices
4   leeks, white and light-green parts only, split lengthwise, cut crosswise into thin slices and washed well
4   cloves garlic, minced
1   cup dry white wine
3   cups Chicken Stock, page 299, or canned low-sodium chicken broth
2   tablespoons tomato paste
1   cup black olives, such as Niçoise or Kalamata, halved and pitted
1   teaspoon dried thyme
2½   teaspoons salt
4   carrots, cut into 1-inch pieces
2   bay leaves
½   teaspoon fresh-ground black pepper

WINE RECOMMENDATION: MATCH THE PROVENÇAL FLAVORS IN THIS DISH WITH A WINE FROM THE SAME REGION, SUCH AS A CÔTES DE PROVENCE OR A WHITE CÔTES-DU-RHÔNE.

1. Heat the oven to 350°. Remove the skin from the chicken. Dredge the chicken pieces in the flour.

2. In a large ovenproof pot, heat 3 tablespoons of the oil over moderately high heat. Add about a third of the chicken and brown well on both sides, about 8 minutes in all. Remove. Brown the remaining pieces in 2 more batches and remove. Reduce the heat to moderate. Add the remaining 2 tablespoons oil to the pot. Add the fennel, leeks and garlic. Cook, stirring, until the vegetables are very brown, about 10 minutes.

3. Add the wine. Scrape the bottom of the pan to dislodge any brown bits. Stir in the stock, tomato paste, olives, thyme and salt. Add the chicken with any juice that has accumulated, the carrots and bay leaves. Bring to a simmer. Cover and cook in the oven until the meat is tender, about 45 minutes. Remove the bay leaves. Stir in the pepper.
—Grace Parisi

Mediterranean Chicken Stew

The wonderful flavors of the Mediterranean—garlic, fennel, eggplant, tomatoes and black olives—are captured in this savory chicken stew.

SERVES 6

4	tablespoons olive oil
1	small eggplant (about 1 pound), cut into ½-inch cubes
2	3½-pound chickens, each cut into 8 pieces
1	onion, chopped
1	fennel bulb, chopped
2	cloves garlic, minced
1	bouquet garni: 6 parsley stems, 3 sprigs fresh thyme or ½ teaspoon dried, and 1 bay leaf
¾	cup dry white wine
3½	cups canned tomatoes with their juice (28-ounce can), chopped
1	cup Chicken Stock, page 299, or canned low-sodium chicken broth
2	teaspoons salt
¼	cup black olives, such as Niçoise or Kalamata, pitted
¼	teaspoon fresh-ground black pepper
1	teaspoon lemon juice
2	tablespoons chopped fresh flat-leaf parsley

WINE RECOMMENDATION:
A ROSÉ FROM THE CÔTES DE PROVENCE OR A RED WINE FROM ONE OF THE FRENCH SEASIDE TOWNS, SUCH AS BANDOL OR CASSIS, IS IDEALLY SUITED TO THE BOLD MEDITERRANEAN FLAVORS OF THIS DISH.

1. Heat 2 tablespoons of the oil in a large nonstick frying pan over moderately high heat until very hot. Sauté the eggplant until brown on all sides, about 5 minutes. Remove.

2. In a large pot, heat the remaining 2 tablespoons over moderately high heat. Add about a third of the chicken and brown well on both sides, about 8 minutes in all. Remove. Brown the remaining chicken in 2 more batches and remove. Discard all but 2 tablespoons of the fat and reduce the heat to moderate.

3. Add the onion and fennel. Cook, stirring occasionally, until the onion is translucent, about 5 minutes. Add the garlic and cook for 1 minute.

4. Add the bouquet garni, wine, the tomatoes with their juice, the stock and salt and bring to a boil, scraping the bottom of the pan to dislodge any brown bits. Add the eggplant, the chicken with

any juice that has accumulated and the olives. Bring to a simmer over moderate heat, reduce the heat and cook at a bare simmer, partially covered, until the chicken is tender, 25 to 30 minutes. Remove the bouquet garni and stir in the pepper, lemon juice and parsley.

FENNEL SUBSTITUTES

Fennel, the bulb with an anise-like flavor, can be difficult to find, especially in summer. A good substitute is fennel seed, either whole or ground. Use one-quarter teaspoon whole fennel seed or three-quarters teaspoon ground in place of one fennel bulb. Or add a little anise-flavored alcohol, such as Pernod.

Moroccan-Style Chicken and Sweet-Potato Stew

Quick and easy yet with a taste of the exotic, this stew can double as a weeknight and a company dish.

SERVES 6

1	tablespoon butter
1	tablespoon cooking oil
2	3½-pound chickens, each cut into 8 pieces
3	onions, chopped
3	cloves garlic, minced
2	green bell peppers, chopped
1	tablespoon turmeric
¾	teaspoon ground cinnamon
¼	teaspoon cayenne
3	pounds sweet potatoes (about 3), peeled and cut into 1-inch cubes
2½	cups canned tomatoes, drained and chopped
½	cup raisins
3	cups Chicken Stock, page 299, or canned low-sodium chicken broth
2½	teaspoons salt
1½	teaspoons grated fresh ginger

WINE RECOMMENDATION:
LOOK FOR A LIVELY BUT NOT TOO DISTINCTIVE DRY WHITE WINE FROM ITALY TO HANDLE THE SWEETNESS OF THIS DISH. TWO GOOD CHOICES: A SOAVE AND A PINOT GRIGIO.

1. In a large pot, heat the butter and oil over moderately high heat. Add about a third of the chicken and brown well on both sides, about 8 minutes in all. Remove. Brown the remaining chicken in 2 more batches and remove. Pour off all but 1 tablespoon fat.

2. Add the onions, garlic and bell peppers and cook, stirring occasionally, until the onions are translucent, about 5 minutes. Add the turmeric, cinnamon and cayenne and cook, stirring, for 30 seconds.

3. Return the chicken pieces to the pot with any juice that has accumulated. Add the sweet potatoes, tomatoes, raisins, stock and salt. Bring the stew to a simmer over moderate heat. Reduce the heat, cover and cook at a bare simmer, stirring occasionally, until the meat is falling off the bone and the potatoes are done, about 40 minutes. Stir in the ginger.

Coq au Vin

Made with wine, bacon, mushrooms and small onions, this French classic features a dark, rich and flavorful sauce. It usually includes red wine but can just as easily be based on white. In Alsace, for instance, where white wine is king, Coq au Riesling is on every menu.

SERVES 6

¼ pound bacon, chopped

5 pounds chicken parts

2 onions, chopped

8 shallots, minced

4 carrots, chopped

¼ cup flour

5 cups red wine

3 cups Brown Chicken Stock, page 299, or canned low-sodium beef broth

4 cloves garlic, minced

1 bouquet garni: 8 parsley stems, 3 sprigs fresh thyme or ½ teaspoon dried, and 2 bay leaves

2 tablespoons tomato paste

1½ teaspoons salt

1 pound small white onions, about 1 inch in diameter, peeled

4 tablespoons butter

2 teaspoons sugar

1½ pounds mushrooms, quartered

¼ teaspoon fresh-ground black pepper

3 tablespoons chopped fresh flat-leaf parsley

WINE RECOMMENDATION: Look for a rustic young red wine from the Rhône Valley in France to go with the winey flavor of this stew. Two nice selections are a Côtes-du-Rhône and a Crozes-Hermitage.

1. In a large pot, cook the bacon over moderate heat until crisp. Remove. Pour off and reserve all but 2 tablespoons of the bacon fat.

2. Raise the heat to moderately high. Add about a third of the chicken and brown well on both sides, about 8 minutes in all. Remove. Brown the remaining chicken in 2 more batches and remove. Discard all but 2 tablespoons of the fat and reduce the heat to moderate.

3. Add the chopped onions, the shallots and carrots to the pot and cook, stirring occasionally, until browned, about 8 minutes. Add the flour and cook, stirring, for 2 minutes. Stir in the wine, scraping the bottom of the pot to dislodge any brown bits. Add the stock, garlic, bouquet garni, tomato paste and 1 teaspoon of the salt.

4. Return the chicken to the pot with any juice that has accumulated. Bring to

a simmer over moderate heat. Reduce the heat and cook at a bare simmer, covered, until the chicken is cooked through, 25 to 30 minutes.

5. Meanwhile, in a medium saucepan, combine the small onions, ¼ teaspoon of the salt, 2 tablespoons of the butter, the sugar and just barely enough water to cover. Bring to a boil, reduce the heat and simmer until the onions are tender and the water has evaporated, 10 to 15 minutes. Continue cooking, stirring, until the onions are brown, about 7 minutes longer.

6. In a large frying pan, heat 2 tablespoons of the reserved bacon fat with the remaining 2 tablespoons butter over moderately high heat. Add the mushrooms, the remaining ¼ teaspoon salt and the pepper. Sauté until the mushrooms are brown, about 8 minutes.

7. Remove the chicken and reduce the sauce, if necessary, to 4 cups. Discard the bouquet garni. Return the chicken to the pot, add the bacon, small onions and mushrooms and bring to a simmer. Serve the stew topped with the parsley.

PEELING SMALL ONIONS

Little white onions have thin skins that cling tenaciously. To ease the task of peeling, blanch them in boiling water for about 10 seconds. Drain, rinse with cold water and drain again. Cut off the root, pinch the stem end and the onion will slip out of its skin. You can also simply soak the onions in tap water for about half an hour to get much the same loosening effect.

Chicken Stew with Mushrooms and Caramelized Onions

A shot of wine vinegar added near the end of this recipe makes the time-honored combination of chicken, mushrooms and onions especially good.

SERVES 6

3 tablespoons cooking oil

¾ pound mushrooms, quartered

2 teaspoons salt

½ teaspoon fresh-ground black pepper

2 tablespoons butter

5 pounds chicken parts

6 tablespoons flour

3 cups Chicken Stock, page 299, or canned low-sodium chicken broth

¾ pound small white onions, about 1 inch in diameter, peeled

1 tablespoon sugar

6 tablespoons sherry vinegar or red-wine vinegar

2 tablespoons mixed chopped fresh herbs, such as chervil, tarragon, chives or parsley

WINE RECOMMENDATION:
WITH ITS DEEP FLAVORS FROM THE MUSHROOMS AND CARAMELIZED ONIONS, THIS STEW WORKS BEST WITH A SOMEWHAT ELEGANT RED WINE, SUCH AS A CABERNET SAUVIGNON OR MERLOT FROM CALIFORNIA.

1. In a large pot, heat 1 tablespoon of the oil over moderate heat. Add the mushrooms, ¼ teaspoon of the salt and ¼ teaspoon of the pepper. Sauté, stirring occasionally, until golden, about 5 minutes. Remove the mushrooms with a slotted spoon.

2. In the same pot, melt 1 tablespoon of the butter with the remaining 2 tablespoons oil over moderately high heat. Add about a third of the chicken and brown well on both sides, about 8 minutes in all. Remove. Brown the remaining chicken in 2 batches. Pour off all but 1 tablespoon fat. Return the chicken to the pot with any juice that has accumulated. Sprinkle the chicken with the flour and turn the pieces to coat them on both sides. Cook about 1 minute per side.

3. Add the stock and 1½ teaspoons of the salt. Scrape the bottom of the pot to dislodge any brown bits. Bring to a simmer over moderate heat, reduce the heat and cook at a bare simmer for 15 minutes.

4. Meanwhile, in a medium saucepan, combine the small onions, the remaining ¼ teaspoon salt and 1 tablespoon butter, the sugar and just barely enough water to cover. Bring to a boil, reduce the heat and simmer until the onions are tender and the water has evaporated, 10 to 15 minutes. Continue cooking, stirring, until the onions are brown, about 7 minutes longer. Add the vinegar and scrape the bottom of the pan to dislodge any brown bits.

5. Add the mushrooms, the onions with any liquid and the remaining ¼ teaspoon pepper to the chicken and simmer until the chicken is just done, 10 to 15 minutes longer. Serve topped with the fresh herbs.

—Charles Pierce

STORING FRESH HERBS

One of the best ways we know to keep herbs fresh is to wrap them in a paper towel, put them in a plastic bag, close it loosely and keep in the refrigerator. The bag holds in moisture while the paper towel absorbs any excess. If you're lucky enough to find herbs with their roots still attached, put them in a glass with enough water to cover the roots. Cover the tops with a plastic bag left open at the bottom and keep the herbs in the refrigerator. Or wrap the roots in a wet paper towel, put in a plastic bag and refrigerate. Any of these methods should keep the herbs fresh for four to five days.

Indonesian Chicken Stew with Zucchini and Fried Shallots

A spicy curry paste made with garlic, ginger, coriander, cumin, macadamia nuts and black pepper is the base for this delicious stew. Like many curried dishes in Southeast Asia, it's cooked in coconut milk and topped with fried shallots. It has a lot of ground black pepper already, but if you want to increase the heat, add more pepper at the end of cooking.

SERVES 6

2 3½-pound chickens, cut up
¼ cup lemon juice, from about 2 lemons
2¾ teaspoons salt
2 onions, chopped
8 cloves garlic, chopped
½ cup chopped cilantro stems and 3 tablespoons chopped fresh cilantro leaves, plus whole leaves for garnish
6 tablespoons grated fresh ginger
3 tablespoons chopped macadamia nuts, cashew nuts or peanuts
1 cup water
3 tablespoons ground coriander
1 tablespoon fresh-ground black pepper
2 teaspoons sugar
1½ teaspoons ground cumin
2 tablespoons cooking oil, plus more for frying
2 15-ounce cans unsweetened coconut milk
1½ pounds zucchini (about 4), quartered lengthwise, seeded and cut into ¼-inch diagonal slices

2 teaspoons lime juice, plus lime wedges for serving
6 shallots, cut into very thin slices

WINE RECOMMENDATION:
THIS CREAMY CURRIED CHICKEN STEW, WITH ITS SLIGHT BUT NOTICEABLE HEAT, GOES BEST WITH A COLD BOTTLE OF GEWÜRZTRAMINER FROM ALSACE—OR A BOTTLE OF YOUR FAVORITE BEER.

1. Cut each of the chicken wings into 2 pieces. Separate the thighs and drumsticks. Cut each breast into 3 pieces. This will make 14 pieces per chicken. In a large stainless-steel or glass bowl, marinate the chicken with the lemon juice and ¼ teaspoon of the salt, stirring occasionally, for 30 minutes. Drain and dry on paper towels.

2. Make the curry paste: In a blender, puree the onions, garlic, cilantro stems, ginger and nuts with ¼ cup of the water, the coriander, pepper, sugar, cumin and 2 teaspoons of the salt. ➤

3. In a large pot, heat the 2 tablespoons oil over moderately high heat. Add about a third of the chicken and brown well on both sides, about 8 minutes in all. Remove. Brown the remaining chicken in 2 batches and remove. Reduce the heat to low, add the curry paste and cook, scraping the bottom of the pot to dislodge any brown bits, until fragrant, about 1 minute.

4. Spoon off the thick coconut milk from the top of the cans and set aside. Add the remaining coconut milk, ¾ cup water and ½ teaspoon salt to the pot and whisk until smooth.

5. Add the chicken with any juice that has accumulated and stir to coat.

Bring the stew to a simmer over moderately high heat, reduce the heat and cook at a bare simmer, partially covered, for 15 minutes. Add the zucchini and cook until the chicken is just done, 10 to 15 minutes longer. Stir in the reserved thick coconut milk, the 3 tablespoons chopped cilantro leaves and the lime juice.

6. In a small saucepan, heat ½ inch of cooking oil until very hot, about 350°. Add the shallots to the oil and fry until golden brown, about 2 minutes. Drain on paper towels.

7. Top the stew with the fried shallots and the whole cilantro leaves. Serve with the lime wedges.

GRATING TIP

Fresh ginger, or anything else for that matter, tends to get stuck in the fine holes of a hand grater. Try wrapping the grater tightly with plastic film. The grater's little metal nubs will poke right through the wrap. Grate the ginger as usual and then carefully unwrap the grater. Most of the ginger will stay on the plastic wrap. This works well for citrus zest, too. An even easier, though not quite so effective, technique is to simply knock the grater smartly against a cutting board, grating side down.

Chicken Adobo

Stewing in vinegar and soy sauce is a traditional technique in the Philippines. Whether the main ingredient be chicken, beef, pork or seafood, the vinegar acts as both a tenderizer and a tart seasoning.

SERVES 6

2	3½-pound chickens, cut up
1	cup white vinegar
1	cup water
½	cup soy sauce
4	onions, cut into thin slices
20	cloves garlic, minced
3	bay leaves
1	pound tomatoes (about 2), peeled and chopped, or 1¾ cups canned tomatoes (14½-ounce can), drained and chopped
½	teaspoon fresh-ground black pepper

WINE RECOMMENDATION:
VINEGAR, SOY AND LOADS OF GARLIC—THIS DISH IS A VERITABLE FOOD-AND-WINE-MATCHING NIGHTMARE. TRY A CHENIN BLANC FROM CALIFORNIA OR WASHINGTON STATE. OR PLAY IT SAFE AND SERVE BEER INSTEAD.

1. Cut each of the chicken wings into 2 pieces. Separate the thighs and drumsticks. Cut each breast into 3 pieces. This will make 14 pieces per chicken.

2. In a large pot, combine the chicken, vinegar, water, soy sauce, onions, garlic and bay leaves. Bring to a simmer over moderately high heat. Reduce the heat, cover and cook at a bare simmer, stirring occasionally, until the meat is falling off the bone, about 40 minutes.

3. Remove the chicken from the pot and skim off the fat from the sauce. Remove the bay leaves. Bring the sauce back to a boil and cook until reduced to about 4 cups.

4. Return the chicken to the pot with the tomatoes and simmer 10 minutes longer. Stir in the pepper.

Brunswick Stew

A traditional Southern dish that hails from Brunswick County, Virginia, this stew originated in the 1800s as a hunters' meal made with small game—rabbit and often squirrel. Ours is an updated version such as you're more likely to find in the South these days, combining chicken, pork, lima beans and corn, generously spiced with Tabasco sauce. Thick and meaty, it makes a great down-home meal. If you like it hotter, add more Tabasco.

SERVES 6

1	3½-pound chicken
2	tablespoons cooking oil, more if needed
1½	pounds boneless pork shoulder or butt, cut into 1-inch cubes
3	onions, chopped
3½	cups canned tomatoes with their juice (28-ounce can), chopped
4	carrots, chopped
1	baking potato, peeled and chopped
1	cup fresh or frozen lima beans
2	cloves garlic, minced
2	quarts water
¾	teaspoon Tabasco sauce
2	teaspoons dried thyme
2	bay leaves
2½	teaspoons salt
½	teaspoon dried red-pepper flakes
1½	cups fresh (cut from about 2 ears) or frozen corn kernels

WINE RECOMMENDATION: NOT TO SERVE AN AMERICAN WINE WITH THIS CLASSIC SOUTHERN STEW WOULD SEEM INCONGRUOUS. TRY A BOTTLE OF SEYVAL BLANC, A HYBRID VARIETAL GROWN IN MANY NON-WEST COAST VINEYARDS. IF YOU CAN'T FIND IT, AN EASIER-TO-LOCATE CHOICE IS A DRY CHENIN BLANC FROM CALIFORNIA OR WASHINGTON STATE.

1. Remove excess fat from the chicken. In a large pot, heat the oil over moderately high heat. Add half the pork and brown well on all sides, about 8 minutes. Remove. Brown the remaining pork, adding more oil if needed, and remove. Reduce the heat to moderately low.

2. Add the onions and cook, stirring occasionally, until translucent, about 5 minutes. Add the pork with any accumulated juice, the chicken, the tomatoes with their juice, the carrots, potato, fresh lima beans, if using, garlic, water, Tabasco sauce, thyme, bay leaves, salt and red-pepper flakes. Bring to a simmer over moderate heat, reduce the heat and cook at a bare simmer for 2½ hours in all.

3. Remove the chicken when it is cooked through, after about 1 hour. When the chicken is cool enough to handle, remove the meat from the skin and bones and tear it into shreds.

4. After 2 hours of cooking, add the chicken meat, frozen lima beans, if using, and the corn and continue cooking, covered, until the pork is falling-apart tender and the stew is thick and flavorful, about ½ hour longer. Skim the fat from the surface.

—Jan Newberry

CHOPPING CANNED TOMATOES

An easy way to chop canned tomatoes without making a mess is to put them, with or without their juice, depending on the recipe, in a large bowl and mash them with a potato masher. Another technique some people like is to run a table knife back and forth through the tomatoes right in the can.

Grandmother's Stewed Chicken with Parsley Dumplings

Dumplings are at their light-and-fluffy best when the dough is cooked just before serving. The chicken can be stewed in advance, but be sure to bring it back to a simmer before you add the dumpling dough. The trick is to drop the dough into the pot and cover at once so that the dumplings steam.

SERVES 6

2   3½-pound chickens, each cut into 8 pieces
1   quart Chicken Stock, page 299, or canned low-sodium chicken broth
2   onions, chopped
2   ribs celery, chopped
2½   teaspoons salt
1   egg
¼   cup milk
1½   cups flour
1½   teaspoons baking powder
2   tablespoons butter
2   tablespoons chopped fresh parsley
1   cup water
¼   teaspoon fresh-ground black pepper

1. Put the chickens in a large pot with the stock, onions, celery and 2 teaspoons of the salt. Bring to a simmer over moderate heat. Reduce the heat and cook at a bare simmer, partially covered, until the chickens are almost done, 20 to 25 minutes.

2. Meanwhile, prepare the dumplings: In a small bowl, lightly beat the egg and milk. In a medium bowl, combine 1 cup of the flour, the remaining ½ teaspoon salt and the baking powder. Rub or cut the butter into the flour until the mixture resembles coarse meal. Stir in 1 tablespoon of the chopped parsley. Pour the egg and milk into the dry ingredients and stir the mixture into a dough.

3. Drop the dumpling dough in 6 spoonfuls on top of the simmering chicken. Cover the pot and cook 10 minutes longer without removing the lid.

4. Transfer the chicken and dumplings to a large serving bowl and keep warm. Strain the stock. Press the vegetables firmly to get all the liquid. Return the stock to the pot.

5. In a small bowl, whisk together the remaining ½ cup flour and the water. Bring the cooking liquid back to a simmer. Gradually whisk in enough of the flour mixture to thicken the gravy. Bring to a boil, still whisking, and continue boiling for 1 minute. Stir in the remaining 1 tablespoon parsley and the pepper and ladle the gravy over the chicken and dumplings.

FROM DUMPLING TO BISCUIT

After enjoying dumplings steamed on top of chicken stew, we tried baking the dough left over from testing. Voila! The dough made light and delicious biscuit-like bread. So for a change, you might want to serve parsley drop biscuits in place of the dumplings. Or, since dumpling dough makes such good biscuits, you may end up throwing out your old recipe and making dumpling dough whenever you want biscuits. It's the egg that makes them both light and rich at the same time. Drop the 6 spoonfuls of dough onto a buttered baking sheet about 2 inches apart. Bake in a 450° oven until the tops are golden, about 12 minutes.

Cornish Hen Spring Stew with Asparagus and Tarragon

The only trick to preparing these small birds is to avoid overcooking them. They should cook only ten or fifteen minutes after browning or the breasts will be too dry.

SERVES 6

3	Cornish hens, about 5 pounds total
3	tablespoons cooking oil
1	onion, chopped
1	carrot, chopped
1	rib celery, chopped
½	cup dry white wine
3	cups Chicken Stock, page 299, or canned low-sodium chicken broth
½	cup plus 1 tablespoon flour
1½	teaspoons salt
½	teaspoon fresh-ground black pepper
1	tablespoon butter
4	shallots, chopped
1½	pounds asparagus, peeled and cut into 1-inch lengths
1	cup fresh or frozen petite peas
1	cup heavy cream
1	teaspoon grated lemon zest
2	tablespoons chopped fresh tarragon

WINE RECOMMENDATION:
THE CREAMY TEXTURE AND TASTE OF THIS STEW AND THE FLAVOR OF ASPARAGUS BOTH WORK WELL WITH A YOUNG, ASSERTIVE BOTTLE OF SAUVIGNON BLANC FROM BORDEAUX OR THE LOIRE VALLEY IN FRANCE, OR FROM NEW ZEALAND.

1. Cut away the backs from the Cornish hens. Cut each hen into quarters. In a large pot, heat 1 tablespoon of the oil over moderately high heat. Add the backs and cook until very brown, about 8 minutes. Discard all but a teaspoon of fat. Add the onion, carrot and celery and cook 3 minutes longer. Add the wine and simmer 2 minutes, scraping the bottom of the pan to dislodge any brown bits. Add the stock. Bring to a boil and simmer until the stock has reduced to 2 cups. Strain the stock. Press the vegetables and bones firmly to get all the liquid. Set the stock aside.

2. Combine ½ cup of the flour, ½ teaspoon of the salt and ¼ teaspoon of the pepper. Dredge each hen quarter in the seasoned flour. In a frying pan, heat the remaining 2 tablespoons oil over

moderately high heat. Add some of the Cornish hen quarters and cook until brown, about 4 minutes per side. Remove. Brown the remaining quarters.

3. In a large pot, heat the butter over moderate heat. Add the shallots and cook until beginning to turn golden, about 3 minutes. Add the remaining 1 tablespoon flour and cook, stirring, for 2 minutes. Add the hens with any juice that has accumulated, the reserved stock and the remaining 1 teaspoon salt. Bring to a simmer over moderate heat. Reduce the heat and cook, covered, at a bare simmer for 5 minutes. Add the asparagus and fresh peas, if using. Simmer until the hens are just done and the vegetables are tender, about 5 minutes longer.

4. Add the frozen peas, if using, the cream, lemon zest, tarragon and remaining ¼ teaspoon pepper. Bring back to a simmer and serve.

FRESH VS. FROZEN PEAS

Nothing is better than sweet green peas fresh from the garden—as long as they've been picked within twenty-four hours. Once past their day of youth, their sugars convert to starch and they become mealy and hard. Unfortunately, most fresh peas that you can buy are of this vintage. Unless you have a terrific source, like your own backyard or a farmers' market, you're better off using peas frozen at their peak. Especially good are those labeled petite peas. Avoid canned peas, which have little in common with fresh. Though they're processed shortly after picking, these peas are subjected to such high heat during canning that their flavor, texture and color are altered forever.

Cornish Hens with Cabbage and Bacon

Cornish hens take on a hearty note when paired with cabbage, bacon and potatoes. These small birds cook in minutes. Remove the breasts if they're done before the legs and thighs, then put them back shortly before serving to reheat.

SERVES 6

¼   pound bacon, chopped

3   Cornish hens, about 5 pounds total

½   cup plus 1 tablespoon flour

1¾ teaspoons salt

½   teaspoon fresh-ground black pepper

½   cup dry white wine

¾   pound Savoy or green cabbage, cored and cut into 1½-inch chunks

2   onions, each cut into 8 wedges

1   pound boiling potatoes (about 3), peeled and cut into ½-inch cubes

1½ cups Brown Chicken Stock, page 299, or canned low-sodium chicken broth

WINE RECOMMENDATION:
BACON, CABBAGE AND WINE ARE TRADITIONAL INGREDIENTS IN MANY ALSATIAN DISHES. TRY A RIESLING OR PINOT GRIS FROM THAT EASTERN REGION OF FRANCE.

1. In a frying pan, cook the bacon until crisp. Remove and drain on paper towels. Pour off all but 2 tablespoons fat, reserving the extra fat.

2. Cut each Cornish hen into quarters. Combine ½ cup of the flour, ½ teaspoon of the salt and ¼ teaspoon of the pepper. Dredge each hen quarter in the seasoned flour. Put the frying pan over moderately high heat. When the fat is hot, add some of the Cornish-hen quarters and cook until brown, about 4 minutes per side. Remove. Brown the remaining quarters and remove. Add the wine and simmer 2 minutes, scraping the bottom of the pan to dislodge any brown bits.

3. In a large pot, heat 1 tablespoon of the reserved bacon fat. Add the cabbage, onions and potatoes and cook, covered, until the cabbage begins to wilt, about 10 minutes. ➤

4. Add the remaining 1 tablespoon flour and cook, stirring, for 2 minutes. Add the bacon and the Cornish hens with any juice that has accumulated, tucking the hens into the cabbage and potato mixture. Add the wine mixture, the stock and the remaining 1¼ tea-spoons salt. Bring to a simmer over moderate heat. Cover, reduce the heat and cook at a bare simmer, stirring occasionally, until the potatoes are tender and the Cornish hens are done, about 10 minutes longer. Stir in the remaining ¼ teaspoon pepper.

REHEATING POULTRY STEWS

Some people consider it impossible to reheat a poultry stew without making the meat dry, but with care it can be done. Warm the stew in a covered pot over low heat or in a 300° oven, stirring occasionally, just until heated through. Twenty minutes should be enough for a room-temperature stew, slightly more if it's straight from the refrigerator. When making the dish ahead of time and planning to reheat before serving, we like to undercook chicken by about ten minutes and Cornish hens by about three minutes. They'll finish cooking when you reheat them.

Cornish Hen Stew with Leeks, Figs and Orange

The sweetness of figs complements the savory hens and leeks beautifully. You can substitute chicken for the Cornish hens. Use five pounds of chicken parts and lengthen the cooking time to about twenty-five minutes.

SERVES 6

5	3-inch-long strips orange zest
3	Cornish hens, about 5 pounds total
1	tablespoon cooking oil
1	tablespoon butter
4	leeks, white and light-green parts only, split lengthwise, cut crosswise into ¼-inch slices and washed well
1	teaspoon chopped fresh rosemary, or ¼ teaspoon dried, crumbled
⅓	cup flour
½	cup cognac or other brandy
1	quart Chicken Stock, page 299, or canned low-sodium chicken broth
1	pound dried figs, stemmed and cut into quarters
2½	teaspoons salt
	Rustic Croûtes, page 309

WINE RECOMMENDATION:
A RIESLING FROM ALSACE IN FRANCE HAS PLENTY OF STEELY FLAVOR AND ACIDITY TO CUT AGAINST THE SWEETNESS HERE.

1. Stack the strips of orange zest, cut them lengthwise into the thinnest possible strips and then cut the strips in half. Bring a small saucepan of water to a boil. Add the strips. Blanch 1 minute. Drain. Rinse with cold water. Drain thoroughly.

2. Cut each hen into quarters. In a large pot, heat the oil and butter over moderately high heat. Add some of the hen quarters and cook until brown, about 4 minutes per side. Remove. Brown the remaining quarters and remove.

3. Reduce the heat to moderate. Add the leeks and rosemary and cook, scraping the bottom of the pan, until the leeks are golden, about 7 minutes. Add the flour and cook, stirring, for 2 minutes. Add the cognac. Return the hens to the pot with any juice that has accumulated. Add the orange zest, stock, figs and salt. Bring to a simmer, cover and cook until the hens are just done, about 10 minutes. Serve with the croûtes around the edge of the dish.

Duck and Mushrooms in Port

Port adds a pleasant sweetness to this rich duck stew, and crisp cracklings contrast with the silky sauce. Potatoes roasted with herbs make a good accompaniment. Simply cut them in chunks, toss with a few tablespoons of oil, some sage, rosemary, thyme or marjoram, salt and pepper, put them in a small baking dish and roast alongside the carrots, onions and mushrooms that go into the stew.

SERVES 4

2 ducks, about 5½ pounds each
1¾ teaspoons salt
1 onion, chopped
2 carrots, chopped
1 rib celery, chopped
2 tablespoons tomato paste
2 tablespoons tamari or soy sauce
2 cups port
5½ cups water
1 bouquet garni: 6 parsley stems, 3 sprigs fresh thyme or ½ teaspoon dried, and 1 bay leaf
⅔ pound baby carrots, or larger carrots cut into 2-inch pieces
⅔ pound small white onions, about 1 inch in diameter, peeled
⅔ pound mushrooms
½ teaspoon fresh-ground black pepper
2½ tablespoons cornstarch, dissolved in ⅓ cup water

WINE RECOMMENDATION:
THE RICH, SWEET FLAVORS OF THIS DISH ARE PERFECT FOR THE LIVELY BUT SOMEWHAT SWEET FLAVORS OF WINES MADE FROM THE PINOT NOIR GRAPE. LOOK FOR A THREE- TO FIVE-YEAR-OLD BOTTLE FROM ONE OF OREGON'S BETTER PRODUCERS, OR SPLURGE ON A BOTTLE OF VILLAGES-LEVEL WINE FROM THE CÔTE DE NUITS IN FRANCE'S BURGUNDY REGION.

1. Remove the legs from the ducks (drumstick and thigh attached). Cut each breast section off the bone: Cut along the breastbone. Then, holding the sharp edge of the knife against the bone at an angle, slide the knife between the bone and the meat until the breast is removed in one piece. Repeat for the other side and the second duck. Reserve the bones. Remove the skin from the breasts. Cut it into ½-inch pieces and set aside. With a heavy knife or poultry shears, cut the reserved bones and wings into pieces.

2. In a large pot over moderate heat, cook the duck skin, stirring occasionally, until the fat has rendered and the skin is crisp, about 15 minutes. Remove the

cracklings with a slotted spoon and drain on paper towels. Sprinkle the cracklings with ¼ teaspoon of the salt and set aside.

3. Pour off and reserve all but 2 tablespoons of the fat. Add the bones to the pot and cook, stirring occasionally, until brown, about 15 minutes. Stir in the chopped onion, carrots and celery and cook until golden, about 5 minutes longer. Stir in the tomato paste, tamari, port, the 5½ cups water and the bouquet garni. Scrape the bottom of the pot to dislodge any brown bits. Bring to a boil, reduce the heat and simmer 45 minutes. Strain the stock. Press the vegetables and bones firmly to get all the liquid. You should have about 4½ cups.

4. In a large pot, heat 2 tablespoons of the reserved duck fat over moderately high heat. Add the legs to the pot, skin-side down, and brown well on both sides, about 10 minutes in all. Remove the legs from the pot. Add the duck breasts and brown them on both sides, about 8 minutes in all. Remove.

5. Discard the fat from the pot. Add the stock and scrape the bottom to dis-lodge any brown bits. Return the duck to the pot with any juice that has accumulated. Add 1 teaspoon of the salt. The duck should be nearly covered with liquid. Bring to a simmer over moderately high heat, reduce the heat and cook at a bare simmer, covered, until the duck is tender, about 1¼ hours.

6. Meanwhile, heat the oven to 450°. In a large roasting pan, combine the baby carrots, small onions, mushrooms, 1 tablespoon of the reserved duck fat, the remaining ½ teaspoon salt and ¼ teaspoon pepper. Cook the vegetables, stirring occasionally, until beginning to brown, about 25 minutes.

7. Remove the duck pieces from the stock. Skim any fat from the cooking liquid and bring to a boil. Whisk in the cornstarch mixture. Reduce the heat and simmer the sauce until thickened, about 3 minutes longer.

8. Return the duck to the sauce with the roasted vegetables and the remaining ¼ teaspoon pepper and heat through. Serve topped with the reserved cracklings.

—Grace Parisi

Turkey Mole

The traditional recipe for this Mexican specialty requires days of labor and therefore is reserved for special occasions. Here we offer you a delicious short version.

SERVES 6

4	tablespoons lard or cooking oil
6	pounds turkey parts
1½	quarts Chicken Stock, page 299, or canned low-sodium chicken broth
2¾	teaspoons salt
1	stale corn tortilla
2	slices stale white bread
2	onions, quartered
4	cloves garlic, crushed
¼	cup unblanched almonds
3	tablespoons raisins
¼	cup sesame seeds
¼	cup chili powder
1	teaspoon fresh-ground black pepper
½	teaspoon ground cinnamon
½	teaspoon ground coriander
½	teaspoon dried red-pepper flakes
¼	teaspoon ground cloves
½	cup water
1	ounce unsweetened chocolate, chopped

WINE RECOMMENDATION: A SLIGHTLY CHILLED, VERY FRUITY RED WINE, SUCH AS A BEAUJOLAIS FROM FRANCE (OR, DURING THE WINTER, A BEAUJOLAIS NOUVEAU), IS REFRESHINGLY DELIGHTFUL WITH THIS DEEP, SPICY TURKEY STEW.

1. In a large pot, heat 2 tablespoons of the lard or oil over moderately high heat. Add half of the turkey and brown well on both sides, about 10 minutes in all. Remove. Repeat with the remaining turkey. Discard the fat.

2. Return the turkey to the pot and add the stock and salt. Bring to a simmer over moderate heat. Cover, reduce the heat and simmer until the turkey is just done, about 30 minutes. Remove the turkey and reserve the stock. When the turkey is cool enough to handle, remove the meat from the skin and bones and cut it into serving pieces.

3. In a food processor, puree the tortilla, bread, onions, garlic, almonds, raisins, sesame seeds, chili powder, black pepper, cinnamon, coriander, red-pepper flakes, cloves and water.

4. In a large pot, heat the remaining 2 tablespoons lard or oil over moderately

low heat. Add the puree and cook, stirring, until brick colored, about 5 minutes. Add the chocolate and stir until melted.

5. Whisk in the reserved stock until smooth. Simmer, uncovered, stirring occasionally, until slightly thickened, 35 to 40 minutes. Add the turkey, cover and simmer 20 minutes longer.

 VARIATION

Sweeten savory mole with fried plantains. Plantains are the large cooking bananas available at most Mexican markets and are usually still green when sold. When plantains are left to ripen, the skin darkens and the potato-like flesh softens and sweetens. Fry them to add another dimension to Turkey Mole. Peel 2 ripe plantains and cut them into ½-inch cubes. In a large frying pan, heat ½ inch of lard or cooking oil over moderate heat. Add the plantains and fry, stirring occasionally, until well browned, 2 to 3 minutes. Remove with a slotted spoon and drain on paper towels. Stir the plantains into the mole just before serving.

CHAPTER 9 · MEAT STEWS

Veal Stew with Carrots and Dill

Flecks of fresh dill enhance the trio of veal, carrots and small onions. The dill is quite prominent, and you can give the stew an entirely new taste by replacing it with chervil or tarragon. White rice makes an ideal accompaniment.

SERVES 6

3	pounds boneless veal shoulder, cut into 1½-inch cubes
2	ribs celery, quartered
1½	cups dry white wine
3	cups Veal or Chicken Stock, page 302 or 299, or canned low-sodium chicken broth
1½	teaspoons salt
¾	pound small white onions, about 1 inch in diameter, peeled
1½	pounds carrots, cut into 1-inch pieces
5	tablespoons butter
5	tablespoons flour
3	tablespoons chopped fresh dill
¼	teaspoon fresh-ground black pepper

WINE RECOMMENDATION: SERVE THIS ELEGANT STEW WITH A REFINED, SLIGHTLY AUSTERE RED WINE, SUCH AS A CLASSIFIED GROWTH FROM THE MÉDOC REGION OF BORDEAUX.

1. In a large pot, combine the veal, celery, wine, stock and salt. Bring to a simmer over moderately high heat, reduce the heat and cook at a bare simmer, partially covered, until the veal is almost tender, about 1 hour.

2. Add the onions and carrots to the stew. Bring back to a simmer and cook until the meat and vegetables are tender, about 30 minutes longer. Strain the stew. Discard the celery.

3. Melt the butter in a large pot over moderately low heat. Whisk in the flour. Cook, whisking constantly, for 2 minutes. Whisk in the cooking liquid. Bring back to a boil, whisking constantly, and let boil for 2 minutes. Add the veal, onions, carrots, dill and pepper and simmer 5 minutes.

—Charles Pierce

Blanquette de Veau

This is a luscious version of an already delectable French classic. Traditionally blanquette is a "white" stew made with veal, small onions and mushrooms, none of which are browned, and served in a creamy-white velouté sauce. Here béarnaise sauce is stirred into the velouté at the end. Purists might shudder, but we think the béarnaise with its perfume of tarragon and kick of vinegar is an inspired addition.

SERVES 6

3   pounds boneless veal shoulder, cut into 1½-inch cubes
1   clove
2   onions, cut crosswise into halves
1½ quarts Veal or Chicken Stock, page 302 or 299, or canned low-sodium chicken broth
10 peppercorns
1   bouquet garni: 6 parsley stems, 3 sprigs fresh thyme or ½ teaspoon dried, and 1 bay leaf
2   teaspoons salt
10 ounces small white onions, about 1 inch in diameter, peeled
¾   pound mushrooms, quartered if large
3   cups heavy cream
15 tablespoons butter
3   tablespoons flour
5   tablespoons water
3   tablespoons white-wine vinegar
1   tablespoon chopped shallot or scallion
2   tablespoons chopped fresh tarragon, or 2 teaspoons dried
2   egg yolks

WINE RECOMMENDATION: CONTRAST THIS LUSH, CREAMY DISH WITH A FEISTY YOUNG RED WINE WITH PLENTY OF ACIDITY AND TANNIN. LOOK FOR A CLASSIFIED GROWTH FROM THE MÉDOC REGION OF BORDEAUX OR EXPLORE ONE OF THE SATELLITE APPELLATIONS IN THE BORDEAUX REGION, SUCH AS THE CÔTES DE BOURG OR PREMIÈRES CÔTES DE BLAYE.

1. Put the veal in a large pot of cold water. Bring to a boil. Continue boiling for 1 minute. Drain and rinse the meat with cold water. Rinse the pot.

2. Return the blanched veal to the pot. Press the clove into 1 onion half and add to the veal with the remaining onion halves, stock, peppercorns, bouquet garni and 1½ teaspoons of the salt. Bring to a simmer over moderately high heat, reduce the heat and cook the veal at a bare simmer until the meat is almost tender, about 1 hour.

3. Add the small onions and cook 15 minutes. Add the mushrooms and cook until the veal is tender, about 15 minutes longer. Strain the stew. Discard the onion halves, peppercorns and bouquet garni.

4. Return the stock to the pot and boil until reduced to 3 cups. Add the cream and simmer until the sauce is reduced to 4½ cups, about 10 minutes.

5. In a medium saucepan, melt 3 tablespoons of the butter over moderately low heat. Whisk in the flour. Cook, whisking constantly, for about 2 minutes. Whisk in the reduced stock mixture. Bring the sauce to a boil, whisking constantly, and cook for 2 minutes. Add the veal and vegetables to the sauce and set aside.

6. For the béarnaise, melt the remaining 12 tablespoons butter. In a small heavy saucepan, combine 4 tablespoons of the water, the vinegar, shallot and 1 tablespoon of the fresh tarragon or all of the dried. Bring to a boil and

cook until the liquid is reduced to ¼ cup, about 3 minutes. Strain and reserve.

7. In the same saucepan, beat the egg yolks and remaining tablespoon water. Whisk in the reserved vinegar mixture. Whisk over the lowest possible heat until the mixture is thick and frothy, about 7 minutes. Remove from the heat. Add the butter in a slow stream, whisking constantly so that the butter is absorbed by the yolks to form a sauce. Add the remaining ½ teaspoon salt and the remaining tablespoon fresh tarragon, if using.

8. Reheat the stew and stir in the béarnaise sauce. Do not bring the stew back to a boil or it may curdle.

—Christopher Gross
Christopher's

SHORTCUT

Chefs have resources that the home cook can only dream of. One of which, of course, is many hands in the kitchen. A restaurant also generally has several sauces ready for the various dishes on the menu, and combining them is a simple matter. So stirring béarnaise into a stew shortly before sending it to the table is no problem. For this recipe from a fine chef, making béarnaise sauce at the last minute is well worth the effort. If it seems too troublesome, though, you can get close to the same effect by first thickening the blanquette in the traditional way (whisk some of the hot sauce into two egg yolks and then, over the lowest possible heat, whisk the mixture into the remaining sauce) and when you're ready to serve, adding 2 tablespoons tarragon and a teaspoon or so of vinegar.

Italian Veal Stew
with Paprika

Flavored with both hot and mild paprika, this fragrant and spicy veal stew has its origins in the northeast corner of Italy, near the former Yugoslavian border. Beef or pork would be good cooked this way, too. Serve with buttered pappardelle or other egg noodles.

SERVES 6

3	pounds boneless veal shoulder, cut into 1½-inch cubes
3	tablespoons olive oil, more if needed
2	tablespoons mild paprika
4	teaspoons hot paprika
¼	pound pancetta or bacon, chopped
2	onions, chopped
2	carrots, chopped
1	rib celery, chopped
4	cloves garlic, minced
1¾	cups red wine
2¾	cups Chicken or Veal Stock, page 299 or 302, or canned low-sodium chicken broth
2	tablespoons tomato paste
1½	teaspoons dried thyme
1	teaspoon salt
1	bouquet garni: 6 parsley stems, 1 bay leaf and 1 cinnamon stick
½	pound baby carrots, 1 inch of each stem left on, or regular carrots cut into thirds
1	head broccoli, about 1¼ pounds, cut into florets with 2-inch stems
1	pound small white onions, about 1 inch in diameter, peeled

1. Heat the oven to 325°. In a large bowl, combine the veal, 2 tablespoons of the oil and both paprikas. In a large ovenproof pot, heat the remaining tablespoon oil over moderately low heat. Add the pancetta and cook, stirring, until brown, about 8 minutes. Remove the pancetta with a slotted spoon.

2. Raise the heat to moderately high. Add about a third of the veal. Brown on all sides, about 8 minutes, taking care not to scorch the paprika. Remove. Brown the remaining veal in 2 more batches, adding oil if needed. Remove.

3. Reduce the heat to moderately low, add the onions and carrots, the celery and garlic and cook, stirring occasionally, until the onions are translucent, about 5 minutes. Add the wine, stock, tomato paste, thyme and salt and simmer, scraping the bottom of the pot to dislodge any brown bits.

4. Add the pancetta, the veal with any juice that has accumulated and the bouquet garni and bring to a simmer over moderately high heat. Simmer the stew in the oven, covered, stirring occasionally, until the meat is almost tender, about 1 hour.

5. Meanwhile, in a large pot of boiling, salted water, cook the baby carrots for 4 minutes. Add the broccoli and cook 3 minutes more. Drain. Rinse with cold water and drain thoroughly.

6. Add the small onions to the veal, cover and cook until the meat is tender, stirring occasionally, about ½ hour. Discard the bouquet garni. Add the carrots and broccoli. Cover and cook in the oven until heated through, about 10 minutes.
—Bruce Tillinghast
New Rivers

CHOOSING THE RIGHT POT

Long-cooked dishes like stews should be cooked in a heavy pot. The heavier the pot, the better it will maintain constant and even heat. Copper is ideal for cooking, but it does have its drawbacks. A copper pot large enough to hold a stew to serve six is incredibly heavy even when it's empty, not to mention outlandishly expensive. Le Creuset, a brand of enamel-coated cast-iron pots, is our choice for stews. The pots are heavy but not so heavy as copper. They're certainly less expensive and are equally ovenproof. Stainless-steel pots with copper sandwiched between layers of steel in the bottom of the pot is an alternative. The copper provides the desired even heat, but often does not extend far enough up the side of the pan, and the food around the edge burns.

Boeuf Bourguignon

Beef simmered in red wine with mushrooms, bacon and small onions is a classic from Burgundy. Long, slow cooking mellows the wine and produces a dark, rich stew that's even better the next day.

SERVES 6

½	pound bacon, chopped
3	pounds boneless beef chuck, cut into 2-inch cubes
1	onion, chopped
4	shallots, chopped
2	carrots, chopped
3	tablespoons flour
¼	cup cognac or other brandy
3	cups red wine
1½	cups Beef Stock, page 302, or canned low-sodium beef broth
1	tablespoon tomato paste
1¼	teaspoons salt
1	bouquet garni: 12 parsley stems, 6 sprigs fresh thyme or 1 teaspoon dried, and 1 bay leaf
½	pound small white onions, about 1 inch in diameter, peeled
2	tablespoons butter
1	teaspoon sugar
¾	pound mushrooms, quartered
½	teaspoon fresh-ground black pepper
3	tablespoons chopped fresh flat-leaf parsley

WINE RECOMMENDATION:
THE TIME-HONORED AND GEOGRAPHICALLY APPROPRIATE MATCH FOR THIS CLASSIC IS A RED BURGUNDY. SPLURGE ON ONE FROM THE VILLAGE OF BEAUNE OR SANTENAY.

1. In a large pot, cook the bacon until crisp. Remove. Pour off and reserve all but 1 tablespoon of the bacon fat.

2. Raise the heat to moderately high. Add about a third of the meat. Brown well on all sides, about 8 minutes, and remove. Brown the remaining meat in 2 more batches, adding some of the reserved bacon fat if needed. Remove.

3. Reduce the heat to moderate. Add the chopped onion, shallots and carrots and cook until browned, about 5 minutes. Add the flour and cook, stirring, 2 minutes. Add the cognac and wine and simmer 2 minutes, scraping the bottom of the pot to dislodge any brown bits.

4. Add the stock, tomato paste, ¾ teaspoon of the salt and the bouquet garni. Return the meat to the pot with any juice that has accumulated. Bring to a simmer over moderately high heat. Reduce the heat and cook at a bare simmer, covered, until the meat is tender, about 2 hours.

5. Meanwhile, in a medium saucepan, combine the small onions, ¼ teaspoon of the salt, 1 tablespoon of the butter, the sugar and just barely enough water to cover. Bring to a boil, reduce the heat and simmer until the onions are tender and the water has evaporated, 10 to 15 minutes. Continue cooking, stirring, until the onions are brown, about 7 minutes longer.

6. In a large frying pan, heat 2 tablespoons of the reserved bacon fat with the remaining tablespoon butter over moderately high heat. Add the mushrooms and the remaining ¼ teaspoon salt. Cook, stirring, until the mushrooms brown, about 8 minutes.

7. If the sauce is thin, remove the meat and boil to reduce to 2 cups. Discard the bouquet garni. Return the meat to the pot and add the bacon, small onions, mushrooms and pepper. Bring to a simmer and cook 10 minutes. Serve topped with the parsley.

TOO MUCH LIQUID? NOT ENOUGH FLAVOR?

Sometimes when the meat is tender and the vegetables are done the stew is still swimming in liquid that just does not have a whole lot of flavor. When this happens, use a slotted spoon to lift the meat, fish or chicken and the vegetables out of the stew. Bring the liquid to a boil and cook until it's reduced to the amount you want. The recipe on this page specifies the quantity, but many don't. The flavor should be concentrated and the liquid slightly thickened. Return all the ingredients to the pot and reheat.

Boeuf en Daube

The home of this traditional French beef stew is Provence, where numerous versions exist. Daube can be cooked in white or red wine and generally features bacon, mushrooms and Provençal flavorings such as garlic, orange and thyme. Strong black olives are often added. If you like them, stir half a cup of pitted Niçoise or Kalamata olives into the finished stew.

SERVES 6

3	pounds boneless beef chuck, cut into 2-inch cubes
2	cups dry white wine
2	tablespoons olive oil
2	onions, cut into thin slices
3	carrots, cut into thin slices
2	cloves garlic, minced
2	3-inch-long strips orange zest
½	teaspoon dried thyme
2	bay leaves
¼	pound bacon, chopped
1	tablespoon flour
1½	cups Beef Stock, page 302, or canned low-sodium beef broth
3½	cups canned tomatoes (28-ounce can), drained and chopped
1	teaspoon salt
1	tablespoon butter
½	pound mushrooms, sliced
¼	teaspoon fresh-ground black pepper
3	tablespoons chopped fresh flat-leaf parsley

WINE RECOMMENDATION: A RED WINE FROM PROVENCE IS APPROPRIATE FOR THE DISTINCTIVE FLAVORS OF THIS PROVENÇAL CLASSIC. LOOK FOR A SLIGHTLY AGED BANDOL FROM THE COASTAL TOWN OF THE SAME NAME OR A YOUNG CÔTES DE PROVENCE FROM A GOOD PRODUCER.

1. In a glass or stainless-steel bowl, combine the meat, wine, oil, onions, carrots, garlic, orange zest, thyme and bay leaves and let marinate for at least 4 hours. Drain, reserving the marinade. Separate the meat from the vegetables, zest and herbs and dry the meat with paper towels.

2. In a large pot, cook the bacon until crisp. Remove. Pour off and reserve all but 2 tablespoons of the bacon fat. Raise the heat to moderately high. Add about a third of the meat. Brown well on all sides, about 8 minutes, and remove. Brown the remaining meat in 2 more batches, adding some of the reserved bacon fat if needed. Remove.

3. Add the drained vegetables, zest and herbs and cook over moderate heat, stirring occasionally, until the vegetables

are brown, about 5 minutes. Reduce the heat to moderately low. Add the flour and cook, stirring constantly, for 2 minutes. Add the reserved marinade and simmer 2 minutes, scraping the bottom of the pot to dislodge any brown bits. Cook until the marinade reduces to 1 cup.

4. Add the meat with any juice that has accumulated, the stock, tomatoes and ¾ teaspoon of the salt. Bring to a simmer over moderately high heat, reduce the heat and cook at a bare simmer, covered, until the meat is tender, about 2 hours.

5. In a large frying pan, heat 1 tablespoon of the reserved bacon fat with the butter over moderately high heat. Add the mushrooms and the remaining ¼ teaspoon salt. Cook, stirring, until the mushrooms brown, about 8 minutes.

6. If the sauce is thin, remove the meat, onions and carrots and boil to reduce to 2 cups. Discard the orange zest and bay leaves. Return the meat and vegetables to the pot and add the bacon, mushrooms and pepper. Bring to a simmer and cook 10 minutes. Serve topped with the parsley.

 ## COOKING WITH CITRUS ZEST

The citrus zest is the colorful layer of peel on the outside of the fruit. The aromatic oils in the zest have terrific flavor, but the white pith that lies just under the zest is bitter. When cutting strips of citrus zest, take care to get only the outer layer of peel. Check to see that there are no traces of the pith. If there are, cut the white part away with a small paring knife before adding the zest to the dish you're making.

Oxtail Stew with Chianti

A specialty of Rome, this hearty stew redolent of garlic is usually made with white wine. Oxtails, however, are such a full-flavored meat that they stand up well to a red wine, such as the Chianti used in this version. Long simmering makes the meat falling-off-the-bone tender.

SERVES 6

3   tablespoons olive oil, more if needed
6   pounds oxtails
1/3 pound pancetta or bacon, chopped
2   onions, chopped
4   carrots, chopped
1/4 cup chopped fresh flat-leaf parsley
2   bay leaves
2   teaspoons chopped fresh thyme, or
    1 teaspoon dried
    Pinch ground cloves
6   cloves garlic, minced
1   quart red wine, preferably Chianti
7   cups canned tomatoes with their juice
    (two 28-ounce cans), chopped
1½ teaspoons salt
1 to 1½ cups water
8   ribs celery, chopped
½   teaspoon fresh-ground black pepper
    Fried Capers, page 305, optional

WINE RECOMMENDATION: ALTHOUGH THE SAME WINE WITH WHICH IT'S MADE IS A LOGICAL CHOICE, THIS FLAVORFUL STEW IS ALSO WELL MATCHED WITH A WHITE WINE WHOSE PREDOMINANT CHARACTERISTIC IS ACIDITY, THE BETTER TO CUT AGAINST THE HEARTY RICHNESS OF THE MEAT. TRY A YOUNG RIESLING FROM THE ALSACE REGION IN FRANCE.

1. Heat the oven to 325°. In a large, ovenproof pot, heat the oil over moderately high heat. Add about a third of the oxtails. Brown well on all sides, about 10 minutes, and remove. Brown the remaining oxtails in 2 more batches, adding oil if needed. Remove.

2. Reduce the heat to moderately low. Add the pancetta and cook until browned, about 5 minutes. Pour off all but 2 tablespoons of the fat. Add the onions, carrots, parsley, bay leaves, thyme and cloves and cook, stirring occasionally, until the onions are translucent, about 5 minutes. Add the garlic and cook, stirring, 1 minute. Add the oxtails with any juice that has accumulated, the wine, tomatoes, salt and 1 cup of the water or more if needed to

cover the oxtails. Bring to a simmer, cover and put in the oven. Simmer for 2½ hours.

3. Add the celery and pepper and cook, covered, until the meat is very tender, about 30 minutes longer. Discard the bay leaves. Skim any fat from the surface before serving. Top with the capers, if you like.

—Erica De Mane

BROWNING MEAT

The old-fashioned notion that browning, or searing, meat seals in juices is simply not true with long-cooked dishes. Simmering in liquid for an hour or more overrides the effect. Browning is not, however, a step to be skipped. It forms a dark crust on the exterior of the meat, which adds considerable flavor and gives the stew a good, deep color. To brown pieces of meat properly, use a large pot and a small amount of oil, about two tablespoons. Meat browns better in a little bit of oil than a lot. Be sure the oil is hot. Add just enough meat to the hot pot to fit comfortably with some space between the pieces. If the pot isn't hot enough or too many pieces are added to the pot at once, the temperature will fall and the meat will stew in its juices rather than brown.

Old-Fashioned Beef Stew

After testing a myriad of beef-stew possibilities, the talented cook Anne Disrude contributed this, her very best version, to a 1985 issue of *Food & Wine*. You'll appreciate her assiduous work after tasting this wonderfully flavorful stew chock-full of carrots, potatoes, onions and peas.

SERVES 6

2   tablespoons cooking oil, more if needed

3   pounds boneless beef rump or brisket, cut into 2-inch cubes

2   large onions, 1 chopped, 1 cut into eighths

1¼   cups beer or red wine

1¾   cups water

½   teaspoon dried thyme

2   bay leaves

2   teaspoons tomato paste

3   carrots, cut into ¼-inch slices

1   pound boiling potatoes (about 3), peeled and cut into ½-inch cubes

1   teaspoon salt

1   cup fresh or frozen petite peas

¼   teaspoon fresh-ground black pepper

WINE RECOMMENDATION: PAIR THIS STEW WITH THE FRUITY FLAVORS AND SOFT TANNINS OF A YOUNG MERLOT FROM CALIFORNIA OR AUSTRALIA.

1. In a large pot, heat the oil over moderately high heat. Add about a third of the meat. Brown well on all sides, about 8 minutes, and remove. Brown the remaining meat in 2 more batches, adding more oil if needed. Remove.

2. Reduce the heat to moderately low. Add the chopped onion. Cook, stirring occasionally, until translucent, about 5 minutes. Add the beer and simmer 2 minutes, scraping the bottom of the pot to dislodge any brown bits. Return the meat to the pot with any accumulated juice. Add the water, thyme, bay leaves and tomato paste. Bring to a simmer over moderately high heat. Reduce the heat and cook, covered, at a bare simmer until the meat is tender, about 2 hours.

3. Add the remaining onion, the carrots, potatoes and salt. Cook 1 hour. Add the fresh peas, if using, and the pepper 10 minutes before the end of cooking. If using frozen peas, add them 2 minutes before the end. Discard the bay leaves.
　　　　　　　　　　　—Anne Disrude

Carbonnade of Beef

Onions, beef and beer are the essential ingredients in this Flemish specialty. Many cooks use brown sugar to balance the bitterness of the beer, but we find that the sweetness of lots of sliced onions, cooked until soft and golden, does the trick.

SERVES 6

2 ounces bacon, chopped
3 pounds boneless beef chuck, cut into 2-inch cubes
2 pounds onions, about 4, sliced
4 cloves garlic, minced
¼ cup flour
1½ cups beer
1½ cups Beef Stock, page 302, or canned low-sodium beef broth
1 bouquet garni: 6 parsley stems, 3 sprigs fresh thyme or ½ teaspoon dried, and 1 bay leaf
2 teaspoons salt
¼ teaspoon fresh-ground black pepper

WINE RECOMMENDATION:
THE FULL, ROBUST FLAVORS OF BEEF, BACON AND BEER WORK NICELY WITH AN EARTHY RED WINE. LOOK FOR A PINOT NOIR FROM OREGON OR FROM THE CARNEROS REGION OF CALIFORNIA.

1. In a large pot, cook the bacon over moderate heat until all the fat is rendered, about 5 minutes. Remove the bacon with a slotted spoon.

2. Increase the heat to moderately high. Add about a third of the beef. Brown well on all sides, about 8 minutes, and remove. Brown the remaining meat in 2 more batches. Remove. Reduce the heat to moderately low and add the onions to the pan. Cook, stirring occasionally, until the onions are soft and golden, about 15 minutes. Add the garlic and cook 2 minutes.

3. Return the beef to the pan with any juice that has accumulated. Add the flour and cook, stirring, for 2 minutes. Add the bacon, beer, stock, bouquet garni and salt. Bring to a simmer over moderately high heat. Reduce the heat and cook the carbonnade at a bare simmer until the meat is very tender, about 2 hours. Remove the bouquet garni and stir in the pepper.

Hungarian Goulash

The sauerkraut stirred into this goulash toward the end of cooking provides a pleasant tartness that balances the richness of the dish. Use hot or mild paprika depending on your taste, or mix the two.

SERVES 6

2	tablespoons cooking oil, more if needed
3	pounds boneless beef chuck, cut into 1½-inch cubes
2	onions, chopped
2	cloves garlic, minced
2	tablespoons paprika
2	tablespoons flour
½	cup red wine
2	cups Beef Stock, page 302, or canned low-sodium beef broth
2	teaspoons salt
1	pound sauerkraut, drained
¾	cup sour cream
3	tablespoons chopped fresh dill
½	teaspoon fresh-ground black pepper

 MAKE IT AHEAD

Goulash tastes even better made at least a day before serving. Wait to stir in the sour cream and dill, though, until after you've reheated the stew. If you have leftovers, reheat them very gently so that the sour cream doesn't curdle.

WINE RECOMMENDATION:
GOULASH, ENLIVENED BY THE ACIDITY OF THE SAUERKRAUT, IS NICELY PAIRED WITH A LIGHT CABERNET SAUVIGNON FROM HUNGARY. A YOUNG, NOTICEABLY ACIDIC CHIANTI CLASSICO FROM ITALY IS A GOOD ALTERNATIVE.

1. In a large pot, heat the oil over moderately high heat. Add about a third of the meat. Brown well on all sides, about 8 minutes, and remove. Brown the remaining meat in 2 more batches, adding more oil if needed. Remove.

2. Reduce the heat to moderately low. Add the onions and garlic and cook, stirring, until translucent, about 5 minutes. Return the meat to the pot with any juice that has accumulated. Add the paprika and flour and cook, stirring, for 2 minutes. Add the wine, stock and salt and bring to a simmer over moderately high heat. Cover, reduce the heat and cook at a bare simmer for 1¼ hours. Stir in the sauerkraut and cook, covered, until the beef is tender, 30 minutes longer.

3. Stir in the sour cream, 2 tablespoons of the dill and the pepper and cook just until heated through. Do not bring the stew to a boil, or it may curdle. Serve topped with the remaining dill.

Short-Rib Stew
with Horseradish

Short ribs, with their rich beefy flavor, make a particularly succulent stew. Add the horseradish just before serving.

SERVES 6

1	tablespoon butter
1	tablespoon cooking oil, more if needed
5	pounds beef short ribs, trimmed of excess fat
1	onion, cut into thick slices
2	carrots, cut into thick slices
1	rib celery, cut into thick slices
3	tablespoons flour
2	cups Beef Stock, page 302, or canned low-sodium beef broth
3½	cups canned tomatoes (28-ounce can), drained, seeded and chopped
1	cup red wine
1	bouquet garni: 6 parsley stems, 3 sprigs fresh thyme or ½ teaspoon dried, and 1 bay leaf
1	clove garlic, minced
2	teaspoons tomato paste
1	teaspoon salt
4	teaspoons bottled horseradish
¼	teaspoon fresh-ground black pepper
1	tablespoon chopped fresh parsley

WINE RECOMMENDATION:
MEATY AND RICH, THIS DISH WILL BE NICELY COMPLEMENTED BY A HIGH-TANNIN, HIGH-ALCOHOL RED WINE FROM THE SOUTHERN RHÔNE REGION OF FRANCE. TRY A GIGONDAS OR THE LESS EXPENSIVE CÔTES-DU-RHÔNE.

1. Heat the oven to 350°. In a large ovenproof pot, melt the butter with the oil over moderately high heat. Add about a third of the meat. Brown well on both sides, about 8 minutes, and remove. Brown the remaining meat in 2 more batches, adding oil if needed. Remove.

2. Pour off all but 1 tablespoon fat from the pot. Reduce the heat to moderately low. Add the onion, carrots and celery and cook, stirring occasionally, until the onion is translucent, about 5 minutes. Return the beef to the pot with any juice that has accumulated. Sprinkle the flour over the meat and vegetables and stir to coat. Cook 2 minutes. Add the stock, tomatoes, wine, bouquet garni, garlic, tomato paste and salt. Raise the heat to moderately high and bring to a simmer. Cover and put in the oven. Simmer, stirring occasionally, until the meat is tender enough to shred easily, 1½ to 2 hours.

3. Remove the meat from the pot. Discard the bouquet garni. When the meat is cool enough to handle, cut it away from the bones, removing all the fat and gristle as you go. Cut into 1½-inch pieces and return to the pot. Stir in the horseradish and pepper and reheat. Serve topped with the chopped parsley.

—Charles Pierce

ALLOW FOR WASTE

If you buy a whole piece of meat to cut up for stew, or cubes that are not well trimmed of fat and connective tissue, the amount of waste may surprise you. You'll often need to buy four or even four-and-a-half pounds of meat to get three pounds of nice, meaty chunks. When you use very bony meat, as in this recipe, the general rule is to allow about twice as much per person as you would of solid, lean meat.

Portuguese Pork and Clam Stew

Composed of what might sound like an odd combination, this stew is one of the most popular dishes in Portugal. It is meant to be served right out of the pot with the clams still in their shells. Use only the smallest, freshest clams available and be careful not to overcook them, or they'll be chewy.

SERVES 6

3   pounds boneless pork shoulder or butt, cut into 1-inch cubes

3   tablespoons lemon juice, from about 2 lemons

1   onion, cut into thin slices

2   cloves garlic, minced

4   teaspoons chopped fresh thyme, or 1½ teaspoons dried

½ to ¾ teaspoon salt

¼   teaspoon fresh-ground black pepper

3   tablespoons olive oil, more if needed

¾   cup dry white wine

¼   cup flour

2¼ cups Pork or Chicken Stock, page 301 or 299, or canned low-sodium chicken broth

5   cups canned tomatoes, drained and chopped

3   dozen littleneck or cherrystone clams, scrubbed

Wine recommendation:
A young vinho verde from Portugal makes a lot of sense from a geographical standpoint. Fortunately, this tart, refreshing white also contrasts nicely with the rich pork and clam flavors of the dish. It's also quite adept at handling the noticeable taste of lemon here.

1. In a large glass or stainless-steel bowl, combine the pork, lemon juice, onion, garlic, thyme, ½ teaspoon of the salt, the pepper, 1 tablespoon of the oil and the wine. Marinate, covered, in the refrigerator for 12 hours, stirring once or twice.

2. Heat the oven to 325°. Remove the pork from the marinade and dry the pieces with paper towels. Reserve the marinade. In a large, ovenproof pot, heat the remaining 2 tablespoons oil over moderately high heat. Add about a third of the pork. Brown well on all sides, about 8 minutes, and remove. Brown the remaining meat in 2 more batches, adding oil if needed. Remove. Reduce the heat to low, add the flour and cook, stirring, for 2 minutes. Add the

reserved marinade, the pork with any juice that has accumulated, the stock and tomatoes and bring to a simmer over moderately high heat. Simmer, covered, in the oven, stirring occasionally, until the pork is very tender, about 1½ hours.

3. Discard any clams that are broken or do not clamp shut when tapped. Skim off any fat that has risen to the top of the stew. Put the clams on top of the stew and return to the oven, covered, until the clams open, about 20 minutes. Discard any clams that do not open. Taste for salt and, if necessary, add ¼ teaspoon salt.

—Charles Pierce

MARINATE IN A NONREACTIVE CONTAINER

When marinating, choose a glass, plastic, glazed ceramic or stainless-steel container. Marinades usually contain an acid such as lemon juice, vinegar or wine, which reacts with metals like cast iron and untreated aluminum. The reaction often discolors the food and can ruin the flavor.

Stewed Pork and Prunes with Lemon

This rich-tasting stew is inspired. The simple ingredients combine to make a whole that is definitely more than the sum of its parts. Serve with couscous, buttered pasta or sautéed potatoes.

SERVES 6

1	tablespoon butter
1	tablespoon cooking oil, more if needed
3	pounds boneless pork shoulder or butt, cut into 2-inch cubes
⅓	cup dry white wine
2	cups Pork or Chicken Stock, page 301 or 299, or canned low-sodium chicken broth
1½	teaspoons salt
1	lemon
½	pound pitted prunes, about 1½ cups
¾	teaspoon fresh-ground black pepper

Wine recommendation:
THIS STEW'S SWEET, MELLOW FLAVORS ARE BEST MATCHED WITH A FULL, ROUND WINE THAT HAS THE SAME QUALITIES. TRY A PINOT BLANC FROM ALSACE IN FRANCE OR A WHITE MÂCON, WHICH IS BASED ON THE CHARDONNAY GRAPE AND IS ALSO FROM FRANCE.

1. In a large pot, melt the butter with the oil over moderately high heat. Add about a third of the pork. Brown well on all sides, about 8 minutes, and remove. Brown the remaining meat in 2 more batches, adding oil if needed. Remove.

2. Add the wine. Bring to a boil, scraping the bottom of the pot to dislodge any brown bits, and continue boiling until the liquid has reduced to about ¼ cup. Return the pork to the pot with any juice that has accumulated, the stock and salt. Bring to a simmer over moderately high heat, reduce the heat and cook at a bare simmer, covered, for 45 minutes.

3. With a small knife or vegetable peeler, remove only the yellow zest from the lemon, leaving the bitter white pith behind. Stack the pieces of zest and cut

them crosswise into very thin strips. Bring a small saucepan of water to a boil. Add the zest, bring back to a boil and continue boiling for 1 minute. Drain and rinse with cold water. Drain thoroughly. Repeat this process with fresh water. Set the blanched zest aside. Squeeze 1½ teaspoons juice from the lemon and set aside.

4. Add the prunes to the pork, cover and cook, stirring occasionally, until the pork is tender, about 45 minutes longer. Add the pepper.

5. Remove all but 12 prunes from the pot and puree them in a food processor or blender with about ½ cup of the cooking liquid. Return the puree to the pot and stir in to form a sauce. Add half the lemon zest and the lemon juice. Return the pot to low heat until the stew is warmed through, about 5 minutes. Serve sprinkled with the remaining lemon zest.

—Charles Pierce

 MAKE IT AHEAD

By all means make this stew well ahead of time and just reheat before serving. But wait to stir in the lemon zest and juice until the end, or they'll lose their sprightly flavor.

Smoky Pork Stew with Chiles and Black Beans

Ancho chiles and smoky chipotles flavor this medium-hot, chili-like stew. Serve with rice, warm flour tortillas or crusty bread.

SERVES 6

½   pound (about 1 cup) dried black beans

6   cloves garlic, 1 left whole, 5 minced

1   meaty smoked ham hock (about ¾ pound)

2½   quarts water

3   dried ancho chiles

1   dried or canned chipotle chile

2   tablespoons cooking oil, more if needed

2½   pounds boneless pork shoulder, cut into 1-inch cubes

1   onion, minced

3   tablespoons ground cumin

½   teaspoon ground cinnamon

1   teaspoon dried thyme

3½   cups canned crushed tomatoes (28-ounce can)

¾   cup tomato paste

2   tablespoons Worcestershire sauce

1   tablespoon sugar

2½   teaspoons salt

3   bay leaves

2   cups canned yellow or white hominy (16-ounce can), drained and rinsed

½   cup chopped cilantro

4   scallions including green tops, cut into thin slices

WINE RECOMMENDATION:
THE SMOKY FLAVORS OF THE HAM AND THE CHIPOTLE CHILE WORK WELL WITH A RICH WHITE WINE. TRY A YOUNG GEWÜRZTRAMINER FROM CALIFORNIA—OR CONSIDER BEER AS AN ALTERNATIVE.

1. Soak the beans overnight in enough cold water to cover by at least 2 inches. Drain.

2. In a medium saucepan, combine the beans with the whole garlic clove, the ham hock and 5 cups of the water. Bring to a boil, reduce the heat and simmer, partially covered, until the beans are tender, about 1 hour.

3. Meanwhile, boil 3 cups of the water. Soak the dried chiles in the boiling water until softened, about 20 minutes. Reserve 1½ cups of the soaking liquid. Stem and seed the chiles. In a blender, puree them with the reserved liquid and strain into a small bowl.

4. In a large pot, heat the oil over moderately high heat. Add about a third of the pork. Brown well on all sides, about 8 minutes, and remove. Brown the remaining meat in 2 more batches, adding more oil if needed. Remove. ➤

5. Reduce the heat to moderately low. Add the minced garlic and the onion and cook, stirring occasionally, until the onion is translucent, about 5 minutes. Stir in the cumin, cinnamon and thyme and cook, stirring, for 2 minutes. Add the remaining 2 cups water, the pureed chiles, the pork with any juice that has accumulated, the tomatoes, tomato paste, Worcestershire sauce, sugar, salt, bay leaves and hominy and bring to a simmer over moderately high heat. Reduce the heat and cook at a bare simmer, partially covered, until the pork is tender, about 2 hours. Remove the bay leaves.

6. Drain the beans. When the ham hock is cool enough to handle, pull the meat from the bone and cut it into small pieces. Add the beans and ham to the pork and heat. Just before serving, stir in the cilantro and scallions.

—Grace Parisi

Red-Chile and Pork Pozole

The spiciness of this dish depends on the chiles you choose. We suggest the moderately hot dried ancho chiles, which are increasingly available in the produce sections of supermarkets. If you can't find them, though, dried, powdered chiles to taste are fine, too—or even chili powder (a blend of peppers, herbs, spices and salt).

SERVES 6

5	cups water
4	dried ancho chiles
2	tablespoons cooking oil, more if needed
3	pounds boneless pork shoulder, cut into 2-inch cubes
4	cups canned yellow or white hominy (two 16-ounce cans), drained and rinsed
4	cloves garlic, minced
1½	teaspoons ground cumin
1½	teaspoons dried oregano
2½	teaspoons salt
1	small red onion, cut into thin slices

WINE RECOMMENDATION:
POP OPEN A COLD BOTTLE OF BEER WITH THIS MEXICAN-INSPIRED DISH. OR TRY A FRUITY RED WINE, SUCH AS BEAUJOLAIS OR A CALIFORNIA GAMAY-BASED WINE, WHICH CAN BE EVEN FRUITIER, IF LESS COMPLEX, THAN THE BEAUJOLAIS.

1. Boil 1 cup of the water. Put the chiles in a bowl, cover with the water and let soak 20 minutes. Reserve the soaking liquid. Stem and seed the chiles. In a blender or food processor, puree them with the reserved soaking liquid.

2. In a large pot, heat the oil over moderately high heat. Add about a third of the pork. Brown well on all sides, about 8 minutes, and remove. Brown the remaining meat in 2 more batches, adding oil if needed. Return the pork to the pot with any accumulated juice. Stir in the chile puree, the hominy, the remaining quart of water, the garlic, cumin, oregano and salt. Bring to a simmer over moderately high heat, reduce the heat and cook at a bare simmer, partially covered, until the meat is falling-apart tender, about 3 hours. Serve topped with the red onion.

—Jan Newberry

Sausage and Potato Stew in Lemon Rosemary Broth

Appropriate for the summer months as well as the rest of the year, this quick stew sparkles with flavor. You can make the whole thing in just over half an hour.

SERVES 6

2	tablespoons olive oil
12	mild or hot Italian sausages (about 2½ pounds)
6	new potatoes, or 1 pound boiling potatoes, about 3, cut into chunks
3	cloves garlic, minced
¾	teaspoon chopped fresh rosemary, or ¼ teaspoon dried, crumbled
½	cup dry white wine
2	cups Pork or Chicken Stock, page 301 or 299, or canned low-sodium chicken broth
1½	teaspoons salt
1	teaspoon grated lemon zest
1	head escarole (about 1½ pounds), cut into 1-inch pieces
¼	teaspoon fresh-ground black pepper Rustic Croûtes, page 309

1. In a large pot, heat the oil over moderately high heat. Add the sausages and brown well, about 10 minutes.

2. Reduce the heat to moderate. Add the potatoes, garlic and rosemary. Cook, stirring occasionally, until the potatoes are lightly browned, about 5 minutes. Add the wine and simmer until reduced to about ¼ cup. Stir in the stock and salt and scrape the bottom of the pot to dislodge any brown bits. Cover and simmer until the potatoes are tender, about 20 minutes.

3. Add half the lemon zest and the escarole to the stew, pressing the leaves into the broth. Cover and cook until the escarole is soft, about 3 minutes. Add the pepper. Ladle into shallow bowls. Sprinkle with the remaining lemon zest and serve with the croûtes.

—Erica De Mane

Lamb, White-Bean and Sausage Stew

Crisp herbed bread crumbs add a little crunch to this mellow country-style stew.

SERVES 6

½   pound (about 1 cup) dried white beans, such as Great Northern
2   tablespoons cooking oil, more if needed
2   pounds boneless lamb shoulder, cut into 1½-inch cubes
2   onions, 1 chopped, 1 cut in half
2   cloves garlic, minced
½   cup dry white wine
½   cup Beef or Chicken Stock, page 302 or 299, or canned low-sodium chicken broth
½   cup canned tomato puree
1   tablespoon minced fresh rosemary, or 1 teaspoon dried rosemary, crumbled
1¼ teaspoons salt
¼   teaspoon fresh-ground black pepper
1   carrot, cut in half
1   bay leaf
3   sprigs fresh thyme, or ½ teaspoon dried
¼   pound kielbasa or other smoked sausage
½   cup fresh bread crumbs
1   tablespoon chopped fresh parsley

1. Soak the beans overnight in enough cold water to cover by at least 2 inches. Drain.

2. In a large pot, heat 1 tablespoon of the oil over moderately high heat. Add about half of the lamb. Brown well on all sides, about 8 minutes, and remove with a slotted spoon. Brown the remaining lamb, adding oil if needed. Remove.

3. Reduce the heat to moderately low. Add the chopped onion and the garlic and cook, stirring occasionally, until the onion is translucent, about 5 minutes. Add the lamb with any juice that has accumulated, the wine, stock, tomato puree, 2 teaspoons of the fresh rosemary or ½ teaspoon of the dried and the salt and bring to a simmer over moderately high heat. Reduce the heat and cook at a bare simmer, covered, until the lamb is tender, about 2 hours. Then add the pepper.

4. Meanwhile, in a medium saucepan, combine the beans with the onion halves, carrot, bay leaf, thyme and enough water to cover the beans by about 1 inch. Bring to a boil, reduce the heat and simmer for 30 minutes. Prick the sausage with a fork. Add the sausage to the beans and continue simmering until the beans are tender, about 30 minutes. Remove the sausage and slice. Drain the beans and discard the onion, carrot and herbs. Add the beans and sausage to the simmering lamb.

5. In a small frying pan, heat the remaining tablespoon oil over moderately low heat. Add the remaining rosemary, the bread crumbs and parsley and sauté until the bread crumbs are light brown, about 5 minutes. Sprinkle on top of the stew and serve.

—Jan Newberry

Lamb Stew with Eggplant, Peppers and Tomatoes

Be sure to add the eggplant and peppers just half an hour before the end of cooking so that they don't collapse entirely by serving time. Serve this Mediterranean stew with rice or bulgur-wheat pilaf.

SERVES 6

7   tablespoons olive oil, plus more if needed

3   pounds boneless lamb shoulder, cut into 1½-inch cubes

4   onions, cut into thin slices

8   cloves garlic, minced

1   bouquet garni: 6 parsley stems, 3 sprigs fresh thyme or ½ teaspoon dried, and 1 bay leaf

2   cups Chicken Stock, page 299, or canned low-sodium chicken broth

3   pounds tomatoes (about 6), peeled and chopped, or 5 cups canned tomatoes with their juice, chopped

2¾ teaspoons salt

2   red bell peppers, cut into 1-inch squares

2   green bell peppers, cut into 1-inch squares

1   large eggplant (about 2 pounds), peeled and cut into 1-inch cubes

¼   teaspoon fresh-ground black pepper

WINE RECOMMENDATION:

A hearty red wine that has a relatively high alcohol content should accompany this full-flavored stew. Look for a young Côtes-du-Rhône or Châteauneuf-du-Pape, both from the Southern Rhône Valley in France.

1. In a large pot, heat 2 tablespoons of the oil over moderately high heat. Add about a third of the lamb. Brown well on all sides, about 8 minutes, and remove. Brown the remaining meat in 2 more batches, adding oil if needed. Remove.

2. Reduce the heat to moderately low. Add the onions and garlic and cook, stirring occasionally, until the mixture begins to brown, about 10 minutes.

3. Return the lamb to the pot with any juice that has accumulated. Add the bouquet garni, stock, tomatoes and 2 teaspoons of the salt. Bring to a simmer over moderately high heat, reduce the heat and cook at a bare simmer, partially covered, until the lamb is tender, about 2 hours.

4. Meanwhile, in a large nonstick frying pan, heat 1 tablespoon of the oil over

moderate heat. Add the peppers and sauté, stirring occasionally, until they begin to brown, about 10 minutes. With a slotted spoon, remove the peppers. Add the remaining 4 tablespoons oil to the pan. Add the eggplant and the remaining ¾ teaspoon salt and cook, stirring occasionally, until the eggplant is tender and beginning to brown, about 10 minutes.

5. Add the peppers and eggplant to the lamb 30 minutes before the end of cooking. Before serving, discard the bouquet garni and stir in the pepper.

—Jane Sigal

SIMMERING STEW

Cooking meat and chicken at a bare simmer is essential to a good stew. The cooking liquid should move slowly and be broken with a bubble or two occasionally. This slow cooking makes the cubes of meat or pieces of chicken tender without drying them out. For the most part, stews require little attention aside from a stir every so often. But do try to keep an eye on the pot to be sure the liquid does not boil.

Lamb Stew with Chickpeas and Roasted Red Peppers

Marinating the lamb in lemon juice helps tenderize the meat while the thyme and garlic enhance its flavor. If there's time, stir the chickpeas into the stew at least ten minutes before the end of cooking so that they can absorb some of the savory meat juices.

SERVES 6

3   pounds boneless lamb shoulder, cut into 1½-inch cubes
3   tablespoons olive oil, more if needed
2   tablespoons lemon juice
3   sprigs fresh thyme, or ½ teaspoon dried
2   cloves garlic, 1 cut into thin slices, 1 minced
¾   cup dried chickpeas
1   tablespoon butter
2   carrots, chopped
1   onion, chopped
1   rib celery, chopped
3   tablespoons flour
2   cups Chicken Stock, page 299, or canned low-sodium chicken broth
2   teaspoons tomato paste
1   bouquet garni: 6 parsley stems, 3 sprigs fresh thyme or ½ teaspoon dried, and 1 bay leaf
2   teaspoons salt
    Fresh-ground black pepper
1   red bell pepper

WINE RECOMMENDATION:
THIS MELLOW DISH, WITH ITS MEDITER-RANEAN INFLUENCES, IS IDEAL WITH A SIM-PLE, FRUITY, QUAFFABLE RED WINE, SUCH AS A BEAUJOLAIS OR ONE OF THE SOFTER STYLED REDS FROM THE APPELLATION OF CORBIÈRES IN THE SOUTH OF FRANCE.

1. In a large glass or stainless-steel bowl, combine the lamb, 2 tablespoons of the olive oil, the lemon juice, thyme and sliced garlic. Cover and refrigerate, stirring occasionally, for 12 to 24 hours.

2. Soak the chickpeas overnight in enough cold water to cover by at least 2 inches. Drain.

3. Heat the oven to 325°. Remove the lamb from the marinade and pat dry with paper towels. Discard the marinade. In a large ovenproof pot, melt the butter with the remaining 1 tablespoon oil over moderately high heat. Add about a third of the lamb. Brown well on all sides, about 8 minutes, and remove. Brown the remaining meat in 2 more batches, adding oil if needed. Remove.

4. Reduce the heat to moderately low, add the carrots, onion and celery and cook, stirring occasionally, until soft, about 8 minutes. Return the lamb to the pot with any juice that has accumulated and sprinkle the flour over the meat. Cook, stirring often, until the flour is light brown, about 7 minutes. Stir in the minced garlic, stock, tomato paste, bouquet garni and 1½ teaspoons of the salt. Bring to a simmer. Cook, covered, in the oven until the lamb is very tender, about 2 hours.

5. Meanwhile, put the chickpeas in a medium saucepan with water to cover by about 2 inches. Bring to a boil, reduce the heat and simmer, partially covered,

until tender, about 1 hour. Add the remaining ½ teaspoon salt and ⅛ teaspoon pepper and cook 10 minutes longer. Remove from the heat, drain and add to the stew.

6. Roast the red pepper over an open flame or broil 4 inches from the heat, turning with tongs until charred all over, about 10 minutes. When the pepper is cool enough to handle, pull off the skin. Remove the stem, seeds and ribs. Cut the pepper into thin strips.

7. When the lamb is tender, remove the bouquet garni and add ¼ teaspoon pepper and the roasted-pepper strips.

—Charles Pierce

 ## MAKE IT AHEAD

Make this stew days before serving if you like. You'll get double the benefit. The flavors will meld and develop, and the fat will rise to the surface for easy removal.

 ## SHORTCUTS

To save time, use two cups canned chickpeas (about a twenty-ounce can), drained and rinsed, in place of dried ones, adding them to the finished stew. Also, you can use a jarred red bell pepper instead of a fresh one. The jarred variety come already peeled, and so they need no roasting.

Navarin

Traditionally, this French classic is prepared with spring lamb and a medley of baby vegetables. If young turnips, carrots, potatoes, peas and beans are available, by all means use them, but navarin is wonderful any time of year. Don't hesitate to make it with winter ingredients.

SERVES 6

2 tablespoons cooking oil, more if needed
¼ pound bacon, chopped
3 pounds boneless lamb shoulder, cut into 1½-inch cubes
1 onion, chopped
3 cloves garlic, minced
6 tablespoons flour
1 tablespoon tomato paste
1¾ cups canned tomatoes (14½-ounce can), drained and chopped
1½ quarts Veal or Beef Stock, page 302, or canned low-sodium beef broth
2 teaspoons salt
1 bouquet garni: 6 parsley stems, 3 sprigs fresh thyme or ½ teaspoon dried, and 1 bay leaf
2 tablespoons butter
1 pound turnips, peeled and cut into 1½-by-½-inch pieces
1 pound new or other boiling potatoes, peeled and cut into 1½-by-½-inch pieces
1 pound baby carrots, or larger carrots cut into 1½-by-½-inch pieces
10 ounces small white onions, about 1 inch in diameter, peeled
Fresh-ground black pepper
1 pound green beans, cut into 1-inch lengths
1½ cups fresh or frozen petite peas

WINE RECOMMENDATION:
THIS CLASSIC DISH, WITH ITS SURFEIT OF VEGETABLES AND ASSOCIATIONS WITH SPRING, SHOULD BE SERVED WITH A DELICATE, PERFUMED WINE, SUCH AS A PINOT NOIR. TRY ONE FROM CÔTE DE NUITS IN FRANCE OR, FOR A MORE REASONABLY PRICED ALTERNATIVE, FROM SANTA BARBARA IN CALIFORNIA.

1. Heat the oven to 450°. In a large ovenproof pot, heat the oil over moderately high heat. Add the bacon and cook until the fat is rendered, about 5 minutes. Remove with a slotted spoon. Add about a third of the lamb. Brown well on all sides, about 8 minutes, and remove. Brown the remaining lamb in 2 more batches, adding oil if needed. Take the pot from the heat. Return the lamb to the pot with any juice that has accumulated. Stir in the bacon, chopped onion, garlic and flour.

2. Put the pot in the oven and cook, uncovered, stirring once or twice, for 10 minutes. Lower the oven heat to 325°. Return the pot to the stove. Add the tomato paste, tomatoes, stock and 1½

teaspoons of the salt. Scrape the bottom and sides of the pot to dislodge any brown bits. Add the bouquet garni. Bring the stew to a simmer. Cover and return the pot to the oven. Cook until the lamb is almost tender, about 1½ hours.

3. Meanwhile, in a large frying pan, melt the butter over moderate heat. Add the turnips, potatoes, carrots, small onions, the remaining ½ teaspoon salt and ⅛ teaspoon pepper. Cook the vegetables, stirring occasionally, until they begin to brown, about 10 minutes.

4. When the lamb has cooked for an hour and a half, add the browned vegetables to the pot. Bring back to a simmer on top of the stove and return to the oven. Cook until the vegetables are tender, about 30 minutes longer.

5. Meanwhile, bring a saucepan of salted water to a boil. Add the green

beans and cook until tender, about 7 minutes. If using fresh peas, add them to the pan 4 minutes before the beans are cooked. Drain. Rinse with cold water and drain thoroughly. If using frozen peas, there is no need to cook them. Add the green beans, peas and ¼ teaspoon pepper to the stew and simmer until warmed through, about 2 minutes. Remove the bouquet garni.

 ## MAKE IT AHEAD

As with most stews, Navarin simply improves if it is kept overnight, or even several days. But wait to cook and add the green vegetables until the day you serve the stew. Boil, rinse and drain them a few hours ahead if you like and then add them to the stew just a couple of minutes before serving so that they don't lose their bright color.

Creamy Lamb Stew with Lemon

If you choose lamb from the leg for this recipe, you'll save time. Shoulder takes twice as long to tenderize, but it tastes just as good, or even better.

SERVES 6

3   pounds boneless lamb shoulder or leg, cut into 1½-inch cubes
4   onions, chopped
3   carrots, chopped
4   leeks, white and light-green parts only, split lengthwise, cut crosswise into thin slices and washed well
3   cloves garlic, crushed
3   ribs celery, chopped
1   clove
1   bouquet garni: 6 parsley stems, 3 sprigs fresh thyme or ½ teaspoon dried, and 1 bay leaf
1½   teaspoons salt
1½   quarts water
¾   pound small white onions, about 1 inch in diameter, peeled
5   tablespoons butter
¼   teaspoon sugar
¼   cup flour
1¼   pounds mushrooms, quartered
6   tablespoons heavy cream
¾   teaspoon grated lemon zest
1   tablespoon lemon juice
¼   teaspoon fresh-ground black pepper
3   tablespoons chopped fresh parsley

1. Put the lamb in a large pot of cold water. Bring to a boil. Continue boiling for 1 minute. Drain and rinse the meat with cold water. Rinse the pot.

2. Return the blanched lamb to the pot. Add the onions, carrots, leeks, garlic, celery, clove, bouquet garni, 1 teaspoon of the salt and the water. Cover and bring to a simmer over moderately high heat. Reduce the heat and simmer until the lamb is tender, about 2 hours for shoulder or 1 hour for leg.

3. Meanwhile, in a small saucepan, combine the small onions, the remaining ½ teaspoon salt, 1 tablespoon of the butter, the sugar and just barely enough water to cover. Bring to a boil, reduce the heat and simmer until the onions are tender, 10 to 15 minutes. Set aside.

4. Remove the lamb from the pot. Strain the cooking liquid. Press the vegetables firmly to get all the liquid. ➤

5. In a medium saucepan, melt the remaining 4 tablespoons butter over moderately low heat. Whisk in the flour and cook, whisking, for 2 minutes. Gradually whisk in the strained cooking liquid and bring to a boil, still whisking. Reduce the heat and add the meat and small onions, the mushrooms, cream and lemon zest. Simmer until the mushrooms are tender, about 10 minutes.

6. Add the lemon juice and pepper. Top with the parsley.

—Jane Sigal

CLEANING LEEKS

Wash leeks carefully. They tend to bring the garden into the kitchen, literally, with sand and dirt trapped between their layers. The traditional way to clean a leek is to cut off the green top, slit the bulb and light-green part in quarters lengthwise, almost to the root, and then plunge the splayed leek up and down in water. If you like doing this, by all means stick to it. Our recipes instruct to cut the leeks in whatever shape you need and *then* wash them because we find this method easier and more thorough.

Lamb and Shiitake Stew with Fennel and Orange

Rosemary, fennel and oranges give this stew its Mediterranean flair. The orange liqueur and juice just add a pleasant flavor rather than sweetening the stew. Don't be tempted to omit the butter stirred in at the end; it *makes* the dish. Try it before and after adding the butter, and we think you'll agree.

SERVES 6

2	oranges
4	tablespoons olive oil, more if needed
3	pounds boneless lamb shoulder or leg, cut into ½-inch cubes
2	tablespoons orange liqueur
1	cup red wine
2	quarts Chicken Stock, page 299, or canned low-sodium chicken broth
3	cloves garlic, minced
2½	teaspoons salt
1	tablespoon fennel seeds
1	bay leaf
1	tablespoon chopped fresh rosemary, or 1 teaspoon dried, crumbled
6	tablespoons butter
12	new potatoes (about 2 pounds), peeled and quartered, or larger boiling potatoes cut into eighths
12	small white onions, about 1 inch in diameter, peeled
12	baby carrots, or 4 larger ones cut into thirds
1	pound shiitake mushrooms, stems removed, caps quartered
¼	teaspoon fresh-ground black pepper

WINE RECOMMENDATION: A SIMPLE RED WINE FROM CÔTES DE PROVENCE WILL GO NICELY WITH THE FRUITY FLAVORS OF THIS DISH.

1. Grate a tablespoon of the zest from the oranges and squeeze the juice. You should have about ⅓ cup juice.

2. In a large pot, heat 2 tablespoons of the oil over moderately high heat. Add about a third of the lamb cubes. Brown on all sides, about 8 minutes, and remove. Brown the remaining meat in 2 more batches, adding oil if needed. Remove.

3. Add the orange juice, liqueur and wine to the pot and scrape the bottom to dislodge any brown bits. Boil until reduced to about ¾ cup.

4. Return the cubes of lamb to the pot. Add the stock, garlic, 2 teaspoons of the salt, the fennel seeds, bay leaf and the dried rosemary, if using. Bring the stew to a simmer over moderately high heat. Reduce the heat and simmer, partially covered, until the lamb is ten-

der, about 2 hours for shoulder or 1 hour for leg.

5. Meanwhile, heat the remaining 2 tablespoons oil with 2 tablespoons of the butter in a large frying pan over moderately high heat. Add the potatoes, onions, carrots, mushrooms and the remaining ½ teaspoon salt and sauté, stirring occasionally, until the vegetables begin to brown, about 5 minutes.

6. Add the vegetables and fresh rosemary, if using, to the stew and simmer until the potatoes and carrots are tender, about 15 minutes. Remove the bay leaf. Stir in the orange zest and the pepper.

7. Cut the remaining 4 tablespoons butter into 8 pieces. Stir into the stew and serve.

—Michael Chiarello
TraVigne

WHEN IS IT DONE?

Stews should be cooked thoroughly so that the meat is meltingly tender, the vegetables are succulent and the flavors are melded. Depending on the particular piece of meat and the age of the vegetables, cooking time can vary considerably. The best test, as always, is to taste. You can also test by sticking a knife into root vegetables. When it goes in with very little resistance, they're done. Meat is perfectly tender when it no longer clings to a fork. Stab a piece, hold the fork over the pot, tines down, and give it a little shake. If the meat drops back into the stew, it's done.

Curried-Lamb Stew

With mustard seeds as a flavoring, this recipe could only come from South India. It would usually include a small handful of fresh curry leaves, which are available at Indian grocery stores. If you want to add this authentic note, stir in the leaves when the mustard seeds stop popping.

SERVES 6

¼	cup cooking oil, plus more for frying
2	tablespoons mustard seeds
1	3-inch piece fresh ginger, peeled and chopped
4	pounds onions (about 8), halved and cut into thin slices
2	teaspoons turmeric
2	tablespoons ground coriander
1	tablespoon ground cumin
1	teaspoon ground star anise, optional
1	teaspoon cayenne
1½	teaspoons salt
1½	cups water
3	pounds boneless lamb shoulder, cut into 1½-inch cubes
2	pounds small boiling potatoes (about 8), peeled and cut into ¼-inch slices
2	tablespoons chopped fresh cilantro

WINE RECOMMENDATION:
THE CURRY FLAVORS OF THIS INDIAN DISH MAKE THE SELECTION OF A SPICY, RICH GEWÜRZTRAMINER FROM ALSACE IN FRANCE OR FROM CALIFORNIA A NATURAL CHOICE.

1. Put the oil and mustard seeds in a large pot over moderately high heat and cover. When the seeds begin to pop, reduce the heat to low. When they stop popping, uncover the pot and add the ginger and onions. Cook over moderate heat, stirring occasionally, until the onions are tinged with brown, about 15 minutes. Stir in the turmeric, coriander, cumin, star anise, if using, cayenne and salt and cook until fragrant, 1 to 2 minutes. Add the water and scrape the bottom of the pot to dislodge any brown bits. Add the lamb. Cover, bring the liquid to a simmer over moderately high heat, then reduce the heat and cook at a bare simmer until the lamb is tender, about 2 hours.

2. In a large frying pan, heat ½ inch of oil over moderately high heat. Add the potato slices in batches and cook until golden brown, about 2 minutes. Remove. Drain on paper towels. Ten minutes before serving, stir the fried potatoes into the lamb. Serve topped with the cilantro.
—Jane Sigal

Rabbit and Wild-Mushroom Stew

Tomatoes, sage, thyme and lots of garlic announce the Italian heritage of this delectable stew. A good accompaniment is the ear-shaped pasta called *orecchiette*.

SERVES 6

¼	cup olive oil, more if needed
1	pound wild mushrooms, such as shiitakes, chanterelles or portobellos, sliced
2½	teaspoons salt
2	3- to 3½-pound rabbits, cut into legs and boneless loins (see page 294)
2	onions, sliced
2	carrots, sliced
2	ribs celery, sliced
8	cloves garlic, cut into thin slivers
2	pounds tomatoes (about 4), seeded and chopped, or 3½ cups canned tomatoes with their juice (28-ounce can), chopped
½	cup sun-dried tomatoes, sliced
1	cup red wine
2	cups Chicken Stock, page 299, or canned low-sodium chicken broth
2	teaspoons chopped fresh thyme, or ¾ teaspoon dried
2	teaspoons chopped fresh sage, or ¾ teaspoon dried
½	teaspoon fresh-ground black pepper
½	cup chopped fresh flat-leaf parsley
⅓	cup chopped fresh basil, optional

WINE RECOMMENDATION:
MATCH THE HEARTY, AGGRESSIVE FLAVORS OF THIS DISH WITH A SOMEWHAT RUSTIC ITALIAN RED WINE WITH AROUND FIVE TO SEVEN YEARS OF BOTTLE AGE. TRY A GATTINARA OR A SPANNA.

1. In a large pot, heat 2 tablespoons of the oil over moderately high heat. Add the mushrooms with ½ teaspoon of the salt and cook until brown, about 5 minutes. Remove.

2. Heat the remaining 2 tablespoons oil in the pot over moderately high heat. Add several pieces of the rabbit. Brown well, about 4 minutes per side, and remove. Brown the remaining rabbit, adding oil if needed. Remove.

3. Reduce the heat to moderate. Add the onions, carrots, celery and garlic to the pot and cook, stirring occasionally, until the vegetables are beginning to brown, about 5 minutes.

4. Return the mushrooms and rabbit legs to the pot. The loins will be added later. Add the fresh, or canned, and sun-dried tomatoes, wine, stock, thyme, sage and the remaining 2 teaspoons salt. Bring

to a simmer over moderately high heat. Reduce the heat and simmer the rabbit legs, partially covered, until tender, 1 to 1½ hours. Add the loins and cook until just done, about 7 minutes longer. Stir in the pepper, parsley and basil.

—John Ash
Fetzer Vineyards

 ## MAKE IT AHEAD

You can make this stew in advance but take care not to overcook the loins. Unlike rabbit legs, which need long simmering to become tender, the loins, once browned, cook in about seven minutes. Any longer and they'll be dry and uninteresting rather than juicy and delicious. To make the stew ahead, undercook the loins slightly, just about five minutes. Then fish them out and store separately. When you want to serve the stew, reheat it, add the loins to the warmed stew and simmer until just done, about two minutes.

Stewed Rabbit with Pancetta and Baby Onions

Finished with gremolata (a mixture of garlic, lemon zest and parsley), this is clearly an Italian-inspired stew. You can also make both this and the previous stew with chicken parts. Just reduce the cooking time to about half an hour.

SERVES 6

¼	cup olive oil, more if needed
¼	pound pancetta or bacon, chopped
½	pound small white onions, about 1 inch in diameter, peeled
1¾	teaspoons salt
2	shallots, minced
4	cloves garlic, minced
1	pound mushrooms, quartered
½	teaspoon fresh-ground black pepper
2	3- to 3½-pound rabbits, cut into legs and boneless loins (see next page)
2	onions, chopped
2	carrots, chopped
2	ribs celery, chopped
2	cups dry white wine
1	quart Chicken Stock, page 299, or canned low-sodium chicken broth
1	bouquet garni: 6 parsley stems, 3 sprigs fresh thyme or ½ teaspoon dried, and 2 bay leaves
½	teaspoon grated lemon zest
2	tablespoons chopped fresh flat-leaf parsley
	Fried Capers, page 305, optional

WINE RECOMMENDATION:
THE FRAGRANT GREMOLATA IS BEST WITH A PINOT GRIS FROM ALSACE, A RICH BUT ACIDIC WINE.

1. In a large pot, heat 2 tablespoons of the oil over moderate heat. Add the pancetta and cook until brown but not crisp. Remove.

2. Add the small onions and ½ teaspoon of the salt and cook, stirring occasionally, until golden, about 5 minutes. Add the shallots and three-quarters of the garlic and cook for 1 minute. Add the mushrooms and ¼ teaspoon of the pepper and cook, stirring, until the mushrooms brown, about 5 minutes. Remove the vegetables.

3. Add the remaining 2 tablespoons oil and raise the heat to moderately high. Add several pieces of the rabbit. Brown well, about 4 minutes per side, and remove. Brown the remaining rabbit, adding oil if needed. Remove. Add the chopped onions, carrots and celery and cook until the vegetables are light brown, about 3 minutes. Add the wine and stock and bring to a boil, scraping the

bottom of the pot to dislodge any brown bits. Add the remaining 1¼ teaspoons salt, the rabbit legs and bouquet garni and bring to a simmer over moderately high heat. Reduce the heat and simmer, covered, until the rabbit is tender, 1 to 1½ hours.

4. When the rabbit legs are done, add the pancetta, mushroom mixture, rabbit loins and the remaining ¼ teaspoon pepper and simmer until the loins are just done, about 7 minutes. Discard the bouquet garni.

5. Meanwhile, combine the remaining garlic, the lemon zest and parsley in a small bowl. Stir the mixture into the stew. Simmer for 2 minutes. Serve topped with the capers, if you like.

CUTTING UP A RABBIT

Put the rabbit on its back on a cutting board. Cut off the rear legs at the point where they meet the body. Remove the front legs by cutting along the rib cage and behind the shoulder blades. Turn the rabbit over. The meaty portion along the lower back is the saddle, made up of two loins, one on either side of the spine. Remove the loins: Cut along one side of the spine and then, with the blade angled against the bone, cut away the meaty strip. Do the same on the other side. Cut the loins in half crosswise to make eight pieces of rabbit in all. Save the ribs and back for stock, if you like. You can add them to either chicken or meat stock.

Venison Stew
with Roasted Chestnuts

Juniper berries and strips of orange zest add depth to the flavor of this autumnal stew, but they should be discarded before serving. Triangular Croûtes, page 309, are a crisp accompaniment to the tender meat and velvety sauce.

SERVES 6

¼	pound bacon, chopped
3	pounds venison stew meat, cut into 1-inch cubes
2	onions, minced
3	carrots, cut into ½-inch pieces
3	ribs celery, chopped
3	cloves garlic, minced
6	tablespoons flour
2¼	cups Beef Stock, page 302, or canned low-sodium beef broth
2¼	cups red wine
1½	tablespoons tomato paste
3	3-inch-long strips orange zest
4	juniper berries
1½	teaspoons dried thyme
1½	teaspoons salt
2	pounds fresh chestnuts
1½	tablespoons cooking oil
¾	teaspoon fresh-ground black pepper
3	tablespoons red-currant jelly
3	tablespoons chopped fresh parsley
	Triangular Croûtes, page 309

WINE RECOMMENDATION:
THIS SLIGHTLY SWEET, GAMEY STEW IS NICELY MIRRORED BY THE YOUNG, SWEET-SEEMING FRUIT AND GAMEY AROMA AND FLAVOR OF A FINE PREMIER CRU RED BURGUNDY FROM CÔTE DE NUITS IN FRANCE. PINOT NOIR FROM THE CARNEROS REGION OF CALIFORNIA IS A REASONABLY PRICED ALTERNATIVE.

1. In a large pot, cook the bacon over moderate heat until the fat is rendered, about 5 minutes. Remove with a slotted spoon. Pour off all but 2 tablespoons of the bacon fat and reserve.

2. Raise the heat to moderately high. Add about a third of the venison. Brown well on all sides, about 8 minutes. Remove. Brown the remaining meat in 2 more batches, adding more bacon fat if needed. Remove. Reduce the heat to low. Add the onions, carrots, celery and garlic and cook, stirring occasionally, until soft, about 10 minutes. Return the bacon and venison to the pot. Add the flour and cook, stirring, until brown, about 5 minutes.

3. Stir in the stock, wine, tomato paste, orange zest, juniper berries, thyme

and salt. Bring the stew to a simmer over moderately high heat. Reduce the heat and cook at a bare simmer, partially covered, until the venison is tender, about 45 minutes.

4. Meanwhile, heat the oven to 450°. Cut an "X" through the shell on the flat end of each chestnut. Toss the chestnuts in the oil and put them on a baking sheet. Bake in the oven until the shell at each "X" lifts away from the chestnut, about 15 minutes. Peel the chestnuts when they are cool enough to handle.

5. Add the chestnuts and pepper to the stew and simmer 15 minutes longer. Add the red-currant jelly and stir until dissolved. Sprinkle with the chopped parsley and serve with the croûtes.

CHAPTER 10 · STOCKS & GARNISHES

Chicken Stock

Make plenty of chicken stock while you're at it. It's so versatile that it enhances fish and meat, as well as chicken, dishes—a truly all-purpose stock. Boil it down to half, or even less, freeze it in small containers and reconstitute as needed.

MAKES ABOUT 3 QUARTS

7   pounds chicken carcasses, backs, wings and/or necks, plus gizzards (optional)
4   onions, quartered
4   carrots, quartered
4   ribs celery, quartered
15   parsley stems
2   bay leaves
10   peppercorns
4   quarts water

1. Put all the ingredients in a large pot. Bring to a boil and skim the foam that rises to the surface. Reduce the heat and simmer, partially covered, for 2 hours.

2. Strain. Press the bones and vegetables firmly to get all the liquid. Skim the fat from the surface if using immediately. If not, refrigerate for up to a week or freeze. Scrape off the fat before using.

  STOCK OPTIONS

Stocks are not meant to stand on their own as, for instance, a clear chicken soup. The idea is that a stock acts as a multi-purpose base, being used for many different soups, stews and sauces. Therefore, stocks are usually rather mild so that they can be boiled down to concentrate flavor or built upon with other ingredients, depending on the dish. For the same reason, they are generally unsalted or at least under-salted.

 VARIATION

Brown Chicken Stock: Make Chicken Stock, above, but first roast the chicken carcasses, backs, wings, necks and gizzards with the vegetables in a 450° oven, stirring once or twice, for 45 minutes. Transfer to a large pot. Pour off all the fat in the roasting pan and add 1 cup of the water. Bring to a boil, scraping the bottom to dislodge any brown bits. Add to the pot with the herbs, pepper and remaining water. Continue with the basic recipe.

Turkey Stock

Don't throw out that leftover turkey carcass. Simmer it into a flavorful stock and use it to supplement your chicken-stock supply, or make our Turkey Soup with Mushrooms and Wild Rice, page 139, or Turkey, Artichoke-Heart and Mushroom Soup, page 140.

MAKES ABOUT 3 QUARTS

	Carcass from a 14- to 20-pound turkey, broken up
2	onions, quartered
3	carrots, quartered
3	ribs celery, quartered
3	sprigs fresh thyme, or ½ teaspoon dried
10	parsley stems
1	bay leaf
5	peppercorns
4	quarts water

1. Put all the ingredients in a large pot. Bring to a boil and skim the foam that rises to the surface. Reduce the heat and simmer, partially covered, for 2 hours.

2. Strain. Press the bones and vegetables firmly to get all the liquid. Skim the fat from the surface if using immediately. If not, refrigerate for up to a week or freeze. Scrape off the fat before using.

STOCK FROM THE TAP

While most soups call for stock as a base, for the sake of convenience many soups can be made with plain old water, and they'll still be excellent. Generally, soups that have plenty of flavorful ingredients are the best to try without stock, such as Beef and Barley Soup with Mushrooms, page 146. Many pureed vegetable soups that call for Chicken or Vegetable Stock also work well with water, and pea and bean soups are another category that will do just fine with water. For any of these, adding extra onions, garlic and herbs boosts flavor. The only soups for which you should never use water in place of stock are simple combinations that rely on the stock for much of the flavor, such as French Onion, page 38, or Avgolemono, page 131, and most seafood soups since the short cooking time of fish allows for only minimal flavoring of the broth. Certainly you shouldn't hesitate to supplement stock with water or to add plain water if a soup gets too thick.

Pork Stock

Often overlooked as a soup or stew base, pork stock has a delicious flavor that works especially well with Asian dishes. You can make two versions—Western with onions, garlic, carrot and celery, or the Asian variation with onions, garlic and ginger. Pork neck bones are a logical choice because they're relatively inexpensive, but they can be hard to find. A bone-in pork-shoulder roast makes wonderful stock, too.

MAKES 1½ QUARTS

1   tablespoon cooking oil
3½ pounds pork neck bones or a 3½-pound bone-in pork-shoulder roast
2   onions, quartered
2   cloves garlic
1   carrot, quartered
1   rib celery, quartered
3   quarts water
6   parsley stems
3   sprigs fresh thyme, or ½ teaspoon dried
1   bay leaf
5   peppercorns

1. In a large pot, heat the oil over moderately high heat. Add about a third of the pork bones or the roast and brown well on all sides, about 8 minutes. Remove. Brown the remaining bones, if using, and remove. Put the vegetables in the pot and cook, stirring, until browned, about 5 minutes. Return the meat to the pot and add the remaining ingredients. Scrape the bottom of the pot to loosen all the brown bits. Bring to a boil and skim. Reduce the heat and simmer, partially covered, for 3 hours. Remove the roast, if using.

2. Strain. Press the bones and vegetables firmly to get all the liquid. Skim the fat from the surface if using immediately. If not, refrigerate for up to a week or freeze. Scrape off the fat before using.

  WASTE NOT

You can use a pork roast in myriad ways after simmering it to make stock. Give the roast a final browning in the oven and serve it as is; shred it and heat with barbecue sauce; cut it into dice and toss with onions and vinaigrette for a main-dish salad; or make pork fried rice.

  VARIATION

Asian Pork Stock: Omit the carrot, celery, parsley, thyme, bay leaf and peppercorns. Add three ¼-inch slices of fresh ginger and brown the meat only, not the vegetables.

Beef Stock

Because of their strong, meaty flavor and gelatinous quality, beef bones make an excellent, full-bodied stock. While this stock takes about five and a half hours from start to finish, the actual preparation time is minimal—less than 20 minutes. And what a difference from canned beef broth.

MAKES 1½ QUARTS

3   pounds beef bones, cut into pieces
2   onions, quartered
4   carrots, quartered
4   ribs celery, quartered
3½ quarts water
3½ cups canned tomatoes (28-ounce can), drained
12 parsley stems
6   sprigs fresh thyme, or 1 teaspoon dried
1   bay leaf
5   peppercorns

1. Heat the oven to 450°. Put the bones in a large roasting pan. Brown in the oven for 40 minutes, stirring once or twice. Add the vegetables and continue cooking until the bones and vegetables are well browned, about 20 minutes longer.

2. Put the bones and vegetables in a large pot. Pour off all the fat in the roasting pan and add 1 cup of the water. Bring to a boil, scraping the bottom of the pan to dislodge any brown bits. Add to the pot with the remaining 13 cups water, the tomatoes, parsley, thyme, bay leaf and peppercorns. Bring to a boil and skim the foam that rises to the surface. Reduce the heat and simmer the stock, partially covered, for 4 hours.

3. Strain. Press the bones and vegetables firmly to get all the liquid. Skim the fat from the surface if using immediately. If not, refrigerate for up to a week or freeze. Scrape off the fat before using.

 VARIATION

Veal Stock: Milder in flavor than beef stock, veal stock is made in exactly the same way, with veal bones in place of beef. Make either a light-colored stock, by omitting the first step, or a dark one.

Fish Stock

Ask for bones at your fish store. They're often free, and you can get a wealth of flavor from them in minutes.

MAKES ABOUT 3 QUARTS

5   pounds fish bones, heads and trimmings
1   onion, chopped
1   carrot, chopped
3   quarts water
2   cups dry white wine
12   parsley stems
3   sprigs fresh thyme, or ½ teaspoon dried
1   bay leaf
10   peppercorns

1. Remove any gills from the fish. Rinse the bones, heads and trimmings well and cut them into pieces.

2. Put all the ingredients in a large pot. Bring to a boil and skim the foam that rises to the surface. Reduce the heat and simmer, uncovered, for 30 minutes.

3. Strain. Press the bones and vegetables firmly to get all the liquid. If not using immediately, refrigerate for up to a week or freeze.

Vegetable Stock

A nice, light base for vegetable soups, this stock is also an alternative to meat, chicken or fish stock in both soups and stews.

MAKES 3 QUARTS

8   onions, chopped
12   carrots, chopped
4   ribs celery, chopped
1   medium bunch parsley
6   sprigs fresh thyme, or 1 teaspoon dried
3   bay leaves
1   tablespoon peppercorns
3½   quarts water

1. Put all the ingredients in a large pot. Bring to a boil. Reduce the heat and simmer, partially covered, for 45 minutes.

2. Strain. Press the vegetables firmly to get all the liquid. If not using immediately, refrigerate for up to a week or freeze.

Aioli

From Provence comes this garlic-flavored mayonnaise. A last-minute addition to fish soups, it also accompanies the famed poached vegetable platter, *le grand aioli*. The sauce is a major player in the traditional Provençal soup, Bourride, page 107.

6   cloves garlic, chopped
½   teaspoon salt
2   egg yolks
1¾ cups olive oil

1. Put the garlic, salt and egg yolks in a food processor.

2. With the food processor running, add ¼ cup of the oil very slowly and then the remaining 1½ cups oil in a thin stream. The mixture will thicken as you add the oil.

Rouille

Full of garlic and hot with chile peppers, this thick mayonnaise-like sauce is added to fish soups for thickening and flavoring and also spooned onto croûtes to drop into the bowl. It is the traditional final touch for Bouillabaisse, page 105, but anyone who tries it loves it so much that they find many places to use it—on sandwiches, in potato salad, with grilled fish or chicken.

MAKES 1½ CUPS

1   3-inch-long piece French baguette (or equivalent quantity of another white bread), about 1 ounce, crusts removed
4   cloves garlic, chopped
2   small, fresh red chile peppers, seeds and ribs removed, chopped
2   egg yolks
½   teaspoon salt
1¼ cups olive oil

1. Soak the bread in a little water until soft and then squeeze out the water.

2. In a food processor, puree the bread, garlic and chile peppers with the egg yolks, salt and ¼ cup of the oil. With the machine running, add the remaining 1 cup oil in a thin stream. The mixture will thicken as you add the oil.

Pesto alla Genovese

Pesto has a wonderful effect on soup. Stir a little into a vegetable or bean soup and something special happens. This Ligurian sauce has recently enjoyed a great vogue in this country, and we now make it with a variety of herbs and even vegetables, such as red bell peppers. But somehow none of the innovations has the magic of the original.

MAKES ½ CUP

1   clove garlic, chopped
¾   cup lightly packed fresh basil leaves
½   teaspoon salt
¼   cup olive oil
2   tablespoons pine nuts
¼   cup grated Parmesan cheese
1½   teaspoons butter, at room temperature

1. In a food processor, puree the garlic and basil with the salt.

2. With the food processor running, add the oil in a thin stream and continue processing until well blended. Add the pine nuts, Parmesan and butter and process just long enough to chop the nuts.

Fried Capers

When they're fried, tangy capers, the buds of the *Capparis spinosa* bush, open up to look like crisp little flowers. Use them to garnish soups or stews, or toss them into your next Caesar salad.

2   tablespoons drained capers
     Cooking oil, for frying

1. Dry the capers completely on a paper towel.

2. In a small, heavy saucepan, heat 1 inch of oil until hot, about 350°. Add the capers and cook until crisp, 30 to 60 seconds. Remove with a slotted spoon and drain on paper towels.

Croutons

Golden-brown croutons add a crunchy contrast to soups. We call for white bread with the crust removed, but you can use another type, such as sourdough or country bread, and, if you want, leave the crust on. Croutons are a great way to use stale bread. They're easy to prepare and keep for several weeks in an airtight container.

MAKES ABOUT 3 CUPS

2   tablespoons cooking oil
2   tablespoons butter
3   cups ½-inch cubes of bread, from about ½ medium loaf day-old French or Italian bread, crusts removed
¼   teaspoon salt

1. In a large frying pan, heat the oil and butter over moderate heat.

2. Add the bread and sprinkle with the salt. Reduce the heat to moderately low and sauté, stirring frequently, until the bread is crisp and golden brown, about 8 minutes. Drain on paper towels.

VARIATIONS

◆ ONE-INCH CROUTONS: Substitute an equal quantity of bread cut into 1-inch cubes for the ½-inch cubes.

◆ OVEN-BAKED CROUTONS: Heat the oven to 300°. In a medium bowl, toss the bread cubes with the oil, melted butter and salt. Put them on a baking sheet and bake, stirring occasionally, until crisp and golden brown, about 20 minutes.

◆ HERB CROUTONS: Add 1 teaspoon each dried thyme and oregano and a pinch of fresh-ground black pepper to the browned croutons and sauté for 2 minutes longer.

◆ CHEESE AND HERB CROUTONS: Make Herb Croutons, above. Remove the pan from the heat and cool slightly. Toss with ¼ cup grated Parmesan cheese.

◆ GARLIC AND PARSLEY CROUTONS: Add 1 tablespoon olive oil and 1 clove minced garlic to the browned croutons in the pan and sauté for 1 minute longer. Add 1 tablespoon chopped fresh parsley and sauté for 30 seconds.

◆ BLACK-PEPPER CROUTONS: Add ½ teaspoon fresh-ground black pepper to the browned croutons and sauté for 2 minutes longer.

Miniature Croutons

Chef Spicer serves these tiniest possible croutons with her Garlic Soup, page 26. We found that the crunchy bits were an amusing addition to all of our smooth soups. They get lost in chunkier soups.

MAKES ABOUT 1 CUP

6   slices fresh white bread
¼   cup cooking oil
1   clove garlic, lightly crushed, optional
⅛   teaspoon salt

1. Cut the crusts from the bread. Put one piece of bread on a work surface and flatten it with a rolling pin. Repeat with the remaining slices. Stack the slices and cut them into ⅛-inch-wide strips. Gather the strips together and cut them crosswise into ⅛-inch squares.

2. In a large frying pan, heat the oil over moderate heat. Add the garlic clove and bread and fry, stirring frequently, until the bread is crisp and golden brown, about 3 minutes. Remove and drain on paper towels. Sprinkle with the salt.

—Susan Spicer
Bayona

NO STALE BREAD?

If you're fresh out of stale bread for Croutons, opposite page, cut fresh, firm bread into ½-inch cubes and let them dry at room temperature for an hour. A quicker way is to bake the cubes in a 300° oven for about 10 minutes.

Polenta Croutons

In Italy, polenta—cornmeal cooked in water—is usually an accompaniment to the main course. It's either served warm right out of the pot or cooled, sliced and then sautéed or grilled. Here we've cut it into small cubes and fried it to use as a delicious garnish for soups.

MAKES ABOUT 2 CUPS

3   cups water
1¼ teaspoons salt
1   cup coarse or medium cornmeal
4   tablespoons butter, at room
       temperature
¼   cup grated Parmesan cheese
       Cooking oil, for frying

VARIATION

Polenta and Herb Croutons: Stir 1 teaspoon dried sage or 1 tablespoon chopped fresh parsley into the polenta with the butter. Include the Parmesan or omit it, whichever you prefer.

1. Oil an 8-inch-square cake pan. In a medium saucepan, bring the water and salt to a boil. Add the cornmeal in a slow stream, whisking constantly. Reduce the heat to moderate and simmer, stirring frequently with a wooden spoon, until the polenta is very thick and pulls away from the sides of the saucepan, about 20 minutes. Stir in the butter and Parmesan.

2. Spread the polenta in the cake pan in an even layer and refrigerate for 30 minutes or more. Unmold the polenta and cut into ½-inch cubes.

3. In a large frying pan, heat ½ inch oil over moderate heat. When hot, add the polenta cubes and fry, stirring once or twice, until golden brown, 3 to 4 minutes. Remove and drain on paper towels.

Triangular Croûtes

Make these as you like: round, diamond or even heart shaped. Croûtes cut into shapes look a little fancier than plain ones and are traditionally placed around the edge of stews.

MAKES 12 CROÛTES

4   ⅜-inch slices from a large loaf of French or other good-quality bread, crusts removed

1   tablespoon cooking oil

1   tablespoon butter

¼   teaspoon salt

1. Cut each slice of bread diagonally into 4 triangles.

2. In a large frying pan, heat the oil and butter over moderately low heat. Add the bread and cook until crisp and golden brown on both sides, about 5 minutes in all. Drain on paper towels. Sprinkle with salt.

Rustic Croûtes

Delicious plain, croûtes—really just large croutons—can also be rubbed with a cut clove of garlic after they're cooked. Brushing the croûtes with oil helps them stay crisp in soups.

MAKES 12 CROÛTES

12 ½-inch slices French baguette, or an equal quantity of halved or quartered slices from a larger loaf

1   tablespoon cooking oil

¼   teaspoon salt

1. Heat a broiler or grill. Brush both sides of the bread with the oil.

2. Broil or grill on both sides until golden brown, about 4 minutes in all. Sprinkle with salt. Serve warm or at room temperature.

VARIATION

Low-Fat Garlic Croûtes: Though less resistant to liquid, croûtes made without oil or butter still taste good. Make Rustic Croûtes, omitting the oil. After broiling or grilling, rub each croûte on both sides with a halved garlic clove.

Index

Page numbers in **boldface** indicate photographs

D

H

HALIBUT. *See also* Fish
  Bouillabaisse, **104**, 105-6
  Bourride, 107-8
HAM
  Potato Soup with Ham and
    Scallions, 43
  20-Minute Black-Bean Soup, 73
Hazelnuts. *See* Nuts
Hearty Cabbage Soup with Bacon, 48
HERBS, 24, 227. *See also specific
    kinds*
  Cheese and Herb Croutons, 306
  Herb Croutons, 306
  Polenta and Herb Croutons, 30
Home-Style Italian Chicken Soup
    with Tiny Meatballs, **126**, 127-28
HOMINY, 72
  Red-Chile and Pork Pozole, 273
  Smoky Pork Stew with Chiles
    and Black Beans, 271-72
  20-Minute Black-Bean Soup, 73
Horseradish, Short-Rib Stew with,
    264-65
Hungarian Goulash, 263

I

Indian-Style Curried Fish Stew, 197
Indonesian Chicken Stew with
  Zucchini and Fried Shallots,
  228, 229-30
Italian Veal Stew with Paprika,
  252-53

K

KIDNEY BEANS, 65
  Southwest-Style Bean Soup with
    Avocado Salsa, **74**, 75
KIELBASA
  Lamb, White-Bean and Sausage
    Stew, 276-77
  Sour-Rye Soup with Kielbasa,
    158-59
KWAS
  Sour-Rye Soup with Kielbasa,
    158-59

L

LAMB
  Creamy Lamb Stew with Lemon,
    285-86
  Curried-Lamb Stew, 289
  Lamb, White-Bean and Sausage
    Stew, 276-77
  Lamb and Barley Soup with
    Mushrooms, 167-68
  Lamb and Shiitake Stew with
    Fennel and Orange, 287-88
  Lamb Stew with Chickpeas and
    Roasted Red Peppers, 280-81
  Lamb Stew with Eggplant,
    Peppers and Tomatoes, 278-79
  Navarin, **282**, 283-84
LEEKS, 286
  Asparagus and Leek Soup, **28**,
    29-30
  Bouillabaisse, **104**, 105-6
  Bourride, 107-8
  Butternut Squash and Leek
    Soup, 49
  Chicken Noodle Soup with Root
    Vegetables, 118-19
  Cock-a-Leekie, 136-37
  Cornish Hen Stew with Leeks,
    Figs and Orange, 241
  Creamy Lamb Stew with Lemon,
    285-86
  Provençal Chicken with Fennel
    and Olives, 219
  Scallop, Leek and Potato
    Chowder, 99
  Shellfish Stew with Red-Pepper
    Sauce, **198**, 199-200
  Three-Fish Stew with Leeks and
    Carrots, 206-7
  Vichyssoise, 179
LEGUMES, 67, 70, 72. *See also*
  Beans, dried; *specific kinds*
  soups, 55-80
LEMONS
  Avgolemono Soup, 131
  Creamy Lamb Stew with Lemon,
    285-86
  Sausage and Potato Stew in Lemon
    Rosemary Broth, **274**, 275
  Stewed Pork and Prunes with
    Lemon, 269-70
  Zucchini and Lemon Soup with
    Couscous, 27

L

LENTILS, 58, 61, 67, 70, 72
  Curried Red-Lentil Soup, **56**,
    57-58
  Lentil Soup, 59
  Mulligatawny Soup, 135
  Mushroom and Lentil Soup, 60-61
  Oxtail and Lentil Soup, 152-53
LIMA BEANS
  Barley, Split-Pea, Lima-Bean
    and Dried-Mushroom Soup,
    79-80
  Brunswick Stew, 232-33
  Spicy Catfish Stew, **210**, 211
Lithuanian Borscht, 177-78
LOBSTER, 87, 194
  Lobster Bisque, 86-87
Low-Fat Garlic Croûtes, 309

M

Macadamia nuts. *See* Nuts
Manhattan Clam Chowder, 100-101
Marinating, containers for, 268
MASCARPONE
  Wild-Mushroom Minestrone with
    Mascarpone Cappelletti, **16**, 17-
    18
  Yellow-Pepper and Mascarpone
    Soup, **174**, 175
Matzo-Ball Soup, Grandma's, **120**,
  121-22
MEAT, 156, 260, 265. *See also
    specific kinds*
  soups, 141-68
  stews, 247-96
Meatballs, Tiny, Home-Style Italian
  Chicken Soup with, **126**, 127-28
Mediterranean Chicken Stew, 220-21
Melon. *See* Cantaloupe
Mexican Chicken Soup, **114**, 115-16
Mexican Potato Soup, 44
Mexican Tortilla Soup, 117
Middle Eastern Chicken Stew, **216**,
  217-18
MINESTRONE, 14-15
  Wild-Mushroom Minestrone with
    Mascarpone Cappelletti, **16**,
    17-18
Miniature Croutons, 307
Mole, Turkey, 245-46
MONKFISH. *See also* Fish
  Bouillabaisse, **104**, 105-6
  Bourride, 107-8

N

O

P

Minestrone with Pesto, 14-15
Tuscan Mussel Soup with
White Beans and Garlic, **90**,
91-92
White-Bean and Sausage Soup
with Sage, 64-65
White-Bean Soup with Pesto,
62, 63
White kidney beans, 65. *See also*
White beans
Wild-Mushroom Minestrone with
Mascarpone Cappelletti, **16**,
17-18
Wild mushrooms. *See* Mushrooms
Wild Rice, Turkey Soup with
Mushrooms and, **138**, 139
WINE, 189, 209. *See also specific
kinds*
Boeuf Bourguignon, 254-55
Boeuf en Daube, 256-57
Cold Peach and Ginger Soup
with Peach Sorbet, 188-89
Coq au Vin, 224-25

Rabbit and Wild Mushroom Stew,
290, 291-92
Salmon and Red-Wine Stew,
208-9
Stewed Rabbit with Pancetta and
Baby Onions, 293-294
Venison Stew with Roasted
Chestnuts, 295-96
Winter squash. *See* Butternut
Squash

Y

YELLOW BELL PEPPERS
Cod and Sweet-Pepper Stew with
Tarragon Aioli, **204**, 205
Yellow-Pepper and Mascarpone
Soup, **174**, 175
YOGURT
Black-Bean Soup with Cilantro
Yogurt, 71-72

Chilled Fresh-Tomato Soup with
Summer Relish, **180**, 181
Cold Curried Zucchini Soup with
Cilantro, **170**, 171

Z

ZUCCHINI
Cold Curried Zucchini Soup with
Cilantro, **170**, 171
Home-Style Italian Chicken
Soup with Tiny Meatballs,
126, 127-28
Indonesian Chicken Stew with
Zucchini and Fried Shallots,
228, 229-30
Mexican Chicken Soup, **114**,
115-16
Minestrone with Pesto, 14-15
Zucchini and Lemon Soup with
Couscous, 27

Thanks to

ABC Carpet & Home, 888 Broadway, New York, NY 10003: soup plate, page 22; soup plate, small bowl and spoon, page 126; soup plate and wine glass, page 258. Wallie Festa-Hammer, The Crowsnest Pottery, Branford Craft Village, 779 E. Main Street, Branford, CT 06405: bowls by Wallie Festa-Hammer, cover. Balitique CWL Imports, 200 East 10th Street, #493, New York, NY 10003: napkins, pages 228 and 236. Felissimo, 10 West 56th Street, New York, NY 10019: soupspoon, page 22; bowls and plate by Dan Levy, pages 28, 148, 154 and 198; bowls and plates by Fred Rose, pages 110, 138, 192, 210 and 266; bowls and plates, pages 82 and 96; soup plate, page 222; plate, page 228. Henri Bendel, 712 Fifth Avenue, New York, NY 10019: placemat, page 138; glass, page 192; placemat and glass, page 204. Aletha Soule for The Loom Company, New York, NY: bowls, pages 10, 16, 35, 42, 74, 170, 174 and 180; platter, page 290. Takashimaya, 693 Fifth Avenue, New York, NY 10022: bowls, pages 132 and 204; tureen, page 248; soup plate, page 274. Terrafirma Ceramics, 152 West 25th Street, New York, NY 10001: bowls, pages 248 and 282. Wolfman-Gold & Good Company, 116 Greene Street, New York, NY 10012: soup plates and wine glasses, pages 50 and 242; soup plate and tablecloth, page 56; soup plates, pages 62 and 216; soup plate, underplate and wine glass, page 90; soup plates and underplates, pages 104 and 186; bowl, soup plate and napkin, page 142; placemat, page 154. Zona, 97 Greene Street, New York, NY 10012: bowl, page 160; shawl, page 216. Sara Abalan: backgrounds, pages 10, 16, 28, 34, 68, 96, 110, 114, 120, 148, 154, 170, 174, 180, 186, 210 and 298.

CONTRIBUTORS

Ann Chantal Altman is the corporate executive chef for J. E. Seagrams and Co., a food writer and cooking teacher in New York City.

John Ash is the culinary director of Fetzer Food & Wine Center at Valley Oaks in Hopland, California. He co-authored *American Game Cooking* (Addison Wesley) and is working on *John Ash's Wine Country Cuisine* (Dutton), to be published in the fall of 1995.

Paul Bartolotta is the executive chef at Spiaggia in Chicago.

Richard Benz is the executive chef at Gautreau's in New Orleans.

Bob Chambers is the executive chef for Lancôme/L'Oreal Inc. in New York City. He is also a food writer and food stylist.

Julia Child, renowned cookbook author, television personality and co-founder of The American Institute of Wine and Food, is also a contributing editor for *Food & Wine*.

Michael Chiarello is chef/owner of Tra Vigne and the culinary director of Napa Valley Kitchens, both in St. Helena, California.

Ann Clark is a Texas-based food writer whose most recent book is *Quick Cuisine* (Dutton). She also wrote *Ann Clark's Fabulous Fish* (NAL).

Scott Cohen is the executive chef at The Restaurant, The Stanhope Hotel in New York City.

Erica De Mane is a chef and food writer in New York City who specializes in Italian cooking and the history of Italian food.

Anne Disrude is a New York-based food stylist.

Georgia Chan Downard is a food consultant, teacher and stylist and the author of *The Big Broccoli Book* (Random House).

Susan Feniger and **Mary Sue Milliken** are co-owners and co-chefs of Santa Monica's Border Grill and have co-authored *City Cuisine* and *Mesa Mexicana* (Morrow).

Joyce Goldstein is chef/owner of Square One in San Francisco and the author of *Back to Square One* (Morrow), *The Mediterranean Kitchen* (Morrow), and *Mediterranean the Beautiful* (Collins).

Christopher Gross is chef/owner of Christopher's and Christopher's Bistro, both in Phoenix, Arizona.

Hubert Keller is chef/owner of Fleur de Lys in San Francisco, California. He is writing a cookbook to be published in 1996.

Gray Kunz, the executive chef at Lespinasse in The St. Regis Hotel in New York City, is working on a cookbook.

Annette Lantzius is an avid home cook in Vancouver, British Columbia.

Jan Newberry is a food writer and recipe developer in Bedford, New York.

Charles Palmer is chef/owner of two restaurants, Aureole and Alva, both in New York City. He is the author of the forthcoming *Great American Food: Cooking with Charles Palmer* (Random House) and is co-owner with Jonathan White of Egg Farm Dairy in Peekskill, New York.

Grace Parisi is a chef, food writer and food stylist in New York City.

Charles Pierce is a food writer, editor and recipe developer in New York City.

Don Pintabona is the executive chef at New York's Tribeca Grill. He also teaches at The New School and is featured in *The Tribeca Cookbook* (Ten Speed Press), due out in December 1994.

Shirley Salzman is a home cook with over fifty years cooking experience.

Tracey Seaman is the recipe tester-developer of *Food & Wine* magazine's test kitchen and the author of *The Tunafish Gourmet* (Villard).

Jane Sigal is a cooking editor at Macmillan Publishing and the author of *Normandie Gastronomique* (Abbeville) and *Backroad Bistros, Farmhouse Fare* (Doubleday).

Hiro Sone is chef and co-owner with his wife, Lissa Doumani, of Terra in St. Helena, California. He is writing a cookbook, *Terra: The Land and the Restaurant*, to be published in late 1995.

Susan Spicer is the executive chef at Bayona in New Orleans.

Judith Sutton is a food writer and freelance chef in New York City.

Bruce Tillinghast is chef and co-owner with his wife, Pat Tillinghast, of New Rivers in Providence, Rhode Island.

Ming Tsai is the corporate executive chef at Ginger Club in Palo Alto, CA.

Andrew Ziobro is the director of food and beverage, Restaurants Associates at The Harvard Business School, and also a food writer.